I0620071

RITES OF PASSAGE

THE LEGACY OF ADVENTURE CLIMBING IN THE SIERRA NEVADA

E.C. JOE

Foreword by
VITALIY MUSIYENKO

Rites of Passage: The Legacy of Adventure Climbing in the Sierra Nevada

© 2022 E.C. Joe

ISBN: 978-0-578-99548-9

E.C. Joe

vertical2o@gmail.com

First Edition, 2022

DEDICATION
GODSPEED RICHARD LEVERSEE

The climbing community and many friends were saddened, by the passing of Sierra Climbing Icon, Richard Leversee on January 12, 2022. Fittingly and correctly, this book is dedicated to Richard — since he was such wonderful friend, and an inspiring and decisive force, across the Southern Sierra Nevada and beyond. Although the term Stonemaster is somewhat over used, Richard embraced the ethos, and will be sincerely remembered as one. Thankfully, Richard's first ascents are still with us. This lasting memory and fine legacy is now ours to embrace and discover, as he did — following your heart with dynamic energy, to do what you love.

Richard's climbing passion began in the early 1970s, in concert with the clean climbing revolution of that time. This core ethic created a bold and enduring commitment, that took Richard on many fine and epic adventures, across the decades. Richard has left us a timeless inheritance of first ascents in the Sierra Nevada, that remain envious and prized.

The memory of Richard's adventurous enthusiasm will always be a brilliant and haunting force — challenging us to up our game. No matter in tempest, diamond sky, calming starlight, or enchanted cloud, the rock eternally remembers, as well. It too has been forever changed by Richard's touch and passing – quietly whispering back, if you listen.

Godspeed Richard Leversee! 1958 - 2022
— E.C. Joe and David Ohst

"The marriage of adventure and climbing together just became my mantra and my reason to live." — Richard Leversee

CONTENTS

ACKNOWLEDGMENTS

I MUST EXPRESS my deepest gratitude to the following people for their various contributions that included the sharing of ideas, information, stories, and images, to tireless proofreading, and unwavering support. This book would not have been complete without their contributions: Steph Abegg, Linda Adams, Kathy Allison, René Ardesch, Lee Aulman, Janet Banner, Fred Beckey, Alan Boyle, Carol Burkert, Ron Carson, Malinda Chouinard, Gary Clark, Amos Clifford, Moises Cordero, Kevin Daniels, Greg Epperson, Ron Felton, Trish Ferenz, Grant Gardner, Kim Grandfield, Ed Hartouni, Shawn Hayes, Bruce Hildenbrand, Randy Jewett, Christy Joe, Guy Keesee, Herb Laeger, Richard Leversee, Lulu, Bill Cobb, David Hickey, Joel Matta, Joe Metz, Sally Moser, Vitaliy Musiyenko, Ed Noringer, Dave Ohst, David Peck, Randy Powers, Patrick Paul, Dory Ptak, Ed Sampson, Michael Sewell, Kris Solem, Lotus Steele, Randy Steele, Brandon Thau, Sarah Thaves, Nick Todd, Gary Weber, John Vargas, Todd Vogel, and Brad Young.

FOREWORD

A burning sensation started to ignite my left forearm. I kept my hips close to the slightly overhanging section of the wall as I quickly retrieved a cam and jabbed it into an opening in the crack above my head. It goes in, but it doesn't quite fit. My last piece of placed gear, a slotted offset nut, was a distant, thirty feet below. The lactic acid burn then continued to build up in my left hand and progressed to a feeling of weakness. Vulnerable, I hung to a hold just wide enough for a single pad, and my foot started to shake. I held the rejected cam in my teeth while I rifled through the rack for a larger offset cam. Will it fit in the crack with the damned irregularity? IT DOES! Miraculously, I felt stronger, adjusted my position into a wide stem, and caught my breath. The terrain above the bulge looked just as sustained, with no apparent cracks that would take protection. Twenty-four miles in the backcountry, my friends and I were here to climb a wall larger than Mount Watkins' South Face for the first time in known history. Will we find a three-hundred-foot handcrack around the corner? Is the crack I'm trying to follow going to pinch to nothing twenty feet higher? I don't know. Before proceeding, I look back towards the serene wilderness below, the river snaking up the valley that led towards the tallest granite dome in the contiguous United States – Tehipite Dome. I wondered about the stories that the participants of its first ascents would share at a campfire. What were the memorable moments they experienced? Many of these stories may be lost to history. I woke up from my brief daydream because of the burn in my calves. It was already late afternoon, with over a thousand feet of

*difficult climbing ahead and no apparent bivy ledge in sight; I had to make
upward progress...Into the uncertainty, I went.*

The warm orange rays of sunrise over the Sierra Nevada Crest illuminate the jagged east-facing peaks like a massive picket fence. Their
vertical rise from the Owens Valley – the deepest valley in the United
States – in spots reaches well over 10,000 feet. The Sierra Nevada is
unique, even when compared to the Himalayas. The imposing view of
rock faces along the eastern crest continues for 200 miles. Below the
high mountains are countless cliffs and boulders that are host to world-
class climbing and attract people worldwide. Lying in the shadow of the
Eastern Sierra, the western slope is a unique territory unto itself. The
magnificent treasure trove of granite domes and walls west of the crest is
home to legendary high-quality rock, classic climbs, and spectacular
terrain.

Tehipite Dome, Moro Rock, Angel Wings, Bubbs Creek Wall, Castle
Rocks, Shuteye Ridge, Charlotte Dome, and the jaw-dropping spires of
the Needles, aside from containing a lifetime of world-class alpine climbing, all these have one thing in common – backcountry adventure. If a
mountain is a metaphor for life, exploration is its soul. A few climbers
had the vision, drive, and courage to climb these backcountry walls,
which seemed too demanding to other climbers. Romantic Warrior,
Crystal Bonsai, Silver Lining, Rapunzel, Valkyrie, Archangel, Despairadoes, El Niño, and In the Niche of Time are among those routes and
remain test pieces for climbers able to escape the Siren Call of Yosemite
Valley or the Eastern Sierra.

Since rock climbing diverged from mountaineering and became a
separate discipline, what people sought from it changed, too. Climbers
were presented with an open canvas of seemingly infinite unclimbed
cliffs and, with new tools to protect the leader on 5th class, were drawn
to quest into the unknown. Climbers met the challenges by advancing
their skills, innovating superior gear, eventually pushing the limits far
beyond what has been thought possible. Presently, the exploration of
unclimbed walls isn't in vogue; the walls ripe for the picking aren't close
to the road. Yet, the ever-increasing interest in climbing and readily available training facilities continue to breed talent that has pushed the limits
of what was considered physically and mentally impossible. Who would

have thought it was possible to free solo El Capitan, solo the Corkscrew link-up on Cerro Torre, or summit K2 in winter?

Our current generation of climbers is standing on the shoulders of giants who set the foundation necessary to advance climbing to where it is today and to the future levels we can't begin to imagine. One of these giants is E.C. Joe. In this book, he has gathered his own stories and those of other adventurers, procuring wisdom, knowledge, and retrospect, accounts of courageous ascents, and ground-up ethics that will continue to inspire future generations to explore their limits. Even though some of the tales in this book would be impossible to truly relate to without following the path of self-discovery on the same rock, with the same tools, gathering these stories in one piece of literature might be the most significant contribution gifted to the climbing community by the author. As my knees receive more damage than I am willing to admit, and as the armor becomes heavier to carry, I am delighted to have the ability to sit down in a comfortable chair and read the stories written by those whose paths I have followed closely. These stories piqued my curiosity and interest in documenting their contributions for my own comprehensive guidebook to the High Sierra, *High Sierra Climbing-Technical Rock & Ice*. The hope is that these books will capture the imaginations of all kinds of climbers to participate in their own "New Golden Age" of exploration. Respect the environment, leave no trace, and leave the best mountain range on the planet, the Sierra Nevada, pristine for the next adventure.

— Vitaliy Musiyenko

Vitaliy Musiyenko is genuinely a master backcountry climber of this generation. He has come a long way since his teenage years, having weighed in at 300 pounds. First visiting the Sierra in 2010, he has established over 100 new routes. Most recently, Vitaliy soloed the visionary Goliath Traverse, which is likely the most technical ridge traverse in the Western Hemisphere, crossing summits of over 60 peaks between 13,000 to over 14,000 feet in elevation and is 32 miles long. He loves long alpine climbs, cruxy boulder problems, big walls, ice climbing, hiking, photography, and any way to enjoy an adventure in nature. He believes that helping people and challenging personal limits with friends is heaven on earth.

PROLOGUE

LIGHTNING IN A BOTTLE

THE SOUTHERN SIERRA NEVADA is a unique mountain range with countless crags, domes, and magnificent walls across many climates. The extreme southern end of the range is semi-arid with a mix of sage, pine, and Joshua Trees. The wooded expanse of the Kern Plateau to the north gradually blends into the alpine vistas, massive walls, and high peaks of Kings/Sequoia National Parks, Sierra and Inyo National Forests. Until the early 1970s, the Southern Sierra sat largely untouched by climbers, and the documentation of technical routes established was rare. The climber who recognizes the area's potential for climbing partakes in an exclusive experience. As a neophyte climber, I became immersed in that experience. I was able to embrace adventure head-on.

Growing up as a kid in the suburbs of Bakersfield, large doses of imaginative play had a role in developing that perspective. As a teenager, the social vacuum of the Southern San Joaquin Valley fostered urban claustrophobia only to be cured by Boy Scout campouts and wandering the undeveloped foothills east of town. Like most parents of the fifties and sixties, my parents were not outdoor people, and unlike most parents, both were of Chinese descent. My grandfather was a pioneer of Bakersfield's Chinatown;[1] raising my father in the trappings of Chinese and American culture. Mom and Dad had enlisted during the Second World War and became part of a unique group of Chinese American veterans.[2] My Dad served as a tail gunner flying over Germany, getting shot down during his 54th mission. He spent seven months in a Nazi prison camp after evading capture for a week in the countryside.[3] My parents' relatively benign "American Dream" life they had created for my siblings and me belied everything they had been through. They were hard-working, self-made business owners who embraced the freedom for which they had fought. In turn, they allowed me the freedom to find my path, despite their typical parental doubts about my judgment. In my parents' defense, I hold them inculpable for all of the crazy shit I had participated in as a kid that almost killed me in the process.

Early on, I figured that any endeavors that would substantiate their doubts were best not shared with them. Most parents would never have allowed their sixteen-year-old son and other teens to go on a two-week backpack trip across the Sierra with no adults. Mine did. It wasn't supposed to be a death-defying trip. They must have had faith in my budding adolescent mountain sense. Undaunted, my Mom dropped David Mahan, Mike Stanley, Russell Rowe, and me off at the trailhead near Lone Pine, CA and said, "Have fun!" and drove off down the road in a cloud of dust.

After the trip, my parents never asked how we got home. They were just glad to see that we made it back safe. Keeping to the script, I never did bother to tell them when we had collectively decided to hitchhike home after reaching pavement. One ride became death-defying. Swerving wildly down the Kern Canyon Road, we fearfully gazed out of the open windows of our ride, a Plymouth Valiant. As the car swayed from side to side, we viewed the abyss of the canyon and raging river looming far below the edge of the road, while on the other side, there was the threat of oncoming traffic. It appeared evident our successful two-week adventure was about to end with our deaths in a car flying off the edge of the road into the talus and raging river below. While we white-knuckled the upholstery, the driver fired up a big fat joint. It became clear that he wasn't just a shitty driver, and it probably wasn't his first joint that day. Trapped, we held on for the ride. Little did I know that I'd become an authority on every niche of the Kern River Canyon, and I became acutely aware that the most dangerous part of an adventure was the return trip.

I frequently backpacked in the Sierra in the years after that. Craig

Collins, my regular backpacking bud convinced me to sign up for a rock climbing class. I was reluctant, but I was curious and showed up. It was Tex Bossier, an employee at Chouinard Equipment in Ventura, California, who introduced us to "the ropes." Tex had been sent to Bakersfield as part of a dealer outreach to instruct an introductory rock climbing class for High Country Mountaineering, a small outdoor shop. The course included an evening at the shop learning knots and belaying, followed by a full-day climbing at Kern Slabs near Kernville, CA. Afterward, I was not smitten by climbing as my classmates were, but I invested in a harness and climbing shoes, content to go along with people fully equipped with ropes, chocks, and carabiners.

Advancing our skills became a quandary for us, as we lacked experience. Climbing was a process that required a leader to "get the rope up there." We had top-roped a few climbs, but the number of top-rope climbs that were easily accessible was limited, as the rocks we wanted to climb were too tall. Someone had to lead. A few of us stepped forward into that role, or maybe it was that the others had stepped back first. Thankfully, some of that pressure was relieved when a handful of local climbers with "experience" showed up looking for partners. Experience sometimes was overstated by a few. Good intentions aside, those few were better suited as armchair climbers, as a trip up the rock would remove all doubt; rock climbing was a veritable truth serum. Provided that any of us suffered a fool and survived, we would warn the others, and word traveled through the climbing community like wildfire.

I was fortunate enough to have Joel Matta as a mentor. Joel had eighteen years of experience but treated me as an equal, even though we both knew who could do the heavy lifting. Being able to follow a pitch that I was incapable of safely leading was indeed a gift, an opportunity to mentally and physically prepare for my turn to be on the "sharp-end" of the rope. It was a gift of immeasurable value, watching Joel read the subtleties in the rock, not merely for holds but for placing anchors for protection. Joel was a master at the art of placing protection. He was skilled in locating the most obscure niches for nut placements. As Joel and I explored new routes in the unique areas throughout the Kern Plateau, it became apparent to us that the possibilities were endless. That's how I became hooked on the adventure of exploring new places and pioneering new routes. We had an empty slate with the opportunity to write our experiences on it. It was like finding lightning in a bottle and we knew what to do with it!

However, we weren't alone. A few climbers from elsewhere likewise discovered exploring the Kern and took advantage of the adventures there. Perhaps Fred Beckey's 1974 article, "The Needles of Sequoia Forest" in *Summit Magazine* or earlier guidebooks to the High Sierra by Hervey Voge[4] or Steve Roper[5] sparked their interests. Our unrelated, and on occasion, competing factions became a feature of climbing in the area. There was not a centralized scene, nor was there a bonafide source for route information. As climbing interests in the Kern slowly grew, route information remained elusive. Information was passed exclusively by word of mouth or in the form of carefully drawn topos on scraps of paper or a napkin over a beer. To share our notes and topos to preserve the area's rich history, Richard Leversee and I published a guidebook for the entire Kern in 1983.[6] In the spirit of their love for the area, John Harlin III,[7] Sally Moser, Greg Vernon,[8] Patrick Paul,[9] David Hickey,[10] Kris Solem,[11] et al. published subsequent guidebooks to continue in that tradition.

It was a means to an end. There's always another summit to conquer, right? Once skilled enough, I made the pilgrimage from the local crags, curious to experience the classic climbs in fantastic places of legends. Those pilgrimages tested my mettle, and touching unfamiliar stone required me to fashion new techniques while refining my current skill set. Experiencing Yosemite's big walls gave me technical prowess and pummeled me into having humility in retreat. The culmination of my newly found skills was put to good use back home. The climbing experience was addictive. It gave me focus. However, that focus was not always on my climbing pursuits. By chance, I got involved in teaching and guiding and did so for many years. Teaching was a satisfying way to share the experience so that others could have their own adventures. I've been on many summits, but I don't recall what most of them even looked like. I could, however, tell you in great detail how I got there. Those were good times of reckless abandon, fueled by the quest for adventure.

The Southern Sierra remains an infinite resource of climbable rock, and new adventures are ripe for the taking. While a climbing guidebook may preserve the list of routes, their physical description, and the pioneers for history, those records seldom, if ever, reveal the stories of the adventures of those journeys. The Southern Sierra, steeped in a history of adventure, has never had a collection of those experiences. This publication contains tales from one campfire, a collaborative effort from a few who have chosen to share their adventures with you. Enjoy! Every trip is an adventure! — E.C. Joe

SECTION I

ADVENTURES

A crystal dawn
where golden rays
slice into our
frozen berth,
blossoms-
a perfect day.
A difficult climb.
Mentally-
physically-
a new climb.
Demanding-
limits-
push.
Go for it!
A hidden hold!
Belay spot-
with a
beautiful vista-
a timeless experience-
exaltation.

1

GENESIS

By Ron Carson

Way of the Intercepted Fist

It was my 28th birthday. It was a good time of my life that I could look back on. I had been camping out at Upper Peppermint Campground as my basecamp to climb at Dome Rock and the Needles. That day I decided to free solo all of the routes that I'd ever free soloed, but do them all in one day. That would be fun! At the time, I was mentally and physically at the peak of my climbing skill. I had never had any close calls or near misses when free soloing, but I knew that falling was not an option. When free soloing, I always felt under control. It was a time when I climbed that I felt connected to everything around me. The rock on the routes was solid, and at the time, it felt like the thing to do. It was mid-summer. I set out in the early dawn hours, and the weather was perfect, cold and clear. And like most days in these woods, there was no one around. Starting at Dome Rock, I climbed many of the classic routes there. After finishing at Dome, I blasted out to the Needles to free solo some more routes for the rest of the day. I even had enough time to do a couple of my favorite climbs, Igor Unchained and Airy Interlude, twice.

The day had been great, pretty uneventful; good climbing, nice weather, just a perfect day. It was now late afternoon. On the drive out the dirt road from the Needles, I was feeling a little pooped-out. It had been a twenty-six route day. As the dirt road approaches the paved Great Western Divide Highway, it curves behind a knoll and limits the visibility of oncoming traffic. I looked both ways as my truck edged out towards the main road. O.K., nobody's coming, great, go! All of a sudden, here comes this group of about a dozen motorcycle riders. I slammed the brakes. Now, I hadn't pulled out into the road or in front of anybody. Everyone seemed fine -- except one guy. The next scene played out as if it was in slow motion. One rider had locked up his brakes and struggled to maintain control of the bike, tires skidding and the bike swerving wildly. Once he got the bike under control, he turned the bike around and drove over to me. Oh, shit. He's stopping. He put the kickstand down, and I'm thinking, "I'm gonna die." I get out of my truck, and I'm thinking, "What I'm gonna do? I'm gonna get my ass kicked right here. After *everything* I did today, I'm gonna *die now*?!" As the biker walks towards me, he's got a look on his face like he's going to carve my liver.

"Look dude, I've gotta scooter myself. I'm real sorry if I spooked, ya." I pleaded apologetically.

By that moment, we were face to face, and he came out of center field with a right hook like he was gonna tear my head off. I was scared, and my adrenaline was pumping, and by reflex, I drew my hand up and caught his fist. In doing so, my chalk-covered hand released a mysterious cloud of dust into the golden beams of the setting sun that filtered through the forest on us. We were both frozen at the moment, except for his eyes. His eyes curiously gazed at the dissipating plume of chalk dust.

Then, his eyes came back to me, "I'd fuck you up, kid, but I've got things to do."

I replied in a squeaky voice, "So do I."

He turned away and walked back to his bike. I sat in my truck and waited until he and all of his companions were long gone before heading back to camp. The day was calm and normal until that last event. And that event was way beyond my control.

As Seen on TV

The first time I saw rock climbing was when I was about ten years old. It was on TV, and it was mountain climbing. These characters had a psychedelic rope with a kernmantle sheath. Wow, being a young country boy from Pixley, California, the only kind of rope I had ever seen was a brown hemp twist.

The climbing TV show got my attention; the fact that this rope had multi-colors and had a kernmantle sheath fascinated me. I had to have one! So, like everything else I wanted, I had to make it. I immediately started to think of a way to create one. Granny was in the middle of knitting a project with a lot of different colored yarn. (My grandparents raised me since my parents never got along.) I commandeered some yarn, got a piece of plywood, and nailed some steeple nails in a circle on it with one in the middle. Then, I started threading a piece of yarn through each steeple nail. I stretched it across the living room with the ends all even and tied an overhand knot to keep them together. Then, I used another piece of yarn and started weaving through, over and under, around the other strands of yarn. Soon I could see that this must be how you get one of those multi-colored ropes. After a day or so of weaving, I had about twenty-five to thirty feet of what I thought must be climbing rope. Hell, the colors were right!

Well, next, I needed a harness. That night, I waited until my grandma and grandpa had bedded down. I snuck out of the house into the yard, and what did I do? I cut all of the webbing straps out of the single lawn chair we ever had. After all, a climbing harness had to be strong. That night I sewed together a climbing harness. I needed a carabiner; the dog leash had a snap-link on one end. "That will work," I said.

The following day bright and early, I went outside before my grandparents were up. I climbed the pine tree that was next to the living room window. I had climbed this tree a hundred times, all the way to the tippy top. I had spent a lot of time up there. Pixley was as flat as a pancake, farmland; I could see a long way. I went up twelve to fifteen feet in the tree, tied my new climbing rope around a good-sized branch. Then, I hooked it up to my new climbing harness. I put it through a small construction shackle, hooked up to the snap-link. I then waited for my grandfather to sit next to the window like he did every morning.

After all, I was going to impress him when he saw me rappelling right by him. I was all set. After double-checking everything, I weighted the rope. It broke like a shoelace. In an instant, I went rocketing by the living room window and landed in a deep pile of alkali powder dirt. A plume of dust went in the air like a meteor had struck Earth. All I could think about was I hope that he somehow did not see this. What the heck happened? Well, when the dust cleared, I stopped coughing and rubbed the pounds of dirt out of my eyes as I looked up at the window. He was looking right at me; he had a look on his face I had never seen before. I could tell that he knew that I was alright, but I wasn't sure if he would kick my butt or pick it up and dust me off. It seemed like an eternity went by as he meticulously folded the paper he had been reading and came out the front door. His eagle eyes saw that the only thing left of the lawn furniture was the frame. His eyes went from that to me without his head moving. He finally walked over and stood over me. My grandfather was not a big man, about 5'8" or so, but without a doubt the biggest man I knew. His hands were as thick as a bull's hide, and he had a neck full of wrinkles as deep as valleys and eyes that you could look directly into you and see your soul.

He paused for a moment, cleared his throat, and asked me where I got my harness. I wasn't about to lie to him. I told him about the lawn furniture last night. He then reached down with one of those rock-hard hands and gently picked me up out of that pile of dirt that I was covered in. He then dusted me off a little, looked at me with my harness on, the tattered ends of the rope of yarn still attached to the shackle, and asked me if I had ever heard of nylon? I answered back, "No."

My grandfather then put his arm around me as we walked back into the house and said, "After we have breakfast we will go into town." He took me to Pixley Hardware and bought me some nylon yellow construction sling and a 3/8" diameter nylon rope. We went back to the house and my grandfather helped me set up my plywood weaving device, with the 3/8" rope in the middle and made another rope. That was 1971; I still have that rope.

To pay for new webbing, he arranged for me to work at the neighbor's farm. I moved surface pipe, dug ditches, chopped cotton, and stacked hay. We repaired the lawn furniture together. I will never forget this lesson or any of the many lessons I learned from him.

I am eternally grateful to my grand-parents. They didn't have to raise me. They just did. "Up with the stars, do your chores, chop wood for the wood stove that keeps our house warm," he would tell me. "Hit it like you live, boy, hit it like you live," and so I did. As I became a man, I tried to apply what-ever I learned from him. You get out of life what you put into it. I'm at the age in life now, as he was when he picked me up out of that dirt pile. Now the skin on my hands is thick, cracked, and calloused.

The Rope. Photo: Ron Carson

Mr. Knapp

As a freshman in high school, my fascination with climbing almost got me in more trouble. During class one day, I was reading Climbing Maga-zine at my desk.

"You gotta see Charlie Knapp," my teacher said, looking over my shoulder. He picked up the magazine, then tossed it back down on my desk, "Right now, we're here to study English."

Charlie Knapp taught Drama and Choir at the school. When I arrived, he was leaning over a bowl of green-something soup. I was too scared to approach him and stayed in the doorway, "Mr. Knapp?"

He looked up from his soup, the spoon plopping back into the bowl. Then he gazed at me. His eyes were like the pointy-ends of eggs. "Who are YOU?"

"I'm Ron Carson. I want to do climbing."

"You're scrawny kid. See that door jam over your head? Go do a pull-up."

Without out saying another word, he wrote down his address and handed it to me, I tried to take it from his hand, but he held it tight, looked me in the eye, and said, "6:00am...Don't be late."

"Yes, sir," I said while walking backwards through the doorway.

Our outing was to Hospital Rock, a small crag located at the southern end of Sequoia National Park. There was Charlie, myself, and an older student, a senior. At the summit, Charlie built an immense anchor consisting of pitons driven by hammer into the cracks in the rock and chocks slotted into the nooks of other cracks. He used the anchor to set up a top rope on a climbing route on the rock face below. The middle of the rope was at the anchor. The ends were at the ground so we could tie into them.

We tied into either end of a Goldline rope, a much different rope than the psychedelic ones I'd seen on TV. Goldline was just that, gold and looked much like ropes used on a truck, but stretchier. Charlie showed me how to belay, a method of protecting the climber with the rope. While I anchored, I had the rope pass behind my back. I'd pretty-much would be holding the rope with my hands in the event of a fall. Charlie rolled a cigarette, lit it up, and it was, climb on! As the other kid scrambled up a ways to a ledge near the top anchor, Charlie commanded me to give him some slack, "No...MORE, MORE!" Once there was a substantial loop of rope on the ground, Charlie told the kid to let go and fall!

I held the fall while getting pulled off the ground, at the expense of some rope burns on my back and hands.

"O.K. Ron, it's your turn!" Charlie ordered, and we reversed roles and repeated the drill.

Charlie rolled and lit another cigarette, "O.K. We're done here. You learned the most important things; how to fall and how to catch a fall."

Afterward, we retreated below to the Potwisha Campground for the evening and practiced our knots. There, Charlie gave us both a hunk of rope, showed us a Bowline Knot, Figure 8, and Clove Hitch. He told us that when we went home, to take it in the shower and practice tying the knots while standing under the shower with only the cold water on, and that I could have hot water only when I had tied them correctly. That night, fueled by cigarettes, wine, and enthusiasm, Charlie enthralled us with epic stories of climbing and its pioneers. Charlie graciously took me under his wing, and we made several more outings to expand my experience. The years went by, and I had met other climbers. However, when my partner prospects dried up, I was always on the look for a recruit; even my grandfather did not escape an occasion to hold the rope for me.

"First" Embrace

Patrick Paul asked me, "You wanna go do an 'f.a.'?" Patrick was probably the first "real" climber I hung out with.

"What the Hell's an 'f.a'? I asked back curiously.

"Well, come on, we'll do a 'first ascent'," said Patrick, and the next thing we were doing was chopping a trail to "Sky Garden Wall." The day we picked to go up there, it was raining like a dog, and we had one poncho between us. One of us would wear the poncho, then trade-off, while the other would hack the vegetation. We finally hacked a trail up there. Whether Patrick liked it or not, I adopted him as a mentor. I embraced the concept of the first ascent, of the adventure being the first one; it sunk in right away.

It was not long until I was able to forge relationships with other notable first ascentionists with similar aspirations, like Tony Yaniro, Mike Lechlinski, and Herb Laeger, that resulted in great routes like the "Titanic," "Terrorvision," and "Silver Lining." Looking back, Mike Lechlinski, hands-down, was the best climber I had hooked up with. Mike was an excellent climber, technically savvy, and had the head for it. Mike was bold. Mike "could do it all." Route-wise, the Titanic was one of the most spectacular and rewarding routes that I had climbed.

Tony was living in Idaho at the time. We talked on the phone about this line on the Warlock Needle that we both had our eyes on. Tony and I agreed that he'd come down so we could do this thing. Tony showed up with some enormous "monster" bolt hangers he had designed. I don't know what the hell he was thinking making those, but whatever. We marched out there, looked at the line. It looked good. I belayed Tony up the "Howling" so Tony could rappel down our proposed line to check for loose rock. Good thing he did, as there were a couple of rocks that would have more than "hurt." We started climbing from the bottom on a crack way down below the face and worked it, taking turns, climbing and drilling all the bolts on lead while balancing from hooks. It took us a while to do it, like four or five days. Afterward, we took a break down in Southern California at Brett Maurer's place for a few days of rest and good food before having Tony or myself lead the entire pitch in one push.

It was morning back at the Needles parking lot. Brett Maurer and

Randy Leavitt joined Tony and me from SoCal. Randy set up to photograph our ascent. Once out at the Warlock, Tony and I flipped a coin to see who would go first. Tony won the coin toss and headed out on the lead. Tony was climbing well and got out onto the main face.

The day went on and on and on. A bunch of time went by. It was late afternoon already. I was feeling like a horse at the gate, and I wanted to go! I became more impatient when Tony fell on the face and was stuck.

Meanwhile, Leavitt was all over with the camera; he's running here, he's running there, telling Tony, "Wait now! Don't go yet! Stop there! Hang out a minute! I gotta get up here!"

At some point, I lost it and yelled up to Tony, "I'd like to get a shot at this BEFORE THE SUN GOES DOWN!"

Tony let me lower him down, and I pulled the cord. I was so amped when I got on the thing; the next thing I knew, I was at the top. The perfect lighting that evening resulted in Leavitt getting a shot of me that made it to the cover of *Mountain Magazine 145*[1]. That was the Titanic.

Mountain Magazine 145

Reflections

That was a critical moment for me. However, I had already realized my true calling while establishing "Rapunzel" (aka Nirvana) at Castle Rocks in Sequoia. Many years had passed since Charlie Knapp showed me the way to the Castles. During that trip, I had seen a crystal band rising up the massive wall of The Fin to a black water streak. I had envisioned a route there. Returning to climb that route was a realization of that dream. That adventure of climbing a first ascent in the wilderness defined who I was as a climber.

As my grandfather had taught me that you get out of life what you put into it, I believe the same goes for climbing. The rewards of accomplishing climbs like the Titanic or Carson-Oma couldn't have happened without training and a firm commitment to a ground-up style of climbing; it was about the adventure and the unknown. It was like, "Man! Am I gonna be able to stand on that thing? It looks like I can stand on it? I hope I can stand on it? I'm gonna go...Oh, watch me! Good God! Watch me! 'Scared to death...then you push through it and you stand on this thing and it's like, O.K., I'm gonna try to drill...I gotta drill. I ain't going any farther!" It made it so much better. You could never feel the same accomplishment by previewing and placing protection bolts from the top down. I think that those that do are cheating themselves.

After many years of climbing, my heart and soul stand firm in the belief of "First Ascent Achievement." The climber that rises to the occasion to do the first ascent, who pulls courage out of their soul to meet the challenge, deserves that their achievement remain unspoiled. A person adding bolts to an established route would rob themselves of that challenge and alter the achievement of that first ascent forever. Adding protection bolts to a previously established route is grand theft of that First Ascent Achievement. The stone stands in mute testimony to their passing, and the route they had created forever becomes the physical record of who they were on that day, at that moment in time. In respect of those moments, preserving the truth is precious; it's all we've got. Don't cheat yourself, and don't cheat the climber who risked it all. If you must, set a top rope on it, but perhaps you may reconsider and wait for another time when you can climb it and rise to the challenge. You must be willing to risk a loss to obtain success and willing to risk a fall to obtain a summit. You get out of life what you put into it. Do another pull up, work harder, work smarter, be your best, your very best. The only thing to fear is dying without truly living fully. BE BOLD, MY FRIENDS!

Ron Carson on the 1st ascent of Chemo Therapy, Dome Rock. Photo: Ron Carson Collection

2

VERTICAL AND WANDERING FLOW

By Dave Ohst

The Quest

To begin, consider a wandering and often confusing collection of tangibles, mysteries, and questions. Risk, technique, trials, fear, euphoria, mindset and confidence, swords, knights, wizards, King Arthur, the Holy Grail, and Spain in the 1600s – all and more are likely seeds of adventure's memories, realities, and dreams – suited uniquely to each of us.

Whether past, just in the moment or beyond – are adventure's tangible experiences the only important outcome or quest? Alternatively, are our experiences random and nebulous interpretations – built on vague combinations of imagination, motivations, and memory? Moving boldly to enable adventure, perhaps all these pull us forward into new quests. These complexities – real, imagined, interwoven, and/or divergent – are also perhaps just an intricate, sporadic, and wandering collection of Flow[1] – both lost and found.

With these uncertainties spinning, what exactly are the vibrant essentials of adventure in the vertical world and elsewhere? Where is the beginning, and where is the end? What's at the core across time, grace, elegant movement, fear, and elation – regardless of beginning or end?

- Are our vertical experiences transitory glimpses of answers never truly found, or
- Do they create a more lasting ethos embedded in our souls, to perpetually draw on, or
- Are they perhaps a complex hybrid, only partially knowable, something in between fleeting and enduring?

No matter the path or the answers, the quest therein provides adventure's endless attraction – a Holy Grail search, at times forming momentary yet indelible diamonds. John Long directly or obliquely catches fragments or essence, with this very fine writing:

Bishop Peak: Where It All Began Jeff Lang in 1978 – Jeff also proved that he could solo 5.6 rotten stairs. Photo: Dave Obst

- *"Through many epics did we find him, having followed the plumb line mostly, but not owing to our route finding skills, but rather because the Stonemaster had sought us all along. By no other means could you find that island, where the young and the strong alight, for a month or a year, and jump as far as they can. Every old Stonemaster knows the place. We too had pushed past fear, in the search for something truly worthy of our love, and we still feel the wind in our faces. Now in other haunts and in other ways we might still jump beyond ourselves. But, only the young can live on those craggy shores, and we would land there no more."[2]*

Flow fits Vertical adventure well. It's partially captured as a focused absorption of bold confidence, born from a delicate and clever balance – of risk, challenge and difficulty, critically poised just a tick greater than

technique and skill. Consequently, jumping beyond is essential and captivating. As well, clever balance is egalitarian and democratic – where
regardless of skill level, preparation and technique meet opportunity.
Therein is the dance – where fleeting Flow creates soaring elation, grace,
and poise in the groove. This is perhaps adventure's core – something
truly worthy of our love – whether in a tempest, sunlight, or anything in
between.

Such quests, a wandering synthesis of various seeds, drew friends and
I to the magnetic Southern Sierra Nevada – on more than one occasion,
in the early years and a bit beyond. These were, of course, but only in
part Quixotic pursuits for Flow and the Grail – mostly in the groping
days, before we even knew what we were after, and when consistent 5.10
remained challenging and never semi-casual. The results of these
escapades were also naturally mixed and rather vague, thus confirming
adventure's start and end as transitory and ephemeral. With much
greater certainty, what also materialized was a partially unexplainable
tenet of sparkling confidence – forever a poignant and indelible emul-
sion. In the joy and fear of the moment, or maybe in retrospect – it eventually dawned on us that this ethos would always be a guiding light and a
foundation of who we were and are.

- *"And still, men who by guts and skill had mastered the farthest
  wilderness, they must have had a way of standing and a look in their
  eyes. While they scanned the faces of white men, their glance took in
  the movement of river and willows, of backdrop and distance. While
  they talked as men talk of nearing home, and meeting someone newly
  come from there, their minds watched a scroll of forever-changing
  images. What they had done, what they had seen, heard, felt and
  feared – the places, the sounds, the colors, the cold, the darkness, the
  emptiness, the bleakness, the beauty. Till they died, this stream of
  memory would set them apart, if imperceptibly to anyone but
  themselves, from everyone else. For they had crossed the continent and
  come back, the first of all."* — Bernard DeVoto, from The Course
  of Empire

A Central Coast Crucible

I first met Tobin Sorenson[3] and Richard Leversee in San Luis Obispo about 1975, give or take. Other than Ed Sampson introducing me to Tobin, the objects of our crossed paths have faded into the mists of time – save for one object – local rhyolite-dacite rock. The Nine Sisters are a string of volcanic plugs spread between Morro Rock and San Luis Obispo, California. Scattered within this group are some climbs – sophisticated and challenging enough to pursue Flow and the Grail. This is only true if you can partially break free from a college education at Cal Poly – easy enough for a small cadre of 20 year-olds. However, this was not simply boisterous collegiate relief. It was arguably more. That is, fine and bold adventures across the following decade were enabled simply by circumstantial luck – a "Right Stuff" mix of time, place, youth, challenge, personalities, and atomic energy – with a touch of Tobin's extraordinary power, acting as contagious encouragement. This courageous energy was the legacy of the Stonemasters spreading in the world. As such, these good vibrations were quickly absorbed and then adapted uniquely – to our own sensibilities, priorities, and new found goals.

Hollister Peak, North Buttress – February 1978. Photo: Dave Ohst

Naturally then, Bishop Peak, immediately bordering San Luis Obispo, became an early crucible. As well, just down the road, other rock soon beaconed – most notably the graceful and virgin North Buttress of

Hollister Peak, one of the best lines on the Central Coast. The trouble was and is that the peak was and is on private ranch land. The draw was too powerful, however, and a clandestine first ascent of the North Buttress was accomplished with Jeff Lang. This adventure became a key pivot for chasing Flow into the Southern Sierra Nevada and beyond – but not for the reason you might expect.

The pivot instead was what became the unexpected final pitch. On the descent of Hollister Peak's easy south side – just as we were passing a very dilapidated and long-abandoned ranch house – two pick-up trucks appeared across the open fields. There was nowhere to hide, except for a quick free solo up partial, rotten, and decaying stairs, to the second story. Worse yet, the trucks drove up to the house, complete with two dogs, and set up a picnic. The dogs soon sniffed us out. They naturally started barking, trying hard to goad the lawless intruders into hopeful flight and a joyous chase for them. Fortuitously, Jeff and I were: well hid, out of reach, very quiet, and not that stupid. Thankfully, neither paws nor cowboy boots could negotiate rotten 5.6 stairs, and no ladder was about. Later, still undiscovered and after a lifetime of gripping uncertainty, the picnic finally ends. Just as it does, and within our hidden view, the rancher's wife trots over to the backside of the house and takes a dump! This was very good news because the dogs were finally put off the scent. As the trucks disappeared over the ridge with dogs obediently in tow, we down climb the last pitch and high tail it to our prearranged and secret ride home. If there has been a second or third ascent, no one has told!

Emboldened by this adventure and also by good climbs with Ed and Richard – soon fresh ideals naively found no rock too imposing. Consequently, the drive for greater Holy Grails took hold, leading us to Dome Rock, the Needles, El Capitan, Homer's Nose, the Sierra Nevada crest, and countless other summits with intriguing, challenging, and magnetic exposures. In all of these vertical wanderings, we were sometimes intelligent enough to uncover impeccable Flow and joy. We were, as well, also stupid and naive enough to create foolish epics in search of it. Therein was and remains the magic of adventure, with both joy and epic necessary for successful progress – a hybrid mix in a different way.

Accordingly, here are three gems, shedding perhaps a bit more light on the mist.

- *"Our doubts are traitors, that make us lose the good we oft might win by fearing to attempt.* — William Shakespeare

- *"Anything done well and with care exempts itself from fear."* — William Shakespeare

- *"All men dream, but not equally. Those who dream by night, in the dusty recesses of their minds, wake in the day to find that it was vanity. But, the dreamers of the day are dangerous men, for they may act their dream with open eyes, to make it possible."* — T.E. Lawrence

Dome Rock Discoveries

As the small world of Central Coast rock became a bit too repetitive, Richard easily convinced us to visit the Needles and Dome Rock, both adjacent to the former hamlet of Quaking Aspen in the Southern Sierra Nevada. Known for his infectious enthusiasm, sometimes very much so, Richard persuaded Jeff and I to join him for a new line on Warlock Needle, for which Jeff and I had zero familiarity. It was October 1977. Engineering school was in full swing and difficult at best. So, not being completely foolish, I convinced Richard that a weekend of warm-up climbing at Dome Rock was in order. This would also enable a reconnoiter of the new Warlock route. I decided to pack a pair of binoculars – thinking that two full and limited weekend days at Dome Rock would not allow any time to hike to the base of the Warlock. I was right.

In 1977, Dome Rock proved instantly contagious, largely because it was still relatively undiscovered and full of fabulous potential for first ascents. So, on that first weekend, we rapidly became familiar with Dome's ubiquitous chicken heads and classic lines. It was an absolute blast – very much a case of white punks run amuck on rock

The Needles & Voodoo Dome from Dome Rock, The perpetrator Warlock is just left of Voodoo Dome. Photo: Kristian Solem

dope. This was so much so that we paid little attention to our Warlock reconnoiter plans.

Then, as things were winding down, I broke out the binoculars and handed them to Richard. From the summit of Dome Rock, there is a clean and uninterrupted view of the Needles. With a careful visual reconnoiter, Richard was very much chagrined in short order. Because he spotted two dots on Warlock – boldly creating one of the finest climbs in the Southern Sierra Nevada, if not far wider – Romantic Warrior.

This sighting prompted an immediate and hell-bent drive from Dome Rock to the Needles road head. We walked and ran to the Needles fire lookout, atop Magician Needle, racing the day. Shouts connected with E.C. Joe and John Peca, with badass encouragement following - wishing Flow and steel. As twilight added enchanted and mystic energy between Magician Needle and the imposing Warlock, we departed. Critical; however, the electric and stunning élan of those moments enabled a new, enlightening and powerful magic. What a very, very fine moment that was for us to observe and indelibly absorb. The first ascent of Romantic Warrior by E.C. and John was – very bold, done with impeccable style, and inspirational. Beyond my imagination and dreams, this image, forever enduring, created an expanding vision, which was to subsequently carry me to El Capitan and far beyond.

Not long after, I was fortunate enough to do about half a dozen first ascents at Dome, with Richard, as part of a splendid upward progression. Those were blissful blue days under a diamond sky, on diamond rock, with Flow found. Among these, I count Close to the Edge, Satyr, and The Lightning's Hand, as three memorable first ascents. By any measure, however, they all paled in comparison to a much finer line. Bravo, E.C., and John for an innovative vision that will remain forever timeless! We need much more of this ethical steel today.

Prehistoric and Timeless Needles Classics – A Yosemite Antithesis

Pristine wilderness has evolved since prehistory – diminishing over time and changing the face of adventure accordingly. Here is a modern example. In the 1970s, climbing in Yosemite Valley was fabulous, in the immediate wake of the bold and captivating routes of the 1960s. Despite the draw and challenge of these climbs and their expanding ideals – education, work, crowds, and regulations tempered my stays to no more than a week or two. As well, exploring beyond Yosemite became increasingly attractive, as familiarity and skill brought success within Yosemite. This was especially so when fantastic and prehistoric routes could be found in the Southern Sierra Nevada and beyond. So, my own development relied on the Valley primarily for long climbs, with the odd short free climb thrown in, as time permitted.

Saytr 1st Ascent - Diamond Rock under a Diamond, Sky Dave Obst on the 2nd Pitch – July 1980. Photo: Richard Leversee, Dave Obst Collection

As a case in point, after a variety of long and progressive climbs around the Valley, some done in one day, the Nose route on El Capitan finally made the agenda. This was a bit in reverse, as the Nose is sometimes a first big wall. Rather, it was my last in the Valley since adventure beyond beaconed. Because the Nose was at the end of the sequence, the climb turned out to be easy and enjoyable. Upon our return to the Valley late in the day, we walked to El Cap Meadow to retrieve my partner's Ford van. In those days of somewhat less regulation, it was possible to park overnight at El Cap Meadow, so long as you were not camping. This was convenient for climbing El Capitan, and that is exactly what we did. We returned to find the van stolen and much of our gear with it. With no choice except to return to Camp 4 – we reported the theft and called friends for a ride. A poor night was then spent bivouacking in the Camp 4 dirt. Idealized by Steve Roper and other 1960s notables, as counter-culture nirvana – our Camp 4 bivouac comically proven otherwise. After which, the draw of alternatives looked even better.

One of the best and beguiling solutions was the Needles in the Southern Sierra Nevada. Mesmerizing Needle magic was enduring because there were very few people and no thieves about. This was not primordial wilderness, but it felt close. The climbs were equal to and most times better than Yosemite – pristine, prehistoric, plumb, and largely undiscovered. Yes, that's right, it was better than Yosemite.

I was also very fortunate, early on, to fall in with Richard Leversee and E.C. Joe, both of whom had the necessary inside knowledge, as there was no Needles guidebook. A very early ascent of White Punks on Dope (WPOD) with Richard was an eye-opening first outing. WPOD was and remains a

The Last Pitch of the Nose on El Capitan – Enjoying the Exposure and Blissfully Unaware of Impending Dirt Doom. Photo: Gary Clark, Dave Ohst Collection

pearl. Sometimes described as the finest moderate route in California — the route required diverse techniques across cracks, overhangs, and faces. This was only the beginning, as the Needles proved ideal to refine the dance – an interesting progression of new techniques learned and bungled. Critical as well, peaceful and remote adventure, the converse of dirt and crowds, added addicting and primeval elegance.

WPOD, Igor Unchained, the S-Crack, Imaginary Voyage, the Spell, Innersanctum, Yellow Brick Road, and many other classics served to refine technique. Reciprocally, advancing technique cemented continuous excitement for our private collection of diamond routes. What a glorious antithesis to Camp 4 this was! As a result, Yosemite was less and less visited, and then only rarely. Yet, at the same time, mental comparisons to Yosemite standards and test pieces were a constant and indispensable part of technique evolutions. As these comparisons gradually faded, we realized that our technique was rather honed and no longer

A De Rigueur Rugby Shirt Summiting Warlock Needle after the S-Crack. Photo: Kim Grandfield, Dave Ohst Collection

required Yosemite peer pressure to improve. This was a very good thing because we had escaped the trap of comparison with all of its shortcomings.

We became impulsive and independent, very grateful to have experienced Yosemite's tests, but glad to be free of them. Plus, the solitude of the Needles created an atmosphere similar to an

upper-crust London club – not snobbish in any way, but rather magical, a lucky honor – befitting the Sorcerer's vibrations found there. By a combination of luck and meticulous technique, King Arthur's Wizard, Merlin, had invited us to the Round Table, and we gratefully accepted. The resulting evolution empowered the acceleration of noble adventure in many dimensions. Now with both Excalibur and the Holy Grail as Flow objectives, the horizon expanded again.

Heart of Gold, a short first ascent on Magician Needle with Richard Leversee, was a modest example. The second pitch began with moderate face climbing – quite run out to a first bolt,

Witch Needle – Igor Unchained Drop-Dead Blonde Stone Matches Gold Joy. Photo: Gary Clark, Dave Ohst Collection

in order to maximize clean style and ethics. Past this first bolt, upward progress was out of the question. Traversing right and then up was the only option. On continuously decreasing thin edges and small pockets, it was soon impossible to retreat – a classic case of overload and overcommitment. Of course, this medieval sword was precisely what we were after – another fine and private route for the Round Table collection. 40 feet out from the first bolt, desperation took hold. The drill came out to place a second bolt. Balancing precariously, the drill only just came out. In the days before sticky rubber footwear, my right foot continuously oozed off a small edge, the only hold preventing dire consequences. To quote John Long, "Thank God I didn't rip!" An eternity later, after many manual hammer blows on the drill, the bolt was finally in – making for a very morally solid two-bolt pitch. Richard loudly and continuously announced expletives prior to arriving at the second bolt because the traverse created ripper potential for him, as well. Then Richard cried out, upon arriving at said bolt, "You drilled from this edge — F—ME!" Subsequently, Heart of Gold proved average compared to other Needles diamonds. However, the joy of refined technique and unwavering clean principles created another bright benchmark.

Flow was found again, but the swords extracted from the side of Magician Needle and other spires were never Excalibur, and the Grail remained missing. Despite perceived Round Table knighthood, questions remained. Where was this all leading? Knight-errant confusion mocked us, as it had Don Quixote in Spain over 300 years before. Were we correct in our adventures and conservative society not so? Was a transitory and mythical Merlin simply of our own making? Similarly, were we merely arrogant and egotistical?

- *"Nothing Venture, Nothing Win"*— Sir Edmund Hillary KBE – Knight Commander of the Order of the British Empire – and a modern rather than an errant one.

In Hillary's case, the Queen properly conferred knighthood. We were confident about our skills, but risks and uncertainties remained, knighthood included. In the end, the circumstantial "Right Stuff" luck, born on California's Central Coast, proved more powerful than any old Spanish questions – perhaps brazenly so. We carried on, and in hindsight, correctly. Judgment was progressively refined, and risk was very carefully calculated – to craft occasional Flow, intrepid aces, and fine wins from time to time. At the same time, questionable and idealistic knighthood lingered and goaded, and then eventually faded, along with self-doubt. Perhaps, after all, it was properly conferred, and we had, in fact, sighted Merlin. This was subsequently confirmed by cold steel, a fine example of which was Keeler Needle.

Keeler Needle – Cold Steel, Dave's Story

Sublime and Spectacular Alpine Gems – Unnamed Pillars above the North Fork of Lone Pine Creek. Photo: Dave Obst

Deciding on and then committing to any significant climb usually takes a little time, sometimes more and sometimes less. It is a mental negotiation of perhaps dreams. Is the challenge/skill mix appropriate and dead-on now, is my partner equally solid, et cetera? As youthful exuberance slowly or maybe never yields to a different maturity, decision and commitment evolve, regardless. Such was the case with Keeler Needle. By 1980, after a host of adventures and misadventures, the negotiation was easier – because the previous clean confidence matured to cold steel – becoming colder and harder as time passed. Thus, risk became easier to judge but never certain. Keeler Needle twisted all of this and raised the bar once again, which was really the whole point.

Alpine environments challenge more, as opposed to predictable, modest, and easy access roadside crags, such as El Capitan. True wilderness always adds a great bit of extra spice – remote, weather, altitude, rockfall, et cetera. This was certainly the case with Keeler Needle. However, the largest unknown was simply the route itself. In 1976, Steve Roper authored a guidebook to the Sierra Nevada, including a plethora of technical climbs, missing from the previous 1972 peak bagger guide. Note, in the adjacent photos, two key words

in the titles – *Climber's* and *Mountaineer's*, respectively. In other words, the all-encompassing power of 1960s Yosemite chutzpah rapidly eclipsed the peak bagger generation. Note also that Day and Keeler Needles are just left of Mount Whitney's summit on Steve Roper's cover. Thus, legacy and reputation were conferred and implied – adding motivation.

Also, in the early and mid-1970s, a similar and parallel eclipse was about. The power of the 1960s Yosemite pioneers – Robbins, Harding,

Chouinard, Pratt, Roper, et al. – was passing to
the Stonemasters – Bachar, Kauk, Long, Acco-
mazzo, Sorenson, et al. This was simply a
natural progression of generations. So, what did
Steve Roper do? He moved on from Yosemite
Valley to the greater Sierra Nevada, as countless
other old codgers have done as well. The
trouble was – there were so many new climbs
added to the Roper guidebook that descriptions were much abbreviated within 380 small
pages. This was likely on purpose to retain
mystery and support adventure. Cutting to the
chase, here is Steve Roper's voluminous four-
sentence description of the Harding Route on
Keeler Needle.

- *"Although in no way could these formations
  be called separate mountains, their east faces
  contain some of the finest big wall climbs in
  the range. The face of Keeler Needle is rated V
  5.10 A3. This route lies in the obvious crack
  system just right of the Day-Keeler couloir.
  Most of the route goes free and the climb has been done in one day."*

*Generations Pass... Photos:
Dave Obst*

So, Mr. Roper's succinctness was all that we had in 1980. Did we
bother to contact any Bishop, California locals, to ferret out more information? No! By this time – after El Capitan, Mount Watkins, Half
Dome, et cetera, we just knew. Thankfully, this emotional and possibly
rash commitment was without epic.

Consequently, in August, as Kim Grandfield and I hiked up the north
fork of Lone Pine Creek, the whole venture took on the air of a first
ascent. Despite the fact that we just knew – known-unknowns, as well as
unknown-unknowns, spun in our heads. Early the next morning, the
confidence and drive born of icy steel prevailed. Fortuitously the climb
was a diamond, a brilliant example of Warren Harding's bold ambition.
Correctly, and with sixth senses honed on prior big walls, we sorted the
path well when things became less than obvious. The rhythm was unique

and a joy. A big wall feel with big exposure was real. As well, so were moderate pitches, which we romped up at full alpine speed. What a fantastic combination this was and remains.

Shortly afterward, I decided to make a topo of the climb, essentially a diagram of the route. Written descriptions were fine but became rather flawed if the route was long and complex. So, the new topo greatly

The Start of the Harding Route, before Global Warming – August 1980, Complete with GPIW tee shirt as homage. Photo: Kim Grandfield, Dave Ohst Collection

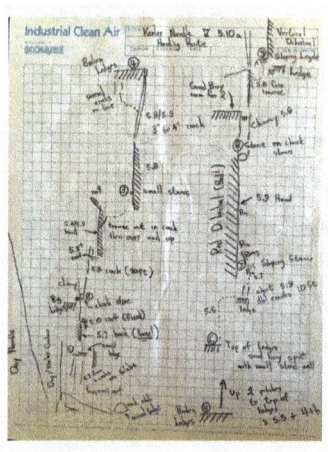

overwhelmed Steve Roper's minuscule and bullshit description. Not to kill adventure with detail, the topo was mostly the result of Richard Leversee's pestering. That is, after he heard of our success, he became rather manic and incessant in a good way, as only Richard could. In the process, I told him a few stories about how bitchin' it was, just to amp up the situation. Richard nearly went berserk! "I am doing that climb. Draw me the topo now, and you better not sandbag me!" I obliged one of my best friends – thinking carefully as I did, to create accuracy.

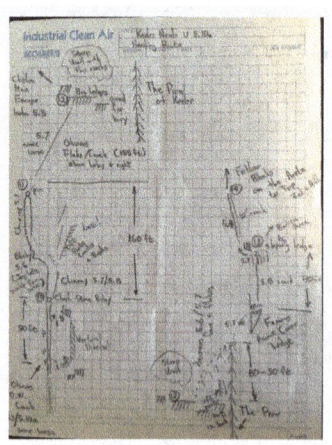

In the process, I also resisted a known and powerful urge to sandbag, something I was infamous for. In the finest traditions of Steve Roper brevity, a few half-truths tempted me in order to maintain some level of mystique and challenge. Richard looked at the topo and was instantly very suspicious, particularly about my description of pitch 14. With a touch of lurking fear, he probed, "How is it even remotely possible, that a clean 12-inch crack can be 5.4 ?" I smiled and said nothing. Richard remained suspicious, having been burned previously. Regardless, drawn to the irresistible sweep of steep arête, he seized the topo and called E.C. Joe. When Richard returned from his success with E.C., the topo was complimented, "Dave Ohst has phenomenal memory !" That is, E.C.'s and Richard's ascent was also born of cold steel, but with a twist.

E.C.'s Story

Richard Leversee and I committed to climb Keeler Needle in 1981 after Dave Ohst infectiously told us what a gem it was – "... one of the finest routes of my life." Plus, with Dave's encouragement, the two of us planned to climb the 2,000-foot wall in one day! "If you toss the bivy gear and use my topo, it will go in one day."

Superb Sierra Granite – the 5.10 Roof on the 3rd Pitch. Photo: Kim Grandfield, Dave Ohst Collection

Keeler Needle's stunning east face is split by an elegant and imposing arête, creating a gorgeous plumb line of a climb – just left of the commanding east face of Mount Whitney. Keeler Needle was also very special because it was – a difficult wilderness free climb with a 14,000-foot summit, was seldom done because of reputation, and had been climbed in one day maybe a couple of times. Plus, as additional motivation Galen Rowell, Warren Harding, and other Yosemite pioneers had been there, thus creating an obligatory and coveted rite of passage.

We camped in the moraine below Iceberg Lake, directly below Keeler Needle's soaring and captivating arête. When we arrived, two guys were already camped out, with the intent of climbing the same route. They had all of their gear organized - like a picture from the 1st ascent of the Salathé Wall on El Capitan: pitons, bivy gear, and all kinds of big wall paraphernalia. Keeler's reputation was definitely in their heads, too much so perhaps. We chatted and shared that we planned to climb the Harding Route. They seemed in no hurry and were unsurprised when we told them that we were leaving very early at O-Dark-Thirty.

The Red Dihedral – Arguably Never Better. Photo: Kim Grandfield, Dave Obst Collection

We were climbing before dawn's light had touched the summit in order to avoid rockfall from adjacent gullies. The climb was magnificent and did not disappoint – soaring hand cracks, an off-width 5.10 crux at 13,000 feet, and more. In the Red Dihedral, Richard yelled with prodigious excitement – "This is what fantastic rock climbing is all about !" Remaining amped up, we soon gained the summit.

We greeted the guys upon our return, late that same day. They were amazed that we had climbed the route in one day. However, they really were stunned after the conversation turned to my new 10mm single rope. "And that's the rope you guys used?" one guy asked. Before this climb, we had never used a single rope as thin, so it was new to us as well. I could see by their expressions, thoughts of "Gulp ...Yikes!" When I mentioned that this was the ONLY rope we brought, they turned pale – as the excess reality of nearly impossible retreat sunk in. Then we casually walked to our moraine camp, fueled up, and sacked out.

The next morning, as we were almost ready to pack out, they peeked around the corner, "Oh, we thought you guys would be hanging-out, polishing your stainless steel testicles."

So, contrasting these two ascents, was the topo a correct choice? Instead, was Steve Roper's abbreviation of Keeler Needle appropriate in preserving mystery and reputation? In one regard, the topo enabled a fine one-day ascent. In another, primeval elegance was lost. Somewhere in between – E.C. and Richard's solid balance of ethics, audaciousness, speed, and proper topo use was vital – to preserve adventure and thus enable a hint of the Grail. Therein, for both ascents, Merlin's conferral of Knighthood was, in fact, no illusion. It was real and correct, after all. Sorcery was well performed, an errant Don Quixote was long dead, and Flow was well

El Capitan – Salathé Wall 1979
Gripping Reality, Poignant Ephemeral
Dreams and Tangible Success. Photo:
Ed Sampson, Dave Obst Collection

found. Instead, as chivalrous knights, should E.C. and Richard have just known and therefore tossed the topo? Nah, they had a fun hog blast with it! Correctly, as medieval duty demanded, they rightfully and perfectly stepped up the game. Plus, that clean 12 inch crack on pitch 14 was, in fact, no harder than 5.4 – thus adding just enough mystery and fear, but also tarnishing an infamous reputation, as well!

Perspectives – A Desperado Philosophy

"As for small difficulties and worrying, prospects of sudden disaster, perils of life and limb – all these and even death itself, seemed to him only sly good natured hits, jolly punches in the side bestowed by an unseen and unaccountable old joker. There is nothing like the perils of wilderness to breed this free and easy sort of genial desperado philosophy." — Herman Melville

Over the years, our wandering searches for Flow, Merlin, Excalibur, The Holy Grail, and Don Quixote – became part of a magnificent and unforgettable collection of wild, vertical, and elegant rock faces, arêtes, and walls – touched by starlight, tempest, diamond sky, wispy enchanted clouds, and occasional transient grace. In hindsight, the climbs were easy enough to find. Uncovering the rest was rather a bit more difficult.

Mt. Athabasca – North Face Ice Instead of Rock in 1981. Photo: Dave Obst

Across time, on some occasions – miraculously, swords were extricated from the rock and ice to successfully slay impending doom – and thus, they continuously honed techniques of cold steel. These weapons, deftly applied to adventure, were never Excalibur. Hence, we never became Kings of the Realm. Knights of the Realm were more than sufficient – since occasional, misty, and transitory glimpses of Merlin, Don Quixote, and the Holy Grail were magically empowering. Across this very broad and complex spectrum of gripping reality and poignant ephemeral dreams, there was also tangible success. Beyond the occasional sword forged, we also forged who we are – a solid and priceless ethos – a concrete way of standing ethically tall across space and time. Vertical adventure had made us forever different. We could very consciously and efficiently differentiate real from fake risk and manage it to stay alive. A core confidence, born of cold steel, calmly made us imperceptibly different to anyone, except ourselves, from everyone else. This never vain or arrogant exception was critical to life well-lived, both in the vertical world and beyond it. There was great depth to draw on in any crisis, different than others perceived or imagined was there. As such, the deeper meanings of risk and adventure – with only intermittent Flow, but with consistent success – became forever an ally.

Very naturally, jumping beyond ourselves became ingrained in our desperado souls. Exploration, victory, epic, and failure evolved beyond the Southern Sierra Nevada and also when the mountains were distant. Therefore, from this story's early question, the more complex hybrid mix proved very solid and correct for answers – never truly found, continuously fleeting, partially knowable, or indelible tenets.

3

SANDBAG OF THE CENTURY

AN ASCENT OF IGOR UNCHAINED

by E.C. Joe

The definition of the term "sandbag" as excerpted from the American Heritage Dictionary:

sand·bag

3. Slang c. *To downplay or misrepresent one's ability in a game or activity in order to deceive (someone), especially in gambling: sandbagged the pool player by playing poorly in the first game when stakes were low*

Needles Dawn. Photo: E.C. Joe

A View from the Top

During a blue-grey dawn, I remember the view of the surreal granite spires of the Needles. The vantage point from the comfort of my sleeping bag atop Dome Rock a few miles away proved to be inspirational and daunting. Indeed, that view was a catalyst for many rock climbers' dreams. However, that view had not prepared me for witnessing the Needles first hand or experiencing their actual intensity and magical beauty.

Curiosity had me taking a closer look via a trail to the upper Needles that started at the end of a narrow dirt road that branched off what was known as the Great Western Divide Highway. The hike was quite remarkable in itself since it garnered views of a neighboring spire, the "Hermit," along with Mount Whitney, Mount Langley, and adjacent fourteen thousand foot peaks of the Sierra crest. Our casual stroll took the better part of an hour to reach our destination.

The Needles Lookout. Photo: E.C. Joe

The Westernmost Needle had a most peculiar structure on its
summit explicitly placed as a fire lookout. Constructed in 1937 with
materials packed in on horseback, this single-room "cabin" sat precariously on top of its summit blocks and defied any practical reasoning
whatsoever. As viewed from the trail, the lookout and its foundation
appeared to be like how Noah's Ark looked up on top of Mount Ararat
after the Great Flood. The end of the trail led us to an airy stairway of
weathered angle iron, adorned with chain link fence, concrete, and
creaky wood planks that wound their way up small craggy buttresses to
the lookout.

I spent a great deal of my time on the lookout tower's catwalk gazing
through the telescope mounted there. The walls were astonishingly beautiful; white granite accented in the colors of gold, black and yellow. The
Needles' vertical spires stunned me with their mysterious shapes, colors,
and surreal beauty.

A few years before my visit, many of the Needles had been climbed
for the very first time. Fred Beckey, famous for pioneering first ascents,
had spent some time amongst these walls and, with various partners,
climbed a new route on every significant escarpment. They too, had been
influenced by the Needles' surreal nature. The names that they had
chosen for the spires truly reflect the Needles' intimidating power: the
Magician, Djin, Sorcerer, Charlatan, Witch, Warlock, and Voodoo Dome.

The seasonal resident of the lookout tower, Dave, the "lookout," was
the unofficial caretaker of a "rudimentary" guidebook to the Needles.
Rudimentary meant an old binder with handwritten drawings and
descriptions of climbs at the Needles that was maintained and utilized by
whosoever felt the need to do so. It was kept in the lookout tower and
was "open source." The guide mainly cataloged the recent first ascents
but not the original "Beckey" routes. Many of the routes had yet to be
repeated, which explained the absence of information about those
climbs. This lack of knowledge helped fuel whatever fears of the
unknown that we may have had, and those fears made us seriously question our motives for climbing there.

I viewed the most striking line that day from the lookout, and someone had recently climbed it. It was on the Witch Needle and was called "Igor Unchained." As seen from the lookout, The Witch appears as a vertical, pyramidal-shaped wall, enhanced with beautiful black and yellow lichens. Igor Unchained consisted of crack systems that took the center stage near the middle of that wall and topped out just left of the true summit.

"What an outrageous line!" I exclaimed. "The guide here shows that it's only 5.8! No Fucking Way! That almost looks like aid from here."

A Safe Haven

After the Needles visit, it was easy to retreat to "The Slabs." Kern Slabs is a small 200+ foot "low angle" slab. Nonetheless, this venue harbored a variety of challenging routes. Many local climbers frequented Kern Slabs on any given weekend. It represented a safe haven for many of us who began our climbing experience there. The Slabs area was a convenient place to climb or boulder and a suitable place to find a climbing partner or share experiences.

While most of us were still figuring out what we were doing on the rock, John McGee had already found his niche. John started climbing at the same time as me. He had a natural talent for climbing and a cool head to back it up. At the time, the rest of us were too timid to share his vision. Whether we liked it or not, some of us were to follow John's example.

John became a regular partner of an experienced local climber, Joel Matta. Right away, they established two challenging test pieces on the Slabs: "A Piece of Cake" and "Cornflakes." I eventually repeated (falling in the process) these routes. Only then I came to realize that the style, spirit,

Kern Slabs. Photo: E.C. Joe

and boldness

John McGee on the 1st Ascent of Just Lovely, Dome Rock. Photo: E.C. Joe

that those climbs represented were to be part of my future. Soon after that, I joined them on some new adventures into the unexplored regions of the Lower Kern Canyon. Then within that first year, John abruptly quit climbing in favor of a new spouse. That was unfortunate for the climbing community to lose his energy. Of course, we did what he would have liked us to continue doing -- and that was to go climbing!

Ordeal by Fire

We learned to climb without the convenience of a guidebook. It was no big deal not to have a guidebook, as none existed for our territory. So, how can you miss what you don't have? For our small band of newbies, the real issue came down to find out who had the willingness and desire to lead. If the tourists only knew when they asked, "How do they get the ropes up there?" that we were wondering the same thing.

Joel Matta. Photo: E.C. Joe

Eventually, our overwhelming desire to climb got us to the base of the rocks. Our skill set was still developing, so it had to be by sheer determination that we got to the top of many of these crags, unfettered by the suffering that comes with wilderness climbing, perhaps because wilderness climbing was the norm and not the exception.

A few excerpts from Doug Robinson's article, *"The Whole Natural Art of Protection,"* published in the 1972 Chouinard Equipment catalog, became our "Mantra." If we held fast to it, everything else was supposed to come together after that:

"Where protection is not assured by a usable crack long unprotected runouts sometimes result, and the leader of commitment must be prepared to accept the risks and alternatives which are only too well defined. Personal qualities - judgment, concentration, boldness - the ordeal by fire, take precedence, as they should, over mere hardware."

-- *"But every climb is not for every climber; the ultimate climbs are not democratic. The fortunate climbs protect themselves by being unprotectable and remain a challenge that can be solved only by boldness and commitment backed solidly by technique. Climbs that are forced clean by the application of boldness should be similarly respected, lest a climber be guilty of destroying a line for the future's capable climbers to satisfy his impatient ego in the present -- by waiting he might become one of the future capables. Waiting is also necessary; every climb has its time, which need not be today."*

-- *"And having the humility to back off rather than continue in bad style - - a thing well begun is not lost. The experience cannot be taken away. By such a system there can never again be 'last great problems' but only 'next great problems.'"*

McEastwood

"New blood" showed up at the Slabs one day. I had never witnessed anyone close the lid of the trunk of their car with their rock hammer before. This was Guy Thompson. Guy had a brash, although likable friendly character. Some of the locals thought Guy, with his "Clint" kinda look, along with his outspoken qualities, reminded them of John McGee and earned him the nickname "McEastwood"...

Joel quit climbing due to a bad shoulder and a new commitment to an orthopedic practice. My pool of local partners wore thin. Many of the group seemed all too content to stay at the Slabs. I was ready for a new partner. Guy was keen to perform his part of climbing duties of trading leads and to drive. We hit it off well, and in short order, we did some repeats of some recent first ascents and made a successful trip to Joshua

Tree. Without a second thought, early that spring, Guy and I hiked into the Needles.

"...it's only 5.8!"

It was early spring of 1977, and the lookout tower was unoccupied. The

tower was locked and boarded up. It was just the Needles and us. The first route we climbed was the long, elegant buttress of the Magician. Due to the lack of sufficient information on the climb, we just started at the very bottom. The extreme toe of the long buttress was not where the existing ten pitch route was supposed to start, but we eventually got back on track. Climbing the additional seven or eight rope lengths up the spine of the Magician made for a pretty long but fun day.

Guy Thompson. Photo: E.C. Joe

Our next objective was "Igor Unchained" on the Witch Needle. The view from the base was wilder than I had imagined. The first two pitches had been entirely hidden from the view from the tower! They were not as steep as the summit pitch and they stood cold, grey, and ominous in the early morning shadows. We were both intimidated. Guy quickly conceded all the leads on Igor to me due to my "experience." We tried to convince ourselves that the route was rated "only" 5.8, so it shouldn't be as tough as it looked.

Carefully, we organized our tools for the task: One 11 mm by 45-meter rope, one set of Chouinard Stoppers, sizes 1 thru 8 (by the way, those are all the sizes that were available back then), one set of Chouinard Hexentrics, sizes 1 thru 11, twenty carabiners, eight 12" by 9/16 slings and ten 24" by 1" slings. Our E.B. climbing shoes were usually the last item to put on since they typically were very uncomfortable.

Nervously, I set forth. The first few moves seemed a bit awkward, and after reaching a tiny stance to rest on, I got in a good Stopper. Assessing the pitch above, I realized that I would have to be very careful in choosing the type and quantity of my protection due to the length and the continuous width of the cracks ahead. Most of the pitch above was a straight-in crack in a left-leaning corner. Even though the angle of the pitch was not too steep, the angle of the corner made for very strenuous climbing; relentless, above the shoulder hand/finger jams and continuous stemming out with my left foot. Hand jam, finger jam, stem, toe jam, hand jam, hand jam, stem, toe jam, finger jam, hand jam, stem, toe jam.

The main crack bottomed out into a shallow groove at a point just about mid-way up the pitch. I used my only #8 Hex in a spot before this section. It was a bittersweet moment. The Hex was a super good piece, but the better crack above the appeared to be #8 size for a long way. I sure would have liked two more #8 Hexes! I struggled to figure out the moves through this section, fearing the impending runout ahead. I was just about to peel off when somehow I stayed on the rock by pinching a bizarre knob that was on the outside edge of the corner. This move allowed me to reach good jams

Rack Du Jour. Photo: Joel Matta, E.C. Joe Collection

above the groove. Fortunately, I still had some energy left. It was a long way before I could get some protection, but the jams were solid, and the moves were not as physical as below. As I approached the belay stance, the crack widened up a bit, forcing me to use up the rest of the big pieces on my rack. At the stance, I had barely enough gear remaining on my rack to build a belay anchor, and I pretty much used up the entire length of the rope. The rusty fixed piton at the belay did not instill much confidence over placing my own gear, but I used it anyway. Guy followed and remarked on how I had appeared to fly up to grasp the knob at the groove. I was just glad I could utilize it at the moment that I had needed it.

"That was one helluva 5.8!" I exclaimed.

Had this been an indication of future events for the next two pitches? Anticipation of what lay ahead was undoubtedly a dreadful thought. I was concerned but kept a "poker face." Guy and I re-racked the gear efficiently, careful not to drop anything. We were still in the cool shadow of the morning while the sun teased us by warming the spires and every-thing else across the way. The second lead was obscured by a three-foot roof directly above the belay stance. The only way of passing this obstacle appeared to be via the straight-in wide crack through the roof. Moving over this giant step required me to throw my right arm and shoulder into the crack, followed by my right foot. I was able to toss a huge Hexentric back in the crack and clip my rope into it for protection. It was as much of a curse as it was a blessing. In wide cracks, the protec-tion and the rope become yet another obstacle to climb around.

"Give me some slack, Dammit!" I urgently ordered Guy, but at the exact moment, I realized that my knee was trapping the rope in the crack, "Shee-it." Remember, be nice to your belayer!

Just as I was turning the lip of the roof, I discovered a tiny black knob out to the left for my foot. It was good to be over that part! The pitch above was a darkish, low-angle ramp. The difficulty eased for many moves; face climbing with some good jams. Eventually, the route appeared to go out left to bypass some small overhangs and a scary loose-looking block. It wasn't easy to place any reliable protection before turning the corner. I had to settle for faith in the one good piece that I set before my traverse. After committing to the moves around the corner, it became apparent that protection possibilities diminished for a distance.

The climbing difficulty in this section did not look trivial, especially with the prospects of a long, tumbling fall back into the corner below. I did my best to stall to assess and re-assess my situation, even though my situation was "only too well defined." Then, as my tunnel vision cleared, I noticed a small seam on the wall of the corner to my right. I used my cleaning tool to remove soil and a couple of loose crystals, discovering a "usable crack." I have to say, that was one of the best #1 Stopper place-ments that I had ever seen. Nonetheless, this didn't instill a morsel of confidence.

At this point, I guess I was either too tired to balance there or too scared to down climb; sometimes, the instinct for survival beats out any higher reasoning, "In all of the excitement, I don't remember whether I placed five pieces or six. That's when you start asking yourself, do you feel lucky...Well, do ya...? Shut-up! You've got protection. Get your ass up there!"

The thin face climbing up the corner, combined with sketchy protection, had been challenging indeed. Above, the reward was some welcome hand jams and easier scrambling to a belay niche at the base of the final headwall pitch. For Guy, following these pitches had not been as remarkable an experience for him as it was for me. There is a significant difference between being on the "sharp end" of the rope versus following the leader. Leading is a climbing experience requiring focus, skill, and wit to deal with nothing else but the moment at hand. Following, with a top rope, no matter how difficult the climbing, is just climbing.

Guy and I were nested in a triangular niche; formed by the intersection of two of the major cracks that split the great wall of the Witch Needle. The final lead on the headwall loomed overhead with a huge granite block that jutted out over the brink. Was it loose? I would soon find out since there was no way around it. I flung the rack out of the way several times as I stemmed up the overhanging wall. I whimpered as I surmounted the evil block, then stood on its top edge. Sticking out like a hound's tooth, I'd have to avoid falling on it too. The protection was excellent, so I set off in a wild vertical layback to a spot where I could then bury my appendages into the crack for not only a physical but psychological rest as well.

The climbing was steep, the moves, for the most part, continuously difficult. However, the excellent crack began to get sparse. I could visualize where I was on the upper wall. If I were to view myself from afar, I was smack dab in the center of the brilliantly yellow lichens-covered wall of the Witch. Unfortunately, while in her grasp, I could not appreciate her beauty, only her obstinacy. Medium-sized Stoppers seem to be solid in the intermittent crack. It was good pro but left barely enough room for my fingertips! There was a scant amount of holds to make my passage; a fingertip jam on my right every four feet or so and the slightest face climbing holds to balance upon the remainder of the section. It was a relief to pass a roof with big jug holds on and around it. There was even a nice stance above it as well! Of course, I had not finished the lead. It was not over yet.

The final cracks to the summit area were thin. The wall was covered in black leafy-like lichens that, when disturbed, tended to blind the perpetrator temporarily. The finger locks were superb, but the footholds elusive, often hiding under the lichens. Then, I realized that I was low on gear—many of the much-needed medium stoppers for this section I had used below. Whatever I left on my rack to place, I had to make the best of it. Above, the primary crack that I was blissfully following soon ended. A tenuous move to another crack that curiously started to the right of where the other had ended got me onto the home stretch. Soon, I heard Guy down below announcing that I was entirely out of rope, just as I placed a belay anchor below the summit slabs. Guy climbed up, retrieving virtually my whole rack from the route below. Once on the summit, we signed the register, a notebook with a pencil in an old cookie tin. There we gazed around at the Needles with newfound respect and reflected on our grand adventure.

Author's Note: *After their first ascent of Igor Unchained in August of 1976, Herb Laeger and Paul Clark had rated the climb 5.8. Today, the route is known for being 5.9+. In my opinion, that was THE Sandbag of the Century.*

4

GOODBYE, YELLOW BRICK ROAD
SOUTHERN SIERRA FOLKLORE

By Randy Powers

Rock climbing in the early 1970s was remarkable. The popularity of climbing and the advancement of the gear were ramping up. Decades ago, I started climbing the granite cliffs in the Southern Sierra. The Needles area was the crown jewel: an esteemed destination for many world-class climbers. For me, these climbing experiences became a mental and physical paradox juiced with adrenaline, fear, and ecstasy.

Recently, I was doing a Google Search: "Climbing at the Needles." One account was about some crack-wedged bottle that contributed to a rescue of a climber. That info got my attention because the legend is incorrect. I know, as my partner and I lived that story 48 years ago. That day, a person we had barely met brainstormed and executed a brilliant solo rescue that saved our butts. But this story really begins earlier, when a young free-spirited rock climber named David Peck introduced me to rock climbing.

David had limited rock climbing experience, and I had none. We managed to scrounge up a sparse array of used climbing gear from dropout climbers and the local Army Surplus store. We didn't even have Stoppers. Our gear rack consisted of a few wedges and chocks from older

European climbing companies, and nothing would fit a crack larger than 2.5 inches wide. One of the most essential items I bought with my slim budget was a used 11 mm kernmantle rope. David's climbing attire consisted of some bohemian threads and Royal Robbins Yosemite boots.

As for me, I climbed in a pair of new E.B.s and some leather knickers I'd scored at a garage sale. We were weekend warriors doing our own thing, climbing established routes at Kern Slabs, Owl Rock, Parker Bluff, Dome Rock, and the Needles. At the Needles, we had even attempted a couple of times to establish a new free climbing route.

Later, David and I approached the upper Needles from the 2.5 mile trail that started at the road's end. The trail ended at the lookout tower atop the Magician Needle. There we met

David Peck, 1971. Photo: Janet Peck, David Peck Collection

Linda Adams, the fire watch attendee, and her boyfriend, John Newman. John was a climber, and he suggested that we climb the "Yellow Brick Road" route on the Wizard Needle. "Yellow Brick Road ascends this via varied, quintessential Needles climbing — face, off-width, thin (splitter) crack, and roof — all in two (or three) pitches."[1]. After we checked out a hand-drawn topo kept in a binder stored in the lookout, we decided to climb it. Being naive about wide cracks, we were clueless that we hadn't the gear to protect such a climb. Undaunted, we proceeded from the base of the lookout stairway, headed down the climbers' trail, and then the 3rd class approach to the base of the route. We both tied into the ends of the rope using a bowline on a coil. David racked up the gear and started leading the pitch while I gave him a hip belay. Higher up, he started flailing and yelling about his boot getting stuck, deep within the off-width crack. He looked desperate and gripped, trapped in the crack with his last protection below him. I thought about my options. I couldn't just leave my sole partner. Our situation was desperate with no solutions. With seemingly no alternatives, David, anchored to nothing except for a solidly planted boot, belayed me so I could climb up to assist him. Soon, I stood in an etrier off of his last piece of protection and wrestled with his boot to no avail. I couldn't free that damn Royal Robbins boot.

Randy Powers. Photo: E.C. Joe

Much time had passed while I continued to struggle to extricate him from the crack. Then, John appeared overhead. John had heard our pleas for help and assessed our predicament. He rappelled down from the summit with a bottle of dish soap. After giving the boot a thorough soaking, John was able to dislodge it from the crack. John returned to the summit and offered his rope to bring us up. Thank God he belayed us to safety. Next, we set up a rappel anchor and knotted our ropes together. After some manly hugs, we each rappelled singly down to the adjacent notch between the spires. This humbling experience weighed heavily on David and me as we hiked out of the Needles.

Thinking back, David and I were a mess. We climbed together for only a couple of years, self-inflicting more harrowing experiences on ourselves due to our lack of experience. However, by the end of our climbing partnership, we had pioneered routes on Voodoo Dome, the Watchtower, and Moro Rock in obscurity. We just wanted to climb and never thought to report them, adventures that only David and I can appreciate. At some point, David gravitated to San Francisco, where he promoted and managed potential high-level politicians.

As for me, I stuck around and was able to hook up with some fantastic and solid climbers by hanging out at Bigfoot Mountaineering in Bakersfield. I was lucky. That network was a total game-changer. I continued to climb in the Southern Sierra on and off for about 20 years.

In closing, I suggest if you ever climb the Yellow Brick Road and notice that tattle-tale bottle of dish soap laying deep inside the off-width crack, you might want to ponder your situation.

The Bottle. Photo Steph Abegg

5

THE PEARL OF GREAT PRICE
CLIMBING THE OBSCURE

By E.C. Joe

"Again, the kingdom of heaven is like unto a merchant man, seeking goodly pearls: Who, when he had found one pearl of great price, went and sold all that he had, and bought it." — Matthew 13:45-46, King James Version

I t wasn't long into my climbing experience that I had learned the joy and excitement of seeking out the "obscure." The southern-most end of the Sierra Nevada near the South Fork of the Kern River was suitable for such a quest, harboring a bounty of rock climbing spots rarely visited by humans. Its arid climatic environment allowed me to stretch my climbing season into the autumn through the spring months when snow in the high country made it impassable or just too cold. There's nothing like catching warm rays of the sun on a crisp winter day. You know, the lizards were on to something; lazily basking on sunny rocks and cooling off with an occasional set of seemingly effortless push-ups. Some compare the Domeland to Joshua Tree National Park or even a Tuolumne Meadows "in the sage."

The Canebrake. Photo: E.C. Joe

Like those areas, the variety of climbing is intriguing. In contrast, Domeland is isolated and remote, factors making it potentially unforgiving. The areas within and adjacent to the Domeland Wilderness offer only the most committed climbers an endless playground.

Richard Leversee, on the summit of White Dome. Church Domes are visible in the distance. Photo: E.C. Joe

Some of the earliest ascents date back to probably the 1950s. Church Dome and its adjacent area have become quite popular, due to its easy access from a road nearby. Indeed, this is an exception to the rule. Typically, most of these "Pearl(s) of Great Price" are guarded by long trudges into *true* wilderness, where one must seriously assess their risks. The risks were multiple: *where the hell are we, will we find anything of note, can we climb what we find, what if one of us gets injured, or will we lose faith and flame out?* Traveling there was not a big wall adventure in Yosemite or elsewhere; instead, it was an antithesis. The rewards are significant to those who can put forth the effort to venture there.

Steve Brower and I were no strangers to adversity, being employed by the Department of Corrections. Steve supervised an inmate laundry, and I managed the inmate canteen. It was a world unkind to both of our spirits. All it took was Steve, then a non-climber, to show interest in going climbing, to create an escape catalyst from the angst of our jobs. Steve and I worked similar shifts, so we were able to sort our schedules simply enough. Since I was always keen on exploring new areas and rocks, especially with a willing partner, Steve's fate was unwittingly sealed before he even knew what fate awaited. Sometimes being clueless is a good thing.

During an early trial run, I set the hook. We had run out of water on our climb of a new route on Voodoo Dome at the Needles. It was not intentional, but once in motion, the hook came out. We slogged our parched asses and gear over to the Witch/Sorcerer Notch, where I told Steve, "Hold on, man, I'll be right back." I returned with a rusty hulk that once was a large can of Del Monte® sliced cling peaches in syrup that I had cached years before in the woods.

Steve looked at the rusted can with its tattered and bleached label incredulously, "We can't eat *that!*"

"Don't worry, it'll be just like brand new," as I pulled out my P-38, "self-customized" can opener with a 3/32" cable loop for securement on the vertical.

What was that gold-tinged light that Vincent Vega was basking in, emitting from inside Marcellus Wallace's suitcase? It *had* to have been an open can of sliced peaches! I peeled back that rusty lid to reveal a veritable pot of gold, just like new.

Relieved, Steve couldn't contain himself, "Those were the *best* sliced peaches I've *ever* had! You SAVED MY LIFE!"

Steve had been metaphorically speaking. Competent partners must be vigilant to protect each other from risk and danger without flinching. Earlier, the same day, I had gotten myself into a ridiculous situation of an imminent ground fall while forging that new route on Voodoo Dome. Having climbed circuitously above the first protection bolt with no alternative to reverse my moves, I had to continue to the next stance to place another bolt. I could easily do the math; a fall before or at the next stance equaled me crashing to the ground. I alerted Steve, who was belaying on the ground.

"If I pitch off, you need to hold on to the rope and run downhill!" This statement later made for excellent campfire fodder, a memory of our synchronistic experience. We jokingly named the route, "Momma Told Me Not to Come." Hook, line, and sinker, Steve was ready for more in the Domeland.

The only available resources about Domeland climbing at the time were random entries in climbing periodicals like *Ascent*, the *American Alpine Journal*, or token articles in magazines as *Off Belay* or *Summit*. And even then, one would have to be paying attention in the absence of Google Search. Amazingly, from these usually ambiguous descriptions, we were able to find and climb numerous gems and establish a few significant climbs of our own.

The "North Domes," Domeland Wilderness. Photo: E.C. Joe

Naturally, a reasonably benign magazine article, "Climbing in the Domeland Wilderness," sparked my interest in a new route established on Columbia Dome by the authors, Dick Richardson, and his partner Andy Solow. Their adventure was magnetic because they had spent some serious time in the wilderness to establish this technically difficult route. Initial explorations to new territory typically produce a route that is *the* most natural line or the easiest to climb; however, this route did not fit that description. I was curious to see what was "between the lines" of the article.

In the early-'80s, access to Domeland was allowed into the area via a few four-wheel-drive roads. Roads through a wilderness area were perhaps the result of the multi-agency jurisdiction and confusion between the U. S. Forest Service and the Bureau of Land Management. In our case, this was a good thing, since later they extended the wilderness boundary. Once extended, it required serious recalculation of wilderness travel logistics. Even so, we still had a few miles of schlepping our water, food, climbing, and bivouac gear as close to the dome as possible.

We backpacked from around Trout Creek to the north of Columbia Dome, leaving Steve's truck behind. After taking advantage of the freshwater from Trout Creek, we meandered through the sparse pinyon pine and sage landscape to the south towards the dome. The journey was silent save for our heavy breathing and the rhythmic crunching of the granitic soil at our feet. The pilgrimage of the backcountry climber can be full of doubts of the unknown; no guidebook, no beta, no Google, only a few cryptic and vague paragraphs. Near the dome, we ditched all but the essentials for climbing and made for our objective: "Kaopectate Blues." With a name like that, what could go wrong?

Through climbing's lengthy history, anyone establishing a route somehow took license to name the climb to catalog it into the minds of the climbing community, guidebooks, or to define it from other rivaling creations. Traditionally, most used lame monikers that merely depicted a route's position, as "The Northwest Face," et cetera. However, over time, choosing more playful names; a name of a popular song, a state of mind, a play on words to perhaps describe a feature of that particular climb, or something that represented a significant event during the ascent. As we were to discover, Kaopectate Blues was fortunately *not* named for the latter.

Once at the dome's base, a long and prominent crack system elegantly stood out and matched our vague description. Finding where the route went to get to the crack was difficult. I knew that the first ascent team had climbed up the face and placed bolts for protection, but damn if I could spot any. The bolt hangers were challenging to see while looking directly at the face because their color, a tarnished silver, blended in with the surrounding rock. Then, I remembered to use a little "trickery." Standing with my face next to the slab, I scanned with a "lizard eye's view." Bingo! I spotted one, then another, like little shark-fins cutting the surface of the sea of stone.

Wow! Let's climb this thing! The initial face climbing was mid-5.10, and the rock was friable. Above the first few bolts, the slab steepened, and there were two evenly spaced aluminum dowels sticking out in a line going towards a horizontal quartz dike. Here, the original ascent team was not able to free climb past this section. So they drilled a hole, inserted an aluminum dowel, then smashed it with a hammer to deform the dowel into the hole, and then bent the remaining exposed part upward into a crude hook shape -- twice. Dowels are marginal to support a leader's body weight. A "technology" occasionally used on "big aid walls" to advance up blank sections of rock, dowels have a slim chance to be strong enough to hold a fall. The bolts and especially the dowels used back then for drilled anchors were designed for construction, not climbing. Bolts, drills, and dowels were cobbled together from the local hardware store. Only the bolt hangers had been custom designed to work with one's choice of a bolt, so the bolt could be attached to the rope via a carabiner to arrest a fall.

I attempted to free the dowel section multiple times to no avail, taking many falls onto the bolt below the dowels. The steeper angled flakey rock proved impossible for me to negotiate. I begrudgingly resorted to "big wall" mode. Tapping into my El Capitan experience, I hitched a nylon sling to the bolt hanger and stood in it to reach the first dowel. The dowel had loosened over time, and I easily plucked it out of the hole. Yikes! Being careful not to drop it, I reinserted it, slung and stood upon it, then gingerly repeated the task with the second dowel. I had on my big wall pants; stay focused, make no false moves, and once you've got all of your weight onto a piece of shit, "Fuggedaboutit!" and work on your next task. From the second dowel, I could free climb to surmount the dike and secure my rope to another bolt for protection. Beyond that was a long, tricky, and unprotected traverse left on the quartz dike to a bolt belay anchor. Handholds on this section were scant. It required precise footwork on the slimy dike. Carefully, I advanced by crossing one foot around the other, performing a bizarre ballet on the stone. Once at the belay, I could see the glorious crack system on the next lead; it appeared to have no end.

Steve had difficulty following on the crumbling holds, as he tried to rely on his hands too much instead of his feet. During his self-inflicted frustration, I jested several times that he had pried off enough holds that the route probably went up a few grades in difficulty. At the first dowel,

Steve was able to pull up on each sling I had left in place. Once he grabbed the sling on the bolt above the dike, Steve was in flight. Without a sound, the bolt sheared off, and Steve, hardware, and hanger in hand fell in a wild 30+ foot arc from a position almost level with me to hanging directly below the belay. Steve's face expressed sheer terror akin to a "Hans Gruber Memorial Exit." Shaken but unscathed, Steve required lots of rope tension to get him up the blank slab to the belay. We were able to laugh about it afterward, and like the rusty peach can, Steve had yet another souvenir to bring home. On a serious note, this was a grim reminder about the rumored "bad batch" of 1/4" Rawl Drive bolts manu-factured around 1975; they were out there. I'm positive that was one of those bolts.

While climbing the slab below had been a bit punishing, the endless crack became our absolution. The price of entry was fierce. Now, past the threshold, we entered a world of unbe-lievable treasure. Wow, what lay before us was hundreds of feet of moderate finger to hand-width size cracks on near-perfect granite! There was absolutely no other climb like it in the Southern Sierra. After each pitch, I'd sit at

Kaopectate Blues. Photo: Richard Shore

the belay with a "shit-eating grin," having enjoyed climbing every move. Leading, I relished it even more as I had expended nearly every piece of gear of my climbing rack. Our summit visit filled our minds with vistas of future places to explore, and for a moment in time, we were the masters of our universe. Steve and I swaggered our way back to our bivouac site, perhaps feeling as if we had won a "Pearl of Great Price," and maybe we had. The only thing for certain was that our journey to that moment was priceless.

6

BLUES FOR THE WILDERNESS

DOMELAND

By Brandon Thau

"The Domeland Wilderness is known for its many granite domes and unique geologic formations. This semi-arid to arid country has elevations ranging from 3,000 to 9,730 feet. Vegetation is mostly pinyon pine and sagebrush...The Dome Land Wilderness covers 94,695 acres of the southeast part of the Kern Plateau." — *USDA, Forest Service*

What do you take when your tummy doesn't feel right? Or when you need to find a bathroom quick, or will it be a clean-up on aisle #6 incident? Kaopectate®, of course! These two thoughts came to mind when I first read the route name "Kaopectate Blues" in the Domeland guidebook. This route is on Columbia Dome, located in the isolated Domeland of the Southern Sierra. All the information provided by the guidebook was a hand-drawn topo and a distant black and white photo of Columbia Dome, Domeland's largest dome. Besides that, nothing seemed intriguing about this route. It was on an obscure dome that I hadn't visited yet and named after an over-the-counter pharmaceutical. Since there were only two existing routes on this colossal dome, I figured there was ample opportunity to establish a new route. If I walked by Kaopectate Blues and it looked terrible, like the name insinuates, at least I'd have a chance to put up a new route. The trip would be a "win" either way. I called another fellow obscurist, Richard Shore, and we made plans to hike in and visit this dome for a few days.

The Splitter Crack of Return to Forever, Radiant Dome. Photo:Jim Marchesini, E.C. Joe Collection

A previous visit to the north Domeland almost cost me a relationship with my girlfriend. In Spring of 1997, Matt Pollard, Jen Seidman, Greg Vernon, and my then-girlfriend Cris Engel started our eight-mile hike from Kennedy Meadows. The air temperature was warm enough to wear shorts but patchy, and icy snow still covered the ground. Traveling was tedious; as one took a step on the snow, your foot would punch through the crust and scrape your bare calves. Then as an insult to injury, the underlying thorny bushes would stab and scratch them as well. It was not a very enjoyable hike. Matt and Jen were engaged to be married later that year. Matt made the smart move and bailed out on the misery after a few miles. Greg and I pushed on, with Cris justifiably complaining and repeatedly stopping in protest. Greg moved far ahead while I stayed back to try and motivate Cris to keep hiking. She still quotes me saying, "You're not going to make me bail, are you?" Those familiar with the "Ten Commandments of Spousal Communication" will realize that this comment didn't go over well, and the predicted argument ensued. I didn't know until later that she was about to break up with me right there, abandon me and hike out, forever banished to the company of my climbing partner and my gear.

Temporarily resolving our grievances, we eventually made it to Radiant Dome and climbed for a few days. We enjoyed climbing the warm white granite on Radiant Dome. We repeated the awesome Loominosity (5.11) face climb to the "splitter" second pitch finger crack of Return to Forever (5.10). We also completed a new route of our own and were inspired to start on another one. Cris eventually forgave me, and we were married several years later. Despite this emotional roller coaster trip to Domeland, I aspired to return to check out route possibilities on the other domes.

After 22 years, I was finally ready to venture back into the north Domeland with a willing partner. Richard and I loaded up with topo maps, climbing equipment, and food for three days. We started from the trailhead marked on the map but were soon bushwhacking through a trail overgrown with whitethorn and foxtails. After losing the path a couple of times, we were able to regain it by using a map app on my phone. It became apparent that not many people had traveled through here. This aspect made the area more attractive to our experience. The trail was as wide as a dirt road and then almost disappeared into the brush or a creek crossing. After about an hour of hiking, we got a view of a large exposed granite dome that we assumed was Columbia Dome.

It was not one single dome; it had a large main face and a sub-dome to the left. It was not obvious where our chosen route, Kaopectate Blues, was located. We followed the established trails to a point closest to the dome, then broke away and hiked cross-country towards the face. About two hours had passed since we left the car, and we established a camp near a creek at the base of the steep, sandy slope leading up to the dome. It was late September, and the stream was barely flowing. The water had a red tinge to it from the algae growing in it. Fortunately, I brought a water filter to make this a viable water source. After setting up our camp and hanging up our food from the bears, we collected our climbing gear and started heading up toward the base of the dome.

Richard and I arrived at the base of the main dome and scanned for any evidence of the climbing routes. We knew from the topo in the guidebook that Kaopectate Blues (5.10, A1, or 5.11) had bolts on the first pitch and that these should be easy to spot from the ground. However, we found no bolts on the main face. Hoping to locate the route still, we scrambled left towards the sub-dome. As we traversed the base, nothing looked especially noteworthy. Then, we turned the final corner of the sub-dome, and an obvious route appeared. Rising from a bed of pine needles was a steep, white, granite slab speckled with dark lichen that contained a splitter finger to hand size crack that went on for hundreds of feet. Without a doubt, we had found Kaopectate Blues, and it looked fantastic! It was so obvious; maybe that's why there wasn't detailed information about it in the guidebook.

Richard Shore on the 5.11 start of Kaopectate Blues. Photo: Brandon Thau

Kaopectate Blues was first climbed in 1976, the year I was born. The initial slab is virtually blank and lacks easily climbable features. Judging by the topo, the first ascent party free climbed and then used a couple of aluminum dowels for aid, then free climbed again to gain the crack system. Once in the crack, they free climbed the route at a 5.9 difficulty. In 1992, likely the 3rd ascent of the route, a team was able to directly free climb to the start of the crack system. This variation involved difficult slab climbing (5.11), entails smearing on a blank slab with an occasional edge or knob, placing three protection bolts in the process. Richard and I chose to take the free climbing way; it was the apparent natural path to the crack.

I was the first to leave the ground on lead. Being this far in the backcountry, with no other people nearby and no cell signal, was *not* a good place to get injured. Here, one has to climb their best while being mindful of the risks. You have to be aware of which limits to push to maintain a feeling of reckless abandon, climbing freely, with no restraint. This free-variation of the route was very thin, tedious, and sometimes grainy. Upon completing the final thin slab move, I was able to grab the flake that started the crack system. I placed a cam for protection and went for my first finger-lock in the crack. All of a sudden, I felt a sharp pain from my fingertips and under my fingernails. I pulled my digits out of the crack to see multiple dried

pine needles sticking out of them. Since no one had climbed this route for 27 years, dead pine needles now clogged the crack system deposited from an adjacent tree. Pine needles filled the next 30 feet of crack. I didn't want to experience this finger torture anymore, so I hung on a cam while I cleaned the crack ahead of me with a nut tool, all the way to the first belay

Kaopectate Blues. Photo: Richard Shore

spot. Afterward, I lowered down and was able to enjoy climbing a pain-free crack.

Richard led the 2nd pitch, which widened into a perfect, straight-in crack. Fortunately for him, this crack was immaculate. The crack stayed a consistent width for most of the rope length. Richard had to conserve his gear by running out sections to have enough for the whole pitch. It's unusual to have such a continuous, hand-sized splitter crack on granite. This pitch alone makes Kaopectate Blues well worth the hike out to this wilderness. Richard belayed on a small perch while hanging on his belay anchors.

Arriving at the belay, I handed over the backpack, racked up the gear on to my harness, and started up the 3rd pitch. The crack continued as a steep, hand-sized splitter and trended right over the blank face and away from Richard at the belay. About 20 feet up, I encountered a section labeled "loose blocks" on the climbing topo; two torso-sized blocks stacked on top of each other in the crack. They were leaning outwards and didn't look stable at all. I contemplated climbing around them; however, I was concerned my rope would pull against them or acciden-tally touch them. There just wasn't an easy way to climb around them, as I needed to use the crack that was behind the blocks. I know previous parties had climbed past them, but perhaps the blocks had moved out further in the last 27 years. I didn't feel comfortable climbing past the blocks, so I would try and remove them. Luckily, I was not climbing directly above Richard, so there was a low chance these blocks would hit him at the belay. However, I was concerned that these blocks might fall towards me and cut my rope when I pushed them off. Therefore, I placed a cam and tied off to it directly, in case my rope were to be cut. I tried to move my rope and body out of the potential fall zone. I told Richard to tuck into the crack at the belay as much as possible. I mentally double-checked my plan. Domeland was *not* a place to get hurt and need a rescue. Once I felt comfortable, I took my hammer and pried the blocks away from the dome. It didn't take much effort, and I sent hundreds of pounds of granite tumbling to the dome's base. I scraped away some of the dirt and flakes from the rock scar, happy to see that the splitter crack continued—no more concern for loose blocks ahead.

Brandon Thau on Kaopectate Blues. Photo: Richard Shore

Richard and I continued up the final pitches and stood on top of Columbia Dome. We gazed out at the desolate expanse of the Dome-land. It was a dry landscape, with pine trees and occasional clusters of rock. Some of the rock outcroppings are small and low-angle, but others are hundreds of feet tall and steep. The best part of the view is the virtual lack of visible civilization. There is great beauty in this desolation. I could just make out a reflection from a window near Kennedy Meadows and a fire lookout on top of Bald Mountain. We continued to relax and try to identify the other known climbing formations in the Domeland. We could see the backside of Bart Dome, one of the backcountry jewels in the Southern Sierra. Closer to us, we recognized Radiant Dome, Steamship Rock, and Moon Dome, beckoning us to return to the "north domes." We packed up our gear. We encountered a large rattlesnake laid out across our path during our walk down the backside of the dome. We paused to appreciate the snake and reminded ourselves again; this is *not* a place to get hurt. We carefully passed and headed for camp.

The following day, Richard and I hiked up to the base of Columbia Dome, this time to establish a new route of our own. If a route as good as Kaopectate Blues existed on this dome, we would have been happy to find one that was half as good. We spent the entire day climbing a new line called Imodium A0 (5.12-, A0), about a hundred yards to the right of Kaopectate Blues. This four-pitch route followed a mix of crack and face features, with the crux being long reaches between black knobs. I had the pleasure of leading this pitch, which started as moderate climbing on a pleasant face covered in "chickenheads," gargoyle-shaped knobs that remain after the softer granite erodes away. Eventually, the face steepens, the chickenheads disappear, and black knobs become the only feature that links up to the hand crack above. Unable to free climb this section, I stepped into slings to aid up to the crack. I climbed another 60 feet and established a belay. With his 6'5" wingspan, Richard made a much better attempt at connecting the moves between the knobs. I'm sure with some more effort; a subsequent team would be able to completely free climb this pitch. The name of our route was a comical tribute to Kaopectate Blues, and the "A0" acknowledges that our new line doesn't go completely free. Though it had some nice hand crack sections, it couldn't keep up with its neighbor's continuous, quality cracks. Tired from a long day of climbing, we returned to camp for our final night in the wilderness.

In the morning, we hiked to our cars which entailed gaining two thousand feet of elevation to meet Sherman Pass Road. We had a great time climbing the line, and thankfully we didn't feel sick to our stomachs while climbing it. I'm still curious why the route was named Kaopec-tate Blues. I still couldn't rationalize the name, except maybe someone on the first ascent party

Brandon Thau on Immodium Ao. Photo: Richard Shore

didn't bring a water filter and had to drink the stagnant water. Richard and I eventually arrived at the cars and reflected on what a great adventure we had. As Richard drove off, I realized it was still early in the day and decided to check out the one piece of civilization that I spotted from the top of Columbia Dome. I wondered if my low clearance city car would make it to the Bald Mountain fire lookout. Well, I tried to see how far I could get. The road was rough and twisty up the backside of Bald Mountain, and I was able to drive within a quarter-mile of the lookout before the road became impassable. Determined, I hiked the rest of the road up to the top of the peak and ascended the lookout stairs.

The views were incredible; Mt. Whitney far to the north and the entire Domeland Wilderness to the south. I could easily spot Columbia Dome a few miles to the south. The man in the lookout had spent all season living up there and many seasons in the past. He invited me in, and we started to chat. I told him that I had just spent a few days climbing on Columbia Dome and pointed it out to him. He was surprised that people went climbing out there. I pointed out a few more formations to him and asked if he had been hiking out there before. He said that he had only made a few trips out there to fish, even though he scans out over the Domeland every day for his job. Here's someone that looks over that landscape for a living and doesn't know about the fantastic climbing. I was pleased to hear this, reinforcing how lucky climbers are to have an area like the Domeland. It's hard to believe such a place exists for isolated, backcountry climbing adventure so close to the 2nd largest city in the United States, where I could get a hefty dose of adventure by climbing in the wilderness over a weekend.

It's much harder to keep a secret crag with the presence of Google

Earth, Instagram, and social networking on SuperTopo or Mountain Project. However, at least one thing has stayed the same; it takes motivation and hard work to hike into the backcountry to establish a new route or repeat an existing one. This aspect has not been made easier by technology. Technology has probably made it more difficult for people to leave the comfort of their local climbing gym or roadside crag to explore the Southern Sierra backcountry, secret crags hiding in plain sight.

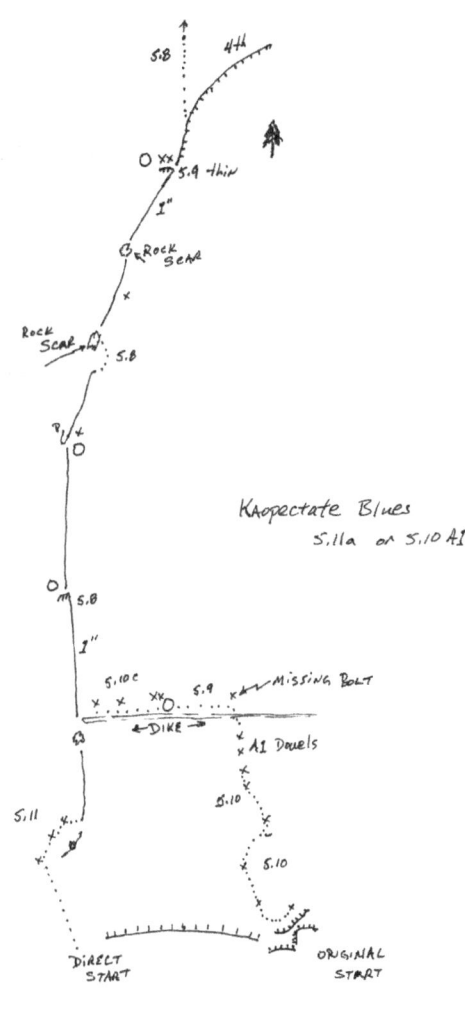

7

KING OF PAIN

By David Hickey

Unlike its world-famous neighbors, the Needles and Dome Rock, Parker Bluff is obscure and seldom visited. Maybe that's a good thing, because we know what happens when a climbing area becomes popular. Why Parker Bluff is obscure remains a mystery despite the fact that it harbors some of the most challenging slab climbs in the area. Parker Bluff's granite is as unique, as it is obscure.

The main escarpment has polished features more typical of crags in Yosemite than the Southern Sierra. The 400-foot high slab stands like a granite windshield adjacent to the defunct logging operation turned funky vacation trailer park of Johnsondale.

It was a clear and crisp day in September when James Cook and I hiked up to Parker Bluff. We carefully navigated the steep brushy trail well to the right side of the bluff, then contoured along the wooded area towards the center of the slab, that makes up the greatest part of the bluff. The terrain along the base was remarkably flat and pleasantly shaded by oak trees; a perfect place to drop our packs and rope up. I had been here about a year before with Eddie Joe after a trip to Bart Dome via Manter Meadow in Domeland was cut short.

I first met Eddie at Kern Slabs, a popular "weekender crag" a few miles up the Kern River from Kernville. He was looking for someone to climb with. I was new to climbing and gladly volunteered, well aware that he and Richard Leversee had co-authored the guidebook on the Kern and the Needles. After that, we climbed together frequently. I introduced him to climbing in Sequoia National Park where we teamed up to establish some fun and exciting first ascents. Eddie was relentless and very focused. He was on the lookout for potential climbs, and continually added them to his list when they caught his eye. It was a great time to be climbing in the Southern Sierra.

Eddie "EC" Joe. Photo: David Hickey

On the trip to Domeland, Eddie had the idea that if we left our sleeping bags and mats in the car and laid out ropes as insulation while sleeping with jackets and our legs in our empty packs, this would allow us to carry more climbing gear. It sounded good in theory. However, in practice, it was flawed, as we froze our asses. Despite the lack of sleep, we still climbed a couple routes. But after two nights of freezing bivouacs, we retreated to the car and the comfort of warm sleeping bags. We quickly recovered and set out to even the score for the lack of climbing in Domeland. Parker Bluff was our next destination with hopes of establishing a new route that Eddie had on his list. That new route became known as "King Of Pain" — led in admirable style by Eddie, and a wide eyed first ascent experience for me.

James Cook was one of those guys who had a natural ability for rock climbing. He had an easy-going personality that made him a good partner. We had been climbing for about the same amount of time and had nearly equal abilities leading on the "sharp end of the rope." James and I sorted though our gear while we contemplated climbing the second ascent of King Of Pain.

A route's mystique can change over time after subsequent ascents; as more information becomes known, the psychological challenge lowers. Seeking climbs in the wake of an original ascent can be curiously inspirational and addictive. Climbing a route's second ascent is not like doing the first ascent, but the experience is rewarding and exciting with fresh challenges. In other respects, the second ascent party gets to unofficially vet the route information for its reported quality, grade of difficulty, route finding, and gear selection.

I had already tried to climb the second ascent of King Of Pain with James, René Ardesch, and Art DeGoede months earlier in June. On that attempt, I took a 30+ foot slider off of the first pitch before the third protection bolt. I launched down the slab and incurred a "nice" road rash on my left thigh and the palm of one hand. I lowered to the ground to tend to my wounds and twisted psyche. James took a crack at it, and climbed to my high point protected by the rope up to the second bolt. Then with an intense effort, James made it to the first belay without falling. Rene and Art both followed the pitch. However, James decided that was enough for him that day, and rappelled back to the base. While packing for home, we discussed the difficult climbing and delved into a mystery: How in the Hell did Eddie stand to drill and place that third bolt? It was an insanely insecure stance, if one were to call it a stance.

James Cook on Moro Rock. Photo: E.C. Joe

Before our dreams of climbing King Of Pain would soon be transformed into procrastination, James rolled and lit a cigarette. He took a deep drag and slowly exhaled a cloud of smoke that hung long in the autumn air. "I'll take the first pitch," he said in an unconvincing tone. I didn't object, given my prior experience with that lead. James appeared solid as he made his way up the first pitch and only once called for the proverbial "Watch me!" before reaching the third bolt. On one delicate edge and smear after another, I felt strong and confident in my ability as I followed the pitch. Of course, being belayed from above didn't hurt! I clipped into the belay anchor and complimented James on a nice lead. James rolled his eyes jokingly, "'just a walk in the park." He added that he was not comfortable in a few spots, especially the runout sections.

Jame Cook on Pitch 1 of King Of Pain. Photo: René Ardesch

As I racked the gear to lead the second pitch, I reflected on Eddie's determination in climbing it. He was a man on a mission to push the climb to the top, a tour de force of concentration, a man on fire. The climbing was entirely on thin edges the size of dimes and quarters. He had placed four bolts on this pitch, all from the tiniest of stances. To place a bolt, Eddie would carefully balance his feet on thin edges at a place where he could have both hands free to work the drill and hammer. Then for 20 or 30 minutes, he would methodically bring the hammer up from a leash, hit the chisel-like drill three or four times, drop the hammer, reposition his feet and start over, "Tap, tap, tap... tap, tap, tap, tap... tap, tap, tap." Eventually, the hole was deep enough so he could place a bolt. Once protected by the bolt, Eddie didn't waste any time moving on, in search of another spot on the virtually smooth slab to repeat the desperate and painful task.

I surveyed the pitch above for the four protection bolts. My memory must have been playing tricks on me since the bolts were much further apart than I remembered, especially the vast distance from the fourth bolt to the belay. Perhaps it was the change in perspective. Now the reality was seriously different, compared to securely following Eddie's bold lead on the first ascent. Thoughts of my prior road rash did not help matters. Climbing with a top rope simply cannot prepare your mind, for leading on the sharp end.

James nodded and gave me a little grin of encouragement, then sealed my fate with, "On Belay." I worked my way up and to the right on thin edges to the first bolt. James focused on my every move just in case he had to pull in any slack in the rope in the event of a fall. Between next three bolts, I had to muster all my skill to climb virtually non-stop, thin move after thin move; edge, crimp, and smear in a ridiculous random order. At the end of each intricate section it was difficult to stand and clip into the protection bolt. I finally reached the fourth bolt, the last bolt before the belay. I peered up to see the belay was 40+ feet above and slightly left — a round, black, sloping, diorite knob set in a sea of white granite. Eddie once relayed to me a pithy climbers' expression,"When in doubt run it out," and no doubt, I *had* to run it out.

E.C. Joe headed for the "Little Black Knob in the Sun Belay," visible left of the center, on the horizon) on the 1st Ascent of King Of Pain.
Photo: David Hickey

Unfortunately, it was no place to hang around and take in the view. It was painful on the toes to remain on these wicked stances and less so to keep climbing. All my thoughts were focused on each move, from one tiny edge followed by delicate fingertip crimps, tenuously inching upward. Before I knew it, the belay was close to 10 feet away. The last delicate moves allowed me to finally get a hand on the black knob. This was hardly a respite, as I had to balance up on a teetering fingertip mantle to surmount the knob while facing a potential 80+ foot fall to meet James and possibly my Maker. I wasted no time and secured myself to the belay bolts. It had been an incredibly insane lead at the very limit of my ability. It was a great day to be alive!

James followed the pitch without any problems. Once he clipped into the anchor, we appreciatively analyzed the consistently thin face climbing. I felt inspired and asked James if I could lead the last pitch, if it was ok with him. James didn't protest, "That's good with me." The sun dropped behind the ridge and cast us in shadows with a noticeable drop in temperature. I expected smooth sailing to the top and proceeded up and past the first bolt. Instead, the rock steepened with the thinnest moves that day. This is not how I remembered it when I followed Eddie on the first ascent! Wow...once again I'd been deceived by the, "Top Rope Derangement Syndrome."

Climbing one move after another, I was amazed that I had moved upward and my feet stuck to the rock. It's important to focus on what's in front of you and not to look down — but I looked. The last bolt was some 30 feet below — looking was a bad idea, and there was still 15 feet to the next bolt. Damn! Looking down triggered a crazy mind game with emergent rational and irrational fears that temporarily dulled my focus. Compartmentalizing is an important skill for routes like this, if you can. As the angle of the rock started to lessen, I made it to a bolt at a surprisingly good stance and clipped in the rope, "Lucky boy, lucky boy..." I say under my breath. Then with a great sense of relief I shouted, "That was wild!"

The top was about 60 feet away with no protection bolts in sight. Fortunately, the climbing was easy compared to anything below. This runout section was a welcome relief and was quickly over. I set up an anchor and yelled, "Off Belay!" The autumn air became still and cold. I called, "On Belay!" to James who then made his way up the last pitch. Belaying the second was a convenient time for me to mentally detox and I enjoyed the view of the forest while reflecting on our adventure. When James arrived, he exclaimed, "I'm glad you led that!"

It had been a great day. Thinking back about climbing the 2nd ascent of King Of Pain (5.10d) will always bring a smile to my face as well as make my palms sweat. We coiled the rope and made our way down the descent where I could hear Eddie's words ring in my ear, "There must be boldness in climbing."

— Amen

David Hickey in the throes of "Jaws" at Parker Bluff. Photo: E.C. Joe

8

VALHALLA AND CHAOS THEORY

SEQUOIA NATIONAL PARK

By E.C. Joe

In the expansive view of "The Great Western Divide," east from the summit of Moro Rock in Sequoia National Park, one can make it out with the naked eye. The area described as "Valhalla" on the USGS topographic map is more familiarly known by climbers for its most prominent granite wall as "Angel Wings." As most views from afar, it's hard to have any perspective of what realities these distant halls of granite hold beyond the collective journals of the pioneers that had been there. And even with those accounts and the few photographs to tease one's imagination, climbing in Valhalla remains a fantasy to most.

"You Can't Always Get What You Want" — Keith Richards/Mick Jagger

Richard Leversee had been out to Valhalla to climb at least once. In the autumn of 1985, I agreed to travel back out there with him to check out new route possibilities on Angel Wings. Then, there were only three known routes on it, hopefully leaving us with plenty of opportunities to climb a line of our own. The hike to Valhalla is relatively easy, straightforward, however long, but doable in a day. And even if we didn't climb anything, it was a beautiful area to backpack in; an alpine setting of granite, clear lakes, and pine trees. Autumn in the Sierra is exceptionally serene; the air is cold and still in the morning, with a crispness that hints at the winter months to come. On the other hand, the autumn afternoons can be invitingly toasty for lounging and pleasantly devoid of human activity. We settled in at Hamilton Lake and spent the evening scouting our prospects from its excellent vantage point to the wall.

The immense granite wall of Angel Wings is only one of the usual pair, but I figured that it was aptly named because "Angel Wing" doesn't sound right. The wall was a whopping 2,000 feet high. It swept towards the sky, a granite wing terminating in a series of spectacular summit towers rising just like primary feathers on its avian counterpart. It was breathtaking as it was daunting. Perhaps, like the Valhalla of Nordic legend. Death aside, being one worthy for "battle" in the hall of the god Odin would be up to us.

Richard and I had a long history of sharing a rope on occasional climbing projects in the backcountry. I had met Richard while he and a partner were on Dome Rock, up on a climb. I was traveling along the base to climb with friends when Richard dropped the entire bolt kit. I avoided getting nailed by the "stuff sack of doom" and we began our long sporadic relationship on the stone. Revealing that I had recently participated in the first ascent of "Just Lovely" on the south part of Dome Rock sparked our shared interests in pioneering new routes. Richard had the good fortune to have a base camp at his parents' cabin at Camp Nelson near Dome Rock and the Needles. Richard was always excited about climbing, and we inspired each other into many adventures.

Weeks before, we had completed the second ascent of the Silver Lining Route on The Fin at Castle Rocks. Now, Richard was keen on a route on Angel Wings on one of its towers, "It looks like a 1,000 foot hand crack!" A longer route up a crack system near the middle of the central massif caught my eye. I lobbied for us to do that instead. We nicely agreed to disagree on each other's lines, but we also realized that either route would take more time than what we had anyway. We basked in the sun next to the lake, deliberating on what to do. I became intrigued with a beautiful dome above and to the east of the Wings. I was able to sell the idea of a route tracing up a series of cracks and arches on its south buttress to Richard. Off we went. We named the dome "Cherubim" and the route, "Archangel" and it has to be *the* best route I had ever done with Richard. We felt worthy of our efforts and vowed to return.

E.C. Joe on the 1st ascent of Archangel, Cherubim Dome. Photo:
Richard Leversee, E.C. Joe Collection

In the summer of 1989, we returned for that new route on Angel Wings he had chosen years prior. Kim Grandfield, Richard, and I established the first few pitches where Richard discovered that his "1,000 foot hand crack" turned out to be a rope length of a heinous six-inch-wide, off-width nightmare. Kim and I were glad he led that. We fixed ropes from our high point to return the next day for a one-day ascent. We decided to go "light and fast" to the top; one headlamp, a lighter, 3 liters of water, minimal food, and wind/rain jackets stuffed into a couple of daypacks. Going light has its limitations, and it finally took this climb for me to realize how a seemingly benign logistic decision could have enormous consequences.

Richard Leversee and E.C. Joe, Angel Wings. Photo: Ron Felton, E.C. Joe Collection

The initial rope we had to ascend was a 5.5 mm x 50 m Spectra Cord, a genuinely insane and dangerous choice that Richard and I have to cop to. Hey, it holds over 3,000 pounds! We all were reevaluating why we were virtually hanging by a thread a thousand feet above Hamilton Lake. Richard and I had used it on a few occasions on other big climbs, but for some reason, now it seemed WRONG! Maybe, it was looking a bit worn, or it was a case of big wall myopia. I don't know, but a rope cutting over an edge could have been an easy way to get some real angel wings. Above the fixed lines, the climbing was difficult free, aid, mixed, and unaesthetic; a route that we just wanted off of ASAP, and it was easier to go up than down.

After topping out with waning daylight for our descent, we couldn't determine the correct chute to descend back to the base. There were one of two ways; one that ended in a cliff and one that didn't. We stopped right there because one headlamp did *not* work well for three persons scrambling about on varied terrain, especially if you could fall off a cliff! The one decision to have only one light source set off a sequence of memorable events.

O.K., so, a night out under the stars was in order, no problem. Build a fire. Damn! I lost the lighter. It *was* in my jacket pocket! It was chilly that night at that altitude of 9,000+feet. Kim and I huddled together against a lone pine in an attempt to glean cover from the night sky. Richard refused to join the group hug. Instead, he insisted on laying out in the open inside of a vapor barrier sack; water and windproof, but not breathable. In the middle of the night, Richard was wet from condensation and shivering wildly with hypothermia. Kim and I all but dragged Richard over and seated him down in between us to keep him warm. "Homophobia" thwarted!

Then -- the mosquitoes arrived. Without shelter, it was a horrendously miserable onslaught. Our hooded shell jackets helped, but the little bastards bit through our pants and massacred our legs. Unknown to the others, in the cover of darkness, I donned my mosquito head net I had stuck into another pocket at camp. Oh, man, I was so relieved to regain my sanity from those intense ear buzzing kamikazes.

Meanwhile, I heard Kim and Richard going insane. It seemed an eternity for dawn to arrive. I suppose I had slept because both Richard and Kim complained that my snoring kept them awake. They also expressed some disapproval that I had been sporting my mosquito head net (not that I could have shared it). It was evident that this adventure's fun meter had dropped below zero.

We negotiated the correct chute in the daylight, made it back to our base camp, packed up, and began the long hike out. By that evening, we camped at Bearpaw Meadow, a unique place in the wilderness where those who could beat the lottery could stay in tent cabins and have catered grub. In the public campground, we laid out in our sleeping bags. Wow, there's nothing better than being engulfed in a cozy and warm down-filled cocoon. As soon as we had gone to sleep, several pack horses began to stir about, whinnying to a young bear's cries. A juvenile bear had gotten into the tree almost directly over us and was calling for its mother. Momma Bear was calling to her cub and was on the way. It was dark, but we could tell that we were smack-dab in between them. We whispered to each other to freeze. Then, the bears stopped communicating for what seemed like an eternity. What was happening? Where are they? Shit! Curious, I directed my headlamp into the tree. The cub was still there and was startled by the light, and he started crying again! Now, Momma sounded pissed! Kim and Richard shouted, "WTF are you doing?!" as I doused the light. We froze again, like for eternity. Eventually, Momma and her cub moved along. Whew --

The following day, we laid in camp well past dawn, trying to recover from our sleep deprivation from the night before last. The full-on cowboys with the pack horses saw us sleeping out with just our bags, "Gee, that looks mighty rough just sleeping out like that with no tents."

I remarked, "Yeah, but at least we have sleeping bags." They had no fucking idea -- We named our climb "Hell On Wings."

Fred Beckey. Photo: David Hickey

Angel Wings, like other notable walls, has its own stories and legends including a "tale of a lost haul bag." In the course of completing the third new route on the wall, "Wings Over Sequoia," Fred Beckey and crew tossed their bags of gear off the cliff, where they exploded when hitting the base. As the legend goes, the intrepid Fred Beckey, the one human with the most first ascents in North America, possessed a "Little Black Book" that included his notes on all of his intended climbing exploits...and it had been in one of those bags. A veritable "DaVinci Code," possessing the book was thought to be a boon to any climber aspiring to pioneer new routes. Could Fred's book be a "King Maker?"

"...I coulda been a contender.
I coulda been somebody..."
- Terry Malloy, *On the Waterfront*

It was my turn to climb that route I had eyed back in 1985. Returning to Angel Wings in the summer of 1996, we discovered the debris field from the exploded bags strewn along the base near the center of the wall. Richard, Ron Felton, and I gathered as much of what was now mostly trash littering the base; old anti-freeze bottles that they had used for water (yikes!) and tatters of webbing. The only item that appeared salvageable was a sun-bleached Forrest Single Point Hammock. Did we ever find Fred's Little Black Book? If I told you, I'd have to kill you!

The route line was in the center of the main south face in a crack system left of the original Steck Route and started on the left of two ramps that intersect and form an "X" a few hundred feet from the base. Two free pitches brought us to a ledge atop the right side of a huge heart-shaped feature. Here we found evidence of a previous attempt by an unknown party; a fixed piton. Higher up, the crack petered out, and a pendulum to the right off of another ancient piton (an apparent high-point of an earlier attempt) led to two pitches of mostly complex aid, one of which Richard reflected that was the best of his climbing experience. These pitches ended below a sloping ledge.

After fixing 80 feet of aid up and to the left of stance below the ledge, I returned to the stance to bivy in the hammock while Richard and Ron struggled to be comfortable on the sloping ledge above. Later, around midnight, I awoke to the slow, faint sound of "ffff-ffff...ffff" I realized that my head was considerably lower than my feet, and the sound was that of the nylon hammock; tearing open down its entire length! The foam pad I had slipped in to line the hammock was the only thing keeping me from birthing out of the bottom! Squeezing out a spot on the sloping stance, I used the foot section, the only good portion left of the hammock, to keep me from sliding off the stance and into the abyss. I spent the night sitting on that sloping stance with my face "rope-a-doping" with the gear hanging off of the anchor.

Richard, E.C., and Ron, on the summit of Angel Wings: Just a Rock in the Park. Photo: E.C. Joe Collection

The route remained high quality. It was better than I had imagined; steep and clean with many memorable difficult passages reminiscent of the big walls of Yosemite. "Just a Rock in the Park" was a real big wall backcountry climbing at its best, a combination of challenging, quality free climbing and serious aid climbing. This type of climb is seldom sought out these days in the backcountry. However, I'm good with that. It was my fantasy.

SEQUOIA N. PARK
ANGEL WINGS
"JUST A ROCK IN THE PARK"
VI 5.10 A3+, 11 PITCHES (60m ROPES)

FA: RICHARD LEVERSEE, E.C. JOE
& RON FELTON
JUNE 1996

2 ⊕ HOOKS
2 BATHOOKS
10 BEAKS
3 A5 LOST ARROWS
4 LONG THULL BUGS
1 EA. .5"-.75 ANGLES
2 EA. NUT TINY → .5"
1 EA. NUT .5" → 1.25"
2 EA CAMS TO 4"
1 EA CAM TO 7"
10 ASST. HEADS

(11) "5A SLOT
(10)
SLABS 5.7
(9) TERRACE
LOOSE
5.8
"GO BIG   5.10
SOME MO'"   SQUEEZE
CAM (8) XX
(BEST BIVI)   LOOSE BLOCKS
                IN CRACK
"GO BIG   5.10 O/W
OR   5" → 8"
GO HOME"
5.9
5.8

BLOCKY ∧ XX (7) SLOPING
8 ·····   BIVY
5.8 + RUNOUT

5.9+ T.T.
XX (6)   5.8
× BATHOOKS

A3 BEAKS, HEADS, HOOK.
A2   "ON A WING
       + A SCARE"
5.9
A1
CRACK   WET
ON   BEND
INSIDE   A2
WALL   HOOKS
(6)
XX
TTTT

(5)
XX
TTT

"THE
FLEDGLING"   A3 BEAKS, HEADS, HOOKS

T.T. HEADS
×
A2
A2
5.8
BAT HOOKS
MOBY'S   T.T. XX
DICK   (4)
(LOOSE)   SLOPING
BEAKS   BIVY 2+
BEAKS ← T.T. ORANGE
              BULGE/ROOF
              A2
"WINGS
TO THE   A3 BEAKS
WALLS"
            BATHOOKS
            × A3 BEAKS
            × (3)
            5.8
PENDULUM   "LITTLE WING"
(2) T.T.   RAMP A3 HEADS
XX
HEART
LEDGE
5.8 RUNOUT
(1)
3AB   GULLY

9

TRAVELS WITH FRED

By Joe Metz

There is nothing like a crisp autumn morning. They always seem pregnant with impending adventure. The days are cool and dry but still long enough to get in a good day's work – in other words, perfect climbing weather. The summers always seem to go by too fast, yet I still look forward to autumn, when the aspens are turning colors, and the weather is hazy and stable. It often means a trip to the Leap, or maybe somewhere on the east side of the Sierra for some last-minute peak bagging. Winter sets in all too soon in the high country. But then, that's why God created Telemark.

Most climbers don't pick up the phone expecting to hear a living legend inviting them to come out and climb. Yet that's what happened to me this October. I was unemployed, keeping busy by working on a bathroom remodeling project at my ex-wife's house. In the middle of installing a tar-paper membrane in the shower stall, my cell phone rang. I carefully picked it up, trying to keep the roofing asphalt on my hands and off the phone. After several rings, I was finally able to maneuver the phone into position and answer it. An unfamiliar voice was on the other end. "Uh, Joe? Uh, yeah, Fred Beckey here. I heard you might want to get out and do something. I was thinking about going down the east side for a little bit, maybe do the East Buttress on Whitney or a route on Bear Creek Spire or something. You think you can make it?"

Fred had been down in Rock Creek and the Palisades with Eddie Joe earlier in the week and in the Whitney area before that. He hadn't been too successful due to bad weather and trouble with the altitude. Now he was licking his wounds and getting a bit of rest at a friend's house up in the Tahoe Basin. Eddie had mentioned to him that I was interested in doing the East Buttress route, so Fred gave me a call.

I immediately learned a few things about Fred. First, he can't hear worth a damn. The phone conversation was difficult, confused, and required a lot of shouting. Second, he is a real beta hound. He was pumping me for any information I had about the East Buttress. This seemed a bit strange to me, what with Fred's huge reputation as a first ascensionist. I figured he just headed into an area and climbed wherever and whatever he wanted to. Third, Fred was driven by a relentless determination to climb things. He was oh-for-three on Whitney now and that wasn't sitting well at all. After a few days' rest, he would be ready to go at it again.

After talking things over for a while, we made plans to meet at Nicely's in Lee Vining on Sunday morning, October 14. Fred was pumping hard for prognostications about what the weather might be doing. We were already starting into the winter pattern and I felt that an attempt on Whitney this late in the season would have poor odds for success. So we opted to have another go at Bear Creek Spire instead. The approach is shorter and easier, and we would be able to get in and out more quickly.

By sunrise, on Sunday morning, my old red truck and I were across the Central Valley and heading up through Yosemite toward Tioga Pass. There was a lanky hitchhiker at the Cathedral Lakes trailhead with a big pack and a sign that said "395" so I picked him up. This guy worried me. He was heading down to climb North Palisade via the U-Notch, and seemed to be thrilled to meet a "real climber." He saw my gear in the back of the truck and somehow came to the conclusion that I must be a real climber, not some *poseur*, as he put it. Based on his questions and comments, I concluded that the poor guy didn't have a clue about what he was trying to get himself into. He had read *Mountaineering, the Freedom of the Hills*, unlike the *poseurs* who owned lots of gear but had never read the book. He had done a few walk-up peaks, had never climbed on ice before, always climbed alone, and hitchhiked everywhere. Now he was ready to do something harder.

I told the hitchhiker that I would be taking him only as far as Lee Vining because I would be meeting someone there and would be leaving my truck behind. It was my intention to keep quiet about what I was up to. But the hitchhiker was asking a lot of questions about where I was heading and what I was planning to climb. I gave him vague answers, but they only piqued his curiosity. He wanted to know who I was meeting in Lee Vining – someone who lived there? Did I climb with this person often? It seemed pretty cool to have a buddy that you could meet in Lee Vining and climb with...Finally, I told him I was going to meet someone who didn't exist. On the seat next to me was Climbing magazine issue 206, and I pointed the hitchhiker to the paragraphs on page 65, which starts, "Fred Beckey: No such person. Fred was originally invented in the 1940s by climbers in the Pacific Northwest as a sort of campfire tall tale – a 'been everywhere, climbed everything' mountaineering bogeyman..." The hitchhiker didn't really get it. He stared at the truck's headliner and wondered, "Fred Beckey...Name sounds familiar...Should I know this guy?"

We pulled into Lee Vining around 10:30. There, on the corner of Highway 395 and Fourth Street, was a red Subaru station wagon with Washington plates, a huge pile of trash, and a crazy-looking 80-some-thing-year old guy wearing a fleece touc, a huge smile, tennis shoes, and thermal underwear. I found a place to park, wished the hitchhiker good luck, and begged him to turn around if he felt things were getting out of hand on his climb. Then I walked down and introduced myself to Fred.

The pile of trash turned out to be bags of all sorts of provisions. Eddie had warned me about this. Fred was sorting through the stuff, trying to identify the contents of each bag, and trying to decide what was worth taking and what should be left in the car. He divided the bags into two piles, lost track of which pile was which, and started over, all the while going through an endless, circular batch of questions: "What to you think? Do you think we'll need coffee? I got some coffee here. Maybe we should take coffee. You got coffee with you? How 'bout this? What do you think this stuff is?" The bags contained a variety of unidentifiable blobs, goos, and powders. He still had the fossilized orange that had impressed Eddie a week earlier. "You think this is any good? Looks like its getting kind of old. Maybe I'll take it. Naw, let's leave it here. It looks kind of old, doesn't it?"

After several minutes of unproductive bag sorting, we somehow managed to get everything into the back of the Subaru and headed south on 395. Fred kept the car pointed more or less in the same direction that the road was heading, not paying much attention to things like lane markers or his speed, which seemed to vary randomly from 40 to 70 mph. I sat back and tried to enjoy the scenery and gently pry my way into Fred's persona. Did he graduate from college? What did he do for a living? Did he have family up in Washington? But he wasn't much for talking about himself and deflected most of the questions. About all I could get out of him was that he had a degree in geography and that he worked for the State sometimes. Our conversation consisted mostly of Fred pumping for data about one peak or another, followed by my shouted and mostly misunderstood answers. It was frustrating and amusing at the same time. This was nothing like the heroic Fred Beckey of my imagination, but way, way more interesting.

We passed a CHP officer who had stopped a northbound SUV. Fred figured the guy in the SUV must have done something pretty crazy in order to get pulled over on Highway 395. "Yeah, I get pulled over a lot, but they never write any ticket. They say I'm weaving or something, I don't know...Maybe it's the Washington plates." Whatever.

I don't often get to travel down 395 as a passenger. It was a pure delight to be able to look out the window and study the Minarets as they slowly crept by, trying to pick out and name the individual spires. Inside the car, the dashboard was covered with yellow post-it notes with faded random phone numbers and names and dates. There were thick stacks of business cards with similar bits of information, held together with rubber bands and stashed into every nook that could be found within reach of the driver's seat. Fred was asking an endless stream of questions about the weather. I could see high clouds moving in slowly from the southwest. Not good, but at least no lenticulars. "May be changing for the worse, but it should hold for a day or so," I told him.

Rock Creek was gorgeous. The further up the canyon we went, the better things got. The aspens changed from green to gold to yellow to orange. There were lots of tourists out with their video cameras. They were taking home shots of the aspens and their cars and the middle third of their relatives' torsos. Fred aimed more or less up-canyon, bouncing the car from shoulder to shoulder. It was sort of like being on the Autopia ride at Disneyland when you putt-putt along with your foot buried in the gas pedal and your hands off the steering wheel, and the car bounces along from side to side on its guide rail. More than once, he remarked, "Getting up here would sure be tough if they hadn't built this road..."

The upper parking lot at Mosquito Flat was full. So we double-parked next to a trash dumpster and had another bag sorting session. A passerby would have thought we were a couple of dirtbags scrounging through the dumpster's contents. From Ed's description of Fred's cooking and eating habits (which, at first, I had thought to be exaggerations, but later, having thoroughly examined the provisions that Fred insisted on sorting through yet again, decided to be more in line with Ed's tendencies toward understatement), I had decided that I wanted no part in letting Fred prepare the food. I had packed a full cook kit and enough food for the both of us and told Fred in no uncertain terms that I would handle the mess duties. But it was impossible to convince Fred that I had everything covered and that he didn't need to bring any provisions along. So after a lot of thoughtful bag sorting, I helped Fred pick out a random collection of unidentifiable goos, blobs, and white powders, which he happily stuffed into his pack. Then Fred took the Subaru back down the hill to look for somewhere to park. I sat in the autumn sun, ostensibly guarding the packs but mostly just enjoying the view up Little Lakes Valley.

Fred soon came strolling up the road, still wearing his crazy touc, a huge grin, and long underwear. None of the tourists that came up the road had stopped to offer the old gentleman a ride. I can't say I blame anyone for that. He had a small, rather random-looking rack slung over his shoulder on a piece of ancient red webbing. It consisted of a few antique stoppers and hexes and a pair of small Camalots. We lifted our packs and poles and headed up the trail. Fred still had his rack dangling across his chest. I prefer to hike in stealth mode – no gear visible – especially in places where there are a lot of day hikers. I get tired of answering the same questions over and over: "Are you guys climbers?" (No, I just like to carry gear around.) "What are you going to climb?" (If I told you, I'd have to kill you.) "What's the highest you've ever climbed?" (Who cares?) "How do you pee up there?" (Downhill usually.) I asked Fred, "Don't you want to put that in your pack?" He gave me a funny look and said, "Naw."

Fred's pack was battered and ill-fitting. The buckle on the waist belt was missing, so he just carried it on his shoulders. He looked like a hunchback, bent over, and complained endlessly about how much his back was bothering him. He leaned heavily on a trekking pole that Eddie had persuaded him to keep. I insisted that Fred hike in front. I wanted him to set the pace. He didn't move very fast, but he didn't stop, either.

There was a steady stream of burley young couch potatoes carrying fishing gear, shouldering their way past us on the trail. After about a half-hour, we began to find them sitting on logs along the side of the trail, panting and complaining about the altitude. As we trudged on past them, they would ask, "How do you guys carry those big packs up here?" I was, in fact, a bit worried about this. I hadn't been at altitude since June. Only a few hours ago I was crawling out of bed at sea level, and now we were 10,400 feet higher. But so far, so good. Fred's slow but steady pace was comfortable. I was working pretty hard on the steep sections but recovered quickly when the grade let off.

Our plan was to spend the night at Treasure Lakes, at about 11,200 feet. That would leave about 2,500 feet of climbing for the next day. On the previous attempt, Fred and Eddie had hiked up the main trail to Gem Lakes and then cut cross-country to Dade Lake. This turned out to be a horrible four-hour struggle across large talus. Fred wanted nothing to do with repeating that route. The guidebooks mention a climbers' path leaving the main trail at Long Lake and heading up past Treasure Lakes to Dade. I spotted the path cutting across the meadows at the head of Long Lake and steered Fred onto it. The trail led through some willow thickets, boggy meadows, and talus fields and soon deposited us into the slabby canyon that drains the Treasure Lakes.

I was impressed with Fred's route-finding instincts. He had an uncanny ability to discover unlikely-looking routes that avoided the worst of the talus, brush, and steep slabs without needing to deviate from the most direct passage up the canyon. He talked almost constantly, either complaining about his back or his crappy shoes (he kept slipping on the talus) or asking, "Um, well, Joe, what do you think? Should we go up this way or over those slabs? Maybe we should go up the talus. What do you think?" I learned pretty quickly to just let Fred lead the way. My answers were usually wrong, and he seldom heard them correctly anyway.

At about 4:00, we reached the southernmost of the Treasure Lakes. We found a good bivy site sheltered among the slabs on the north shore of the lake, in a patch of sandy, dried-up meadow. There were rodent turds everywhere. The meadow grass was fine and loose like lawnmower clippings. It blew around and got into everything. Soon our clothing was covered with the stuff. Fred kept remarking about how strange and annoying this grass was. I had never seen anything like it either.

The sun was already behind Mt. Mills, and it was getting cold fast. I fired up the stove to boil some water for tea. The high clouds had moved on, leaving a clear blue sky and a light breeze. "Fred, I got some tea here. You want some?" "What?" "I said I got some tea here. You want some tea, Fred?" "Yeah, the weather looks like its holding. But it's damn cold, ain't it?"

Fred and his green bowl, Treasure Lakes. Photo: Joe Metz

Fred has a minimalist approach to equipment. He brought a spoon and a big green plastic bowl with him. It looked as though someone had mixed cement in the bowl at one time. It had hard gray matter stuck all over the inside surfaces. Fred slurped tea out of the bowl, fortified with copious quantities of powdered milk and blowing grass clippings, while I cooked up some ramen and vegetables. He was reclining in his sleeping bag, propped up on one elbow, sorting through a pile of plastic grocery bags. I thought we had left most of that stuff back in the car. The ramen went into the bowl, right on top of the tea and the grass clippings. Fred shoveled the noodles down so fast I thought he would choke. "Damn," he said," I didn't bring a fork. I should'a brought a fork." He started rummaging through the pile of bags. "I got some pudding here. Want some pudding? We could make pudding, but I didn't bring a fork. Can't make pudding without a fork...Hey, I got some salami here." He produced a huge bag of rancid sliced salami, coated white with congealed fat. "We could put some salami in the ramen if you like...What do you think?" I declined his generous offer.

Fred was having a hard time staying warm. I put some more water on to boil and went down to the lake to filter water for the next day's climb. When I came back up to camp, Fred was slurping down more tea. We were in bed by 7:00 more to escape the cold than because of the failing light.

From my sleeping bag, I was looking due south, directly toward Bear Creek Spire. I visually scouted a route up to Dade Lake. It looked like the best way was to begin climbing up the slabs to the east as soon as feasible. They seemed to get steeper further south. As the twilight faded, I evaluated our situation. It was cold, but at least it wasn't windy. We agreed that cold was not a big problem, so long as the climbing didn't get too technical. Wind, on the other hand, has a way of making things miserable or even unbearable. As long as the wind held down, we would be fine. I was pleasantly surprised at how well I was doing with the altitude, considering the fact that I was at sea level only fourteen hours earlier. Maybe Fred's slow and steady pace was helping me, too. Mars appeared in the darkening sky, peering over Bear Creek Spire's eastern shoulder, orange-red. The bright cross of Cygnus was directly overhead. I dozed off. Sleep was fitful in the cold. I marked time through the night by watching Cygnus rotate overhead like a celestial clock. As the sky began to lighten, I saw Orion occupying the place where Mars had been at dusk. Winter would be here soon.

When it was light enough to pick out details on the other side of the lake, I got up and started heating water. Everything was frozen – the water bottles, the used tea bags, the rodent turds in Fred's green bowl.

My camera wouldn't work. I guess it was frozen, too. I rinsed Fred's bowl out with boiling water and gave him some tea. Breakfast was made from the contents of some of Fred's bags of unidentifiable powders.

It was cold – mighty cold. The sky had been clear and still all night. As the sun began to shine on the peaks to the west, brisk little gusts of wind began to blow through our camp. The wind concerned Fred. He was having trouble deciding whether to bring his parka along. I figured the gusts were caused by the sun warming the peaks, and it would settle down once the sun got up over the ridge to the east. I was planning to travel light with a fleece jacket, hat, and windbreaker. I would take a small day pack with us, containing a bit of food and water and fifty feet of 9mm rope, but the parka would pretty much fill it up. So Fred dumped the contents out of his backpack and stuffed his parka into it. We would leave his pack at Dade Lake and either leave the parka with it or take it along once we had a better read on how the weather was going to behave. I had planned to take my camera along, but since it was inoperative, it would just be useless weight. So the camera stayed in camp too.

We cleaned up camp as best we could and headed south, around the east shore of the lake, through a silent frozen pre-dawn world. In the lake basin, everything was subdued blues and grays. Sunrise had already come to the peaks, and they were gaudy pinks and oranges. The only sounds were the crunch of frozen grass and an occasional clack of a trekking pole hitting a rock.

We headed up the slabs to the east and topped out onto a sandy plateau covered by a waist-high pine forest. We picked our way across the plateau and dropped down into the gray, austere, gravel-paved bowl containing Dade Lake. It was cold and silent and still. We left Fred's pack and parka and trekking pole at the base of a huge boulder near the north shore of the lake.

The water trickling between the boulders at Dade Lake's outlet was the first sound we heard that day that we hadn't made ourselves. Fred chose a course that contoured up and around a shoulder south of Dade Lake, then up the eastern side of the basin above. Travel was easy for the most part, mainly over slabs with occasional patches of grass and talus. But I was constantly amazed at Fred's ability to piece together the most efficient small-scale choices while keeping the large-scale strategy firmly in hand. It was like watching a mathematician stringing several small, unobvious, seemingly unrelated proofs together and having a grand unexpected truth leap forward when the last line of the last proof was completed. At exactly 10:00, we were standing on the col separating the Rock Creek and Pine Creek drainages.

We took a rest break here. The warm sun was a welcome pleasure after huffing up the cold, shady basin. There was no wind on the ridge top. Things couldn't have been better. I downed some water and part of a Clif Bar. Air seemed to be sufficient for Fred. From here, the route up the Northeast Ridge was fairly obvious. The ridge started out easy – easier than the approach up the basin, in fact – but gradually steepened as it went up and eventually merged into the east face of the peak.

After climbing about 500 feet, we took another oxygen break. The climbing was starting to get interesting, and I was definitely feeling the altitude now. Two people and a dog appeared at the col below. This was a bit surprising, as I hadn't noticed anyone behind us as we came up from Dade Lake. As we started climbing again, one person left the col and started up toward us. The dog and the other person seemed content to settle down in a sunny spot and enjoy the view.

The climbing was easy third class now, and we each picked our own way upward. The guy who had been in the col just a few minutes ago passed us as quickly as if he were at a full run. He had driven up to Mosquito Flat from Bishop with his girlfriend and his dog that morning. A short way above us, a large tower blocked the ridge. We watched the guy from Bishop attack the tower directly. Soon he was deep into fifth-class territory, whooping from the exposure, and then disappeared over the horizon. Fred suggested we explore around the right side of the tower. Sure enough, this provided an easy path upward.

Shortly after passing the tower, a second guy zoomed past us. He was a big, strong-looking kid from British Columbia. He had also driven up from Bishop that morning.

And so it went. The climbing was beautiful, on solid rock that just kept getting steeper and steeper. We came across a small ledge where the Canadian kid had apparently changed into his rock shoes and stashed his boots. Fred wondered a bit at that: "Sure is a nice pair of boots, would hate to lose 'em...Hope he can find 'em on the way down..." I pointed out that it would be a real drag to walk all the way back to Mosquito Flat in rock shoes. "Naw, no mosquitoes up here. Not enough water."

Fred put on his harness and changed into his rock shoes here as well. I stashed his approach shoes into the daypack. It took a bit of work to pry the shoes away from him. He didn't want to make me carry any more weight. But my fat, comfy rock harness came out of the pack, so there was plenty of room for his shoes to go in. I was wearing my La Sportiva Trangos, which are, in my opinion, just fine for backpacking, approach, and climbing. I didn't feel any need to bring rock shoes with me.

Joe Metz on the Northeast Ridge of Bear Creek Spire. Photo: Fred Beckey, Joe Metz Collection

Fred was enjoying the views, especially back down the Little Lakes Valley. He kept referring to the High Sierra as the Dry Sierra and maybe seeing all those lakes made him feel a bit more like he was back in his home territory. We reached a particularly steep section, where a foot-wide ledge formed by the top of a flake cut out across the face to the right. This obstruction was easily bypassed on its left side, but Fred wanted to get a picture here. So I climbed out onto the flake and followed Fred's detailed instructions on how he wanted me posed. "Uh, yeah, this will make a great picture. Okay, uh, Joe, now look up, like you're going to climb this thing. Yep, got those lakes in the background. Yeah, this should be a nice one…"

The northeast ridge eventually merges into a steep face just below the summit ridge. This was definitely getting into fifth class territory, but we both felt comfortable with where we were. As we had pretty much the whole way up, each of us chose our own path up the rock, taking the face or the crack that made the best sense to our own climbing styles and preferences. We were always within sight of each other, usually less than ten yards apart. At one point, I stopped in the middle of a fist crack to catch my breath. The air was getting pretty thin. I had great feet and a good hand, so it was a comfortable place to hang out and get some air. Fred was concerned that I might be wanting a belay and maneuvered to get himself directly above me. It took a bit of shouting to get him to understand that I was just resting.

We could hear the two speedsters from Bishop whooping it up on the summit. Soon we reached the summit ridge ourselves, although the summit was somewhere off to the left, out of sight. Fred, as always, asked my opinion about the best way to proceed. I suggested heading up the right side of the ridge. It was a bit exposed, but the sight-lines were clear, and it looked like it provided a direct way to the summit area. Fred opted to take the left side, a jumble of wedged blocks that didn't appear to lead anywhere. Of course, I followed his suggestion. We squirmed our way around a corner and saw an easy route ahead. My choice, on the other hand, was revealed to turn into a series of steep, exposed slabs. I began to wonder whether Fred could see through granite.

We worked up the ridge and eventually crossed over to the right side. To our left were increasingly large, monolithic, sloping blocks. It wasn't at all clear where the summit was, but it seemed likely that we would have to get to the top of the blocks in order to find it. I told Fred that I felt ok with frictioning my way up to the top to see where the summit might be. He suggested I rope up and set up a belay at the top.

So out came the fifty-foot rope and Fred's little rack, and up the block I went. I found a crack suitable for an anchor just about where the fifty feet of rope gave out. The anchor was almost built when Fred called up, "Hey, Joe. Am I on belay?" "No!" I shouted back. "Okay, Climbing!" "NO!!!"

The rope went slack. I whipped out my belay device, got some good footholds, started to bring rope in with my right hand, and desperately worked to finish and clip into the anchor with my left. I just about had things under control when Fred pulled up onto the ledge.

The summit was still about fifty feet to the south. The two guys from Bishop were nowhere to be seen. Apparently, they had found a different way down and were probably halfway back to their cars by now.

Fred led a short pitch to a notch at the base of the summit block. The rope didn't feel all that necessary – we had covered more difficult and exposed terrain unroped on the way up. But what the heck. We had an anchor, a rope, and a rack, so we might as well use them, right? I followed up and over the blocks to a steep slab that led down into the notch. In my sticky approach shoes, this final part would have been easy. I just pointed my feet straight down the fall line and kept my chin over my toes. But here is where the soles on my Trangos met their limit. They cut loose, sending me into the notch a bit sooner than I intended to arrive. I ended up with a nice abrasion and bruise on my right leg and got a funny, "Why'd you do that?" look from Fred. We spent some time enjoying the views. In the distance, I could identify Mt. Dana, the Clark Range, Humphreys, Darwin, the Palisades. Nearby were Seven Gables, Hilgard, Gabb, Dade, Abbot. Closer still, crazy geometric shapes, huge boulders, and blocks stacked and precariously balanced. Since I was already on belay, Fred sent me up the final block to tag the exposed summit. We then traded places, and he did the same. Now, all we had to do was get down.

The night I was talking (or trying to talk) to Fred in my ex-wife's bathroom with roofing tar all over my hands, we had discussed the need for a rope. I told Fred I had plenty of ropes and could bring a lightweight fifty-five meter one along. "Naw, that's too heavy. I got a hundred feet of six-mil stuff that we can use in case we need to rappel." Rappelling on a 6mm shoelace didn't sound so cool to me – you can't develop much friction on a skinny rope like that. So we reached a compromise. I would hack off fifty feet from an old 9mm lead rope that was hanging in my closet and bring that along.

From the summit, I suggested, we could reverse the two pitches we had just climbed and end up back where we had left the daypack. I felt comfortable downclimbing everything we had just done and could provide Fred with a belay if he felt he needed one.

(Please, dear reader, don't get it in your mind that I was taking the role of the fearless leader here and that Fred was sniveling for a belay. That couldn't be farther from the truth. I was only thinking that Fred had asked for a belay coming up the first pitch, and I would be glad to provide him with one going back down if he desired it.)

But Fred had in mind to rappel directly off to the west, down to the talus at the base of the summit blocks. The only problem was that the talus was about 75 feet below us, and the rope, when doubled, was only 25 feet long. I spotted a ledge and a flake partway down that looked like it could serve as an intermediate rappel anchor. It looked reachable with the doubled rope. A short distance past that, the rock became less steep, and it looked like a crack would provide an easy downclimb. So we set up an anchor, and down I went. I tied a sling, hung it over the flake, clipped into it, and called Fred down. When he arrived, he seemed a bit surprised that we wouldn't be able to reach the ground in with one more rappel. He also pointed out, much to my embarrassment, that I hadn't left enough tail hanging out of one end of the water knot on the sling I was leaning on.

While he re-tied the knot, I explained my plan to rappel down to the crack and downclimb that to the base. But Fred squinted and measured and squinted and announced that the rope, if it weren't doubled, could reach the talus. I asked him how we would retrieve the rope - not that I cared about the rope at all, but I didn't want to leave it behind as litter if it could be avoided. He told me not to worry about that, so I rappelled down to the talus.

Fred rappelled down to the top of the crack and stopped. He placed a nut there, clipped the rope through it, and started climbing back up to the rappel anchor. As he climbed, he used his rappel brake to self-belay on the anchored rope. The climbing did not look all that easy from where I stood. When he reached the rappel anchor, he tied into the top end of the rope and took the rappel anchor apart, then had me belay him as he down-climbed back to the nut at the top of the crack. This was getting a bit scary. I doubted that the nut would catch Fred before he hit the ground if he fell. Finally, he did a sort of down-lead in the crack, downclimbing sections and placing pro, then climbing back up to retrieve the higher piece. After what seemed like a very long time, he finally joined me on the talus.

I downed some water and the rest of the Clif bar. Fred took in some more air. I volunteered to climb up a gully-chimney to retrieve the daypack. So Fred, the geographer and guidebook author, sat down, produced a notepad and pencil from somewhere, and began to write. He took sightings toward various nearby peaks, noting directions (without a compass, but with pretty good precision, apparently) and distances. As I huffed up a chimney between two big blocks, Fred called up, "Uh, hey, Joe, how long do you think that rappel is?" "Seventy-five feet, pretty close," I huffed back. Fred wrote that down too.

After retrieving the pack, I returned to find Fred having a shouted conversation with yet another climber standing on the summit block. The guy up on the summit had discovered, much to his delight, some brand new green webbing and a carabiner threaded around a block a few feet to the left of where we had rappelled down. While he was busy dismantling this anchor (BOOTY!) Fred was inquiring how he was planning to get down without a rope. The whole conversation was, of course, completely nonsensical and at cross-purposes. The guy on the summit was desperately trying to figure out whether he was stealing the anchor right in front of the people who had constructed it, and Fred, while retrieving his approach shoes from my rucksack, was trying to discern whether the guy was trying to kill himself.

We finally gave up trying to communicate and headed down the west slope of Bear Creek Spire, planning to turn north and cross Cox Col when possible. As we turned to leave, the guy on the summit figured out that he was shouting at Fred Beckey, who he had just happened to have met a few days before at a friend's house near Lake Tahoe. He finished looting the anchor, downclimbed (with frightening speed) the steep face, and soon joined us as we trudged down the talus and scree toward the col.

The conversation was spirited as we walked along. I'm not sure Fred remembered meeting the guy (his name was CJ or something like that...), but it was hard to tell, with all the shouting and misunderstandings going on. CJ noticed my boots and wanted to know what I thought of them. He had apparently owned a pair once and found them to be uncomfortable. Fred began complaining loudly about the shitty soles on his approach shoes again.

We reached the col and marveled at the Spire's beautiful North Buttress (where Rowell's route lies) before heading down the scree toward the basin above Dade Lake. The slope was steep and loose, and we moved slowly and carefully. CJ sent a stack of big rocks down onto Fred, who narrowly escaped getting clobbered. CJ was horrified by this until Fred did the same thing to me a few moments later, perhaps with the purpose of making CJ feel better. At the bottom of this slope, we encountered a stretch of ice. I opted to climb around it on some exposed but solid third class rock. Fred and CJ opted to climb down the ice. Below, we rejoined momentarily. It was getting late, and CJ still needed to get back down to his car before dark and sped off down the basin toward Dade Lake.

Fred seemed to be getting tired. He was really slowing down. We worked across the upper end of the basin, mostly on slabs with scattered bits of talus. I spent a lot of time looking at my footing, so I had plenty of opportunities to study the amazing variety of rock lying about. There were various members of the granodiorite family in black, white, white-with-black-intrusions, black-with-white-intrusions, gray, gray-with-black-intrusions, black-with-gray-intrusions. There were chunks of white quartz, pink quartz, orange quartz, white quartz with rust streaks. There were ruby red metamorphic rocks, purple metamorphics, browns, yellows. There was an intrusive igneous rock with big cubes of white feldspar poking out of it. There were rocks with bands of mica running through it, rocks with crisscrossing bands of quartz. There was granite with the usual random salt-and-pepper grains in it, granite with grains aligned in curious straight patterns, swirly patterns, and layered, marble-like patterns. There were glacier-polished slabs, smooth slabs, coarse-grained slabs, fine-grained slabs, slabs with that curious patina on it that one often sees out in the desert. There was a rock shaped just like a bowling ball that Fred was about to step on – did step on – that rolled, throwing him headfirst down a slab into a pile of talus.

Shit, the way he landed, Fred must have broken an arm for sure.

Maybe both arms, and a collarbone too. I began to think about what I had with me that could be used to patch Fred up. And a second thought came to mind. Now I'll be famous – or, more accurately, infamous – because everyone will be talking about how Fred Beckey got busted up on my watch. No, wait, he's getting back up. Complaining about the shitty soles on his approach shoes. Dusting off. Laceration on his arm, but it's hardly bleeding because he's so dehydrated. Damn, this is one tough guy. Eighty-something and taking a fall like that...I offer him some water and my trekking poles, which are the collapsible kind that don't quite fit inside my daypack. He declines both and starts walking.

Bear Creek Spire from Treasure Lakes: The Northeast Ridge is marked by the sun-shadow line. Photo: Joe Metz

We reached Dade Lake. Fred took a long drink. We retrieved his pack, parka, and pole, then headed through the waist-high forest, back toward the upper Treasure Lake. Fred still asked my opinion on navigational matters, even though it must have been obvious that the only useful input I would provide would be to point out which way not to go. It got mighty cold in a hurry after the sun set behind Mt. Mills. We walked through a silent frozen post-dusk world. The only sounds were the crunch of frozen grass and an occasional clack of a trekking pole hitting a rock.

At last, we stumbled back into camp at 6:00, cold, tired, and hungry after ten and a half hours of hiking and climbing. Fred got right into his sleeping bag and set about his usual evening bag sort. I fired up the stove and got a pot of water boiling for tea, then filtered more water for dinner and overnight use. Fred commenced making dinner while my back was turned. It consisted of (I think) elbow macaroni, powdered milk, rancid salami, oatmeal, dried apricots, grass clippings, and rodent turds. He kindly offered some to me, but I declined. He ate the stuff by moving his spoon from the green bowl to his mouth and back as rapidly as the eye could follow. I have never seen anyone eat faster than Fred Beckey.

After a few cups of tea and some dried fruit, I began to relax and reflect on what a day I just had. An excellent climb on excellent rock in a beautiful location, with – imagine! – someone I worshipped as a hero from my earliest days of reading climbing literature. I allowed that I did surprisingly well with the altitude, considering that I had been at sea level only 38 hours earlier. A long day, a hard day, a day with some strange turns and surprises, for sure, but that's why we go out and do these things, right?

We watched the last of the alpenglow disappear from the peaks, and the stars became visible in the sky. Fred rolled over and started snoring. I wasn't far behind.

Tuesday morning we slept in, sort of, until it got pleasantly warm in our south-facing camp. After breakfast, I made a vain attempt at shaking the grass clippings out of everything I owned. Fred, being wiser, didn't bother trying. We packed up and headed down the valley. Fred made more remarks about the Dry Sierra and how the basic building material here was talus. I couldn't argue with him too much – except to note that it was now October 16, and if we were here on June 16, we would be slogging through deep, wet snow. He also carried on with the usual complaints about his shitty approach shoes, backpack, and equipment in general. He thought having a porter would be a great idea. I tried to make a joke about rounding some up in Porterville the next time he passed through the Needles, but he didn't seem to get (or hear) it. Speaking of the Needles – I mentioned what a great time I had on his South Face route on Hermit Spire back in 1995. Fred seemed genuinely pleased that I thought it was a good climb. He almost blushed.

We joined the main trail at the head of Long Lake and were soon surrounded by day hikers again. Fred was always patient and polite and enjoyed pointing out Bear Creek Spire, which we had climbed just yesterday. Several people expressed amazement that someone so – old – was up here climbing mountains. If they only knew, I thought...

The drive back up 395 was as uneventful (if you can call it that) as the drive down. I enjoyed the Most Beautiful Views on Earth while Fred made comments about the trees and the traffic. He was already thinking ahead to his next project, which was connecting with Ron Felton at Calaveras Dome. I was only paying slight attention to him. Outside the windows, there were ash-gray volcanoes and blue granite peaks. Long streaks of golden aspens marked where water ran down from springs up above. Tiny villages with smoky chimneys nestled in shallow canyons scratched into the desert floor where they could escape from the relentless wind. Long graceful highway curves, jagged mining roads zigzagging up the canyon walls. High peaks, blue-gray sage valleys, yellow grass, grazing cattle, clear, sparkling autumn air. Huge moraines on canyon walls, reaching almost to the desert floor, once pushed aside by ice, now covered by sagebrush. What did the Eastern Sierra look like back then? A cold, dry, desolate place of groaning ice and crackling boulders? Then, when the glaciers melted, for a few generations, a wet paradise of green lake-filled valleys and roaring rivers under rainbow clouds of spray?

Back to Lee Vining. Nicely's is packed for lunch with the Winnebago crowd. We snag a table. Fred orders coffee and pie and flirts with the waitress. Soon it's time to leave. I remind Fred to call if he wants to come back down and try Whitney again next year. We shake hands. Up the humongous Lee Vining Canyon, through the brown alpine meadows at Tioga Pass, past the Tuolumne Domes and the western forests, down Priest Grade, through the thick damp fecund air of the Great Central Valley. Later I hear from Ron – "Fuckin' Beckey tried to kill me, man..." It seems that I was the only person who had a successful climb with Fred on his swing through the Sierra this year. Everyone else had bad weather or bad luck or bad whatever...A few weeks later, Ed gets an envelope in the mail, stationary from the Comfort Inn in Seattle, containing two slides and a yellow post-it note saying FOR JOE METZ. The pictures aren't as heroic as I had hoped, but hey, they are of me, way up on Bear Creek Spire, and they were taken by Fred Beckey. It seemed like the adventure was such a long time ago, and I wondered whether that orange was still in the back of Fred's Subaru.

SECTION II

FIRST ASCENTS

1

ROMANTIC WARRIOR
WARLOCK NEEDLE

By E.C. Joe

Unlikely as it was, now that I think about it, a climbing shop in Bakersfield, CA? It was a bit of a stretch, even though it was my hometown. Outdoor activities unrelated to hunting, fishing, or four-wheelin' in this town were still pretty foreign to most folks here. Then, if you can fathom the chance of two climbing shops in "B-Town"...well, there was for a time.

The few of us at that time who were introduced to the activity of rock climbing could always be found hanging around the local climbing shops. They would be considered quaint when compared to today's super outdoor shops. There was lots of natural wood, gear hanging in every available space, and the merchandising was as if it was some guy's closet. It was the simpleness of it all that I recall that was most appealing. What you saw is what you got. The local shops were the perfect venues to find willing partners and check out new gear. They were the best places to listen to, exchange info on, dream up, or read about anything concerning climbing a climber could ever want. Many trips were conceived while at the shops; crazy ideas woven around bull-shit so deep you needed a snorkel to stay in the room. I hung out at the shops enough to have had my own personal parking spot at each. Unfortunately, it was only a short time until there was only one climbing shop that B-Town could support.

Bigfoot Mountaineering, the remaining shop, is where I got acquainted with one of the owners, John Peca (pronounced: *Pes-sah*). John became part of the local outdoor scene by having his shop. He had a sort of "John Denver look" with his blonde hair and little round glasses. John had a college education but decided not to put his degree to work in the usual fashion. Instead, he chose to be a retailer and constantly put up with us climbing bums in the shop. His mountaineering background kept us coming around and helped brew our interests.

John and I had climbed a few times at the local Kern Slabs and did the South Face Route of Warlock Needle, with mini-epics provided free of charge. We got along well and had good times, John, with his dry humor and my tolerance of it. On one particular visit to the shop, John struck up a conversation with me about his desire to do a climb that he could bivouac on. I had spent the night out on a few walls by this time and was always ready to go at a moment's notice. Without hesitation, I mentioned to John that I had been eyeing a new line out at the Needles on the Warlock Needle. The route was the first on my "must do" list. I informed John that it would be the perfect route that we could spend a few days on.

I encouraged John to prepare the specialized gear that he would need on the ascent. Unique items such as ascenders, etriers, and a hammock were on the list. I stressed the importance of setting up his ascenders correctly ahead of time to be efficient and safe. We got together a double rack of Stoppers & Hexentrics, a small assortment of pitons, carabiners, two ropes, and enough food and water for the both of us for the weekend. All seemed to be in order for our ascent.

We pulled up in the Needles parking area in John's new/used Mercedes sedan that Friday night, a car much too fancy to match our scruffy climbing garb. We were a sight only for ourselves to behold, as the Needles hadn't yet seen the numbers of visitors it does these days. The place was deserted. Then, the Needles was always like this. It was October 1977. We crashed out on the ground in the chill of the Southern Sierra autumn night near the meadow, excited about the adventure in store for us ahead.

In the morning, John and I headed out on the trail to the Needles with our loads. It took some time to negotiate the Witch-Sorcerer Gully and then the tight squeeze through the bushes along the base of the Necromancer. The terrain finally opened up, and the boulders became nearly as big as a house near the base of the Warlock. On one of the boulders, I found a perfect vantage point to view our project.

This was the very first time either of us had been to the base of the intended route. I discovered the line on a recent evening from the summit of Dome Rock a few miles to the South, then from the fire lookout on the Magician Needle. The sight was daunting as we could view all but a short section of the route from our platform on the boulder. The route was so vertical and overhanging it allowed a view of close to 800 feet of stone from the base!

It was a beautiful wall bright with yellow lichens. The rock looked solid and was white & golden granite. The

Warlock Needle. Photo: E.C. Joe

line was simple, elegant, and direct. We were to follow a single crack system straight up the Southwest wall of the needle to a point just short of a huge curving roof. There, a thin crack splintered to the right of the main crack, which appeared to be the most direct path more vertically up to a small stance. This path could allow us easy access to a huge sloping ledge and then a significant corner that would get us to the top. We knew that we had our work cut out for us. I had John choose "odds or evens" to decide who would lead each pitch. He chose "even," and I had him swear that he would hold to it so we could share the burden of the work.

Following the main crack system down the wall, I located its origin at the base. The cracks were intermittent and steep. I opted for aid a few moves since I was wearing Robbins boots, not free climbing shoes. The wisps of cracks accepted small stoppers readily. In a few moves, I was into the main crack system. Free climbing was not difficult here, and I stopped at a small stance about 45 meters up. Here the corner steepened and turned incredibly vivid. It was so alive with yellow lichens that I named it the "Living Corner." As I hauled the bag up, John came up big wall style and "jugged" up with his ascenders. We then realized that we would need more time than planned to complete this project since daylight was short in the autumn. We fixed one of our ropes and rappelled back down to the base. We had just enough daylight to hike out and call it a weekend, excited about the route above.

Returning to the base of the route the following Saturday, we ascended our fixed rope to our high point. John free climbed up the Living Corner, wildly stemming from features on both walls, the haul rope at times hung in space due to the steepness. The crack in the corner was a good size but merely for protection. It was quite an impressive lead that appeared intimidating; however, it was not too difficult. John stopped a full rope length out at a small sloping ledge below a bulging headwall. There he placed an anchor and added a bolt to facilitate the hauling.

Randy Powers on pitch 1, Romantic Warrior. Photo: E.C. Joe

E.C. Joe, pitch 3, Romantic Warrior. Photo: Randy Powers

The next pitch headed out right underneath a huge flake. The rock appeared a little loose and threatening. I stepped out into space, carefully aiding outright and then back left as the crack changed directions. The rock quality turned better as I moved past the overhang and onto a more vertical section. Higher, the cracks got much thinner, but I could secure a suitable belay anchor of nuts, pitons, and two bolts at the point where we had planned to follow the crack that departed up and right. It was a whole hanging affair. I don't believe there's a more exposed position at the Needles than this spot. Like being on a wall in Yosemite, the rock was virtually flawless, steep, and grey. I explored the possibility of continuing left to a huge roof. However, the quality of the rock there appeared of less quality than on the direct crack. The seam appeared to be the shortest line between the points from where we were hanging at and the summit corner above. It took John quite some time to jug and clean the pitch. He was struggling with his ascenders on the steep for the first time ever. The weight of the back-pack on his back didn't help matters either, causing him to claw for his ascenders like a beetle stuck on its back trying to right itself.

John appeared over the lip of the overhang and cried out, "I almost died down there!!"

His ascenders had not been adjusted correctly for use on a steep wall and made his progress below strenuous. I could not share in his terror and made a dry remark on how I had asked him to make sure his ascenders were "right" as I was busy at the anchor. Daylight was now waning, and the October chill began to engulf us. By the time John slugged his way to the belay, I had our bivouac primed.

Bivouacs on the side of a cliff come in many variations. The most welcome is a nice grassy ledge, then in decreasing order, the flat rock ledge, the lumpy ledge, the gently sloping ledge, the very sloping ledge, the butt cheek ledge, a stance, a sloping stance, hanging stance, and then just hanging. It is a matter of degrees where steepness and comfort have a direct relationship to each other. The key to dealing with each situation is to adapt as quickly as possible and remind yourself that it's only a temporary situation. I had our hammocks deployed, food bag ready, and all essential night gear on hand. In this world with no floor, one must be careful not to drop anything, and the most critical items should be on leashes. Carabiners come in real handy securing those items. What a concept! We made short order of dinner, passing our shared food back and forth between hammocks. The night was chilly but mild for October.

We were in full shade in the morning, and it was pretty hard to get much done in the autumn chill before 8 am. We got all our gear packed, and it was now John's turn to forge ahead. The following lead up and right was up an insipid crack. It appeared thinner than the cracks in photos of "The Shield" route on El Capitan that I had seen in *Mountain Magazine 44*.

John stepped up to the plate. He checked his swing and looked back at me, saying, "You know that I've never driven a piton before."

"You're kidding?!" I laughed. "Don't worry, it's just like driving a nail into a board. Just hold 'em steady so they won't vibrate too much," I remarked about the postage stamp size pitons called RURPs (Realized Ultimate Reality Piton) that John had to use for this lead.

John used several RURPs in a row, and when the crack opened up once, he boldly used a Leeper Cam Hook in the maximum possible inverted placement. After two bolts in a blank spot and a couple of tiny Stoppers, John acquired the small stance above.

Randy Powers, original pitch 4, Romantic Warrior. Photo: E.C. Joe

"That was the scariest thing I've ever done in my life!" John reflected.

*The View from Excess Reality Ledge. Photo: Randy Powers, E.C. Joe
Collection*

After he placed two bolts to anchor at the stance, I ascended into
space and up to our new home. The stance measured about one foot by
two feet and was perfectly flat. It was in a position at the very top edge
of the overhanging wall we had climbed up, giving us a clear view of the
base of the route. The walls below were steep, gray, and streaked with
black and yellow lichens. The exposure was so surreal here we dubbed
the stance "Excess Reality Ledge." We were glad to have this small place

to stand instead of hang. The summit corner loomed overhead. I made a few tricky moves above the ledge to gain a vast sloping area that I could traverse right into the corner and belay. As I made the traverse, big updrafts of air blew my cap into oblivion. At that precise moment, I heard some screams coming from the direction of the fire lookout. Immersed in a separate reality, we hailed them back with a wave and continued about our business.

I later had found out that Richard Leversee had appeared on the scene to scope out the route we were on. Richard had been the only person other than John that I had divulged my discovery of the route. In an attempt to recruit partners to climb the route, he showed the climb off to his buddies through the telescope at the fire lookout. Then saw us en route. Timing is everything! John had to muscle and drag the bag on the slab to help me haul it up to the anchor. Our bivy on the sloping slab below the base of the corner was an uncomfortable place indeed. A fully hanging bivouac can be more comfortable than a highly sloping ledge. Laying on a slab while keeping yourself from sliding down or around is an all-night maintenance project.

The Book of Deception. Photo: Randy Powers, E.C. Joe Collection

John climbed up the spectacular, vertical corner above, aiding on nuts and a few pitons. The climbing was straightforward. We felt dwarfed by the enormous walls of the corner. The route's character changed from the wall below. Previously, we had hung precariously and exposed. Now we nestled in the false security of "hiding" in the summit corner. When John finished with the lead it was late, so we decided to fix the rope at his high point and stay at the base of the corner for another miserable night.

We were on the move early the following day. There is a supernatural incentive one can muster to get off of a route. It is as if we could smell the top. I guess that is what's been known as "Summit Fever."

In the years after, I have told many an incredulous neophyte wall climber, "Yeah, you're going to spend all this time making your plans to climb your big route, and even relish the thought of living on it for days. I'll tell you, once you get up a ways, unless you bail off, you're going to do everything in your power to get the Hell off the damn thing as fast as possible. Climbing walls can be like beating yourself on the head with a hammer, only because it feels so good when you stop."

I continued up the corner on aid using mostly nuts and a couple of pitons. We thought we would be up in no time at all, but "The Book of Deception" seemed endless. When the corner did end, I was faced with some tricky face climbing and placed a bolt for protection. I finally reached the southern tower of the Warlock Needle about mid-day and fired in a couple of belay bolts. Once on the summit, we knew that we had just accomplished something special but were too exhausted to revel in the moment. John and I quietly gathered our gear, rappelled down the backside of the spire into the woods, and made the trudge back the car.

2

THE WHIPPER!

PARKER BLUFF

By Patrick Paul

Herb Laeger has a great sense of humor; very dry at times. He has a keen eye for plumb lines on slabs, with plenty of time to explore since he retired at the ripe old age of 41. Herb has a calmly intelligent resolution about him that inspires others to go for it and risk-taking the fall. Along with the lure of fun and challenging climbs, there was also the intellectual stimulation. Whenever Herb and I got together, we had wonderful conversations about non-climbing topics. We'd talk about everything from education in America to world energy consumption, from women's plumbing to waterwheels, and from the anatomy of gnats to the true nature of nanoseconds. We both loved a friendly debate about almost anything, and we were both old enough to have an opinion about everything, so there was never a moment without a spirited discussion between us.

We usually started by greeting each other and catching up on what each of us had been doing. I'd tell Herb about my work, and he'd remind me "teachers are over paid." I'd share lovingly about my little family, and he makes sure to ask questions about my son, whom he has known since birth. I make sure to complain that I am out of shape to make sure Herb understands that I won't be climbing very well. I always make sure that I tell him I am recovering from some injury and make a note of the fact that I am still overweight and have been for the last twenty years. Herb catches me up on his latest fishing trip to Baja, his latest caving adventure to Borneo, Belize, or Mexico, his most recent climbing foray to one of his secret spots, and how his lovely wife Eve is doing. I remind him that his wife is a better climber than both of us put together; he ignores my comments about Eve and tells me about his mischievous cats (his version of kids).

A goodly number of years ago, when Herb and I used to climb together pretty regularly, we decided to meet up at Parker Bluff above Johnsondale, in the Southern Sierra, and do some exploring along the base of the cliff. Parker Bluff is a unique east-facing cliff with only a few crack climbs, and an abundance of steep, blank, face climbs that will test anyone's ability to tip-toe on tiny holds. Most other crags in the area, the Needles, Dome Rock, Elephant Knob, Hermit Spire, and Trilogy all feature a mix of face and crack climbs that, while challenging, have "real," more forgiving features like solid cracks, chicken head knobs, solid edges, and buckets. The word bluff is so ironic in the name of this rock because that is precisely the thing you can't do when you climb there. You have to be totally in sync with delicate face climbing, or you will fall. There is no room for bluffing on these steep, smeary, edgy pitches. Parker has route names like Race with the Devil on Spanish Highway, King of Pain, or White Rabbit. You're definitely going to be on some kind of trip when you climb here.

It was always fun to climb with Herb, even if it meant having to desperately inch your way up some dime-edged face climb, Bosch drill dangling below, and a small rack of hooks at the ready in case there is just no way to hang on with only one hand and drill. It may be that the promise of trying to put up a new route using little more than dried bat crap for holds is one of the main attractions about climbing with Herb. When I really think about it, the terror of anticipating a long fall while discovering new territory is also oddly exhilarating. It feels pretty good if you get where you're headed in one piece without soiling your knickers.

Herb's friend from Los Angeles, Charlie Lai, the person for whom the route "Travels With Charlie," is named on Hermit Spire, joined us on this occasion. Charlie was not a very experienced climber at the time, but he always climbed well and is one of the fittest human beings I've ever met due to his constant working out in the Martial Arts. We put the usual eclectic mixture of climbing gear together to be prepared for any situation, threw in the Bosch and batteries, bolts, hangers, hooks, a haul line, a hand drill, and a few extra microwires, and started skulking up the steep trail to Parker.

As was our habit, once we arrived at the base of the rock, we would drop our packs and cruise along the base, look at the routes that were there, checked out what's changed or is new, and reminisced about our past experiences on the rock. This pre-climb activity was always a good way to warm up our bodies and get our heads into the climbing zone before we actually committed. After our perusal of the existing climbs, we moved along the base of the slab to the area where Herb had something in mind. As we were walking beneath an extremely blank section of the rock, Herb stopped and looked up. I could see the faint hue of rust-colored streaks left behind from millennia of water tumbling down the face above. The rock looked very dark and featureless here. Right above where we stood, there was a slight bulge to the rock, and everything looked much more plausible to the right and left of where we were standing. Of course, Herb said, "This is it. I've been looking at this for years and nobody's done it yet. Someone has put up a route over there (he pointed to the left of where we were). I think this has got to be done now, before they come back and grab this line."

"This line," I was thinking, "is only a line because there is a water streak coming down the rock. There's nothing here to climb on."

I started looking down along the bottom of the rock and examining everything closer to eye level. I found a small foothold near the ground. I found a slight edge for fingertips about head high. There was something else for feet about waste high, and Herb and Charlie began to point and make their observations, and a few moments later, I was standing there, rope in hands, belaying Herb as he levitated up the blank face several feet and placed the first bolt.

When you drill a bolt while standing on thin edges, there is probably nothing more satisfying than the "click" sound of a carabiner gate as it lovingly closes behind your rope, and you know that you are finally belayed through protection at eye level and no longer facing a long fall. When I first started climbing back in the mid-seventies, bolts were all drilled by hand. The drill, a steel shaft that held a rock drill, was carried up in a pouch at one's waist, along with a hammer with a lanyard attached to one's waist with a loop of cord. Drilling was arduous! Get to a stance and balance. Reach down and get the drill with one hand. Reach down and get the hammer with the other hand. Hold the hammer and drill over your head and begin to tap, tap, twist, tap, tap, twist over and over again until you think the hole was deep enough for the bolt. Now wet the drill tip and stick it in the hole. Pull it out to compare the dusty drill tip to your bolt to see if the hole really is deep enough. If not, drill some more. If yes, rewet the drill several times to clear the dust from the hole. Put the drill back in the pouch and retrieve a bolt and hanger. Place the bolt in the hole and pound it down with the hammer until the hanger is tight against the rock.

Don't over pound! Let the hammer fall by your side as you clip a carabiner to the hanger and then clip your rope through the carabiner. Tell your belayer to take some tension on the rope, and now you can relax. This process was exhausting, especially if you were on tiny footholds on a steep face where letting go with both hands was very awkward at best. We were using a Bosch battery-powered drill to do our work. The electric drill was especially great for drilling a bolt hole quickly. Just hold the drill and bit above your head and hit the trigger. The rig would punch a hole in a matter of seconds instead of 20 to 30 minutes with a hand drill. We loved that, but electric drills have their drawbacks too. They're heavy, almost nine pounds. You really can't climb with one hanging off of your waist with a hammer and bolts as well. To drill on lead with a Bosch, you have to leave the drill below as you climb. When you get to a suitable stance, you have to pull the drill up to you with a small rope tied to your waist. Usually, one of your hands is busy hanging on to the rock, so pulling the rope and drill up requires pulling up with one hand, biting down on the rope while you grasp the rope, then repeating the process. Once you start pulling that little rope and drill rig up, you notice a marked difference in your weight. You've suddenly added nine-plus pounds to your stance. When you finally do get the drill to hand, you have to hold the whole rig over your head—which forces you to lean out away from the rock— point in, pull the trigger, and punch the hole. Then you go through the process of checking the hole for depth, etc., hang the heavy drill on your side, pound in the bolt and hanger, and finally, clip the bolt and relax.

Herb had stood there, toe tips seemingly attached to the rock with invisible glue, and placed the first bolt with what looked like no real effort at all. I have watched Herb stand on nothing many times. He sets his feet where he wants them to be, and they stay there. It is weird because nothing moves below his knees. His arms do their work; his body moves slightly left or right, but his calves, ankles, and feet never move. He is the quintessential "rock steady" climber, and it is never really evident that he is burning major BTUs to maintain this solid position. After placing bolt number one, he was ready to lower off.

Whipper Snapper. Photo: David Hickey

"It's great climbing," he said. "And it's not that bad."

He untied from the rope, handed me the sharp end, and clipped the tag line for the Bosch to the back of my harness. Charlie looked at what Herb had just climbed and bouldered a few feet up. He jumped back down and, with a big grin on his face, told me that it would be a great climb if we could just get past the next few moves over the bulging face. I started to strain my way up to Herb's bolt using any of the little finger tweakers I could find along the way. I was trying my best to believe that the fear manifested as severe shaking in my back and legs was excitement. In a short time, I was at the bolt and ready to launch out onto new ground.

I couldn't see any way of continuing straight up and decided to move left on some small holds. I could see a stance out there, but I was not convinced that there was anything between me and what now looked like a ledge by comparison to what I was standing on. I started to crab-crawl my way left and then retreated. There was something to stand on, but the move required a long, "reachy" step over, and it did not feel secure at all. I attempted to move left several times and almost fell. I wasn't happy about the idea that I would swing down and right across the face, and I could tell by the loud silence of Charlie and Herb that they, too, were tense about what I was doing. I convinced myself to try the moves across one last time before I could excuse myself and come down. My muscles strained, fingertips fried trying to hold the weight of my entire body as I moved across, and my smoking toes seemed to squeak along the face with me until I made it to the stance. "Now what?"

I pulled the drill up as fast as I could and punched a hole in the rock. I hung the heavy drill on my waste, fumbled for a bolt and hanger and pounded away, dropped the hammer and let it dangle by my feet, pulled the wrench from the bolt bag and tightened the head of the bolt enough to clip a carabiner and then pulled the rope up and clipped.

"Aaahhhh!"

I weighted the bolt and relaxed as Charlie held me fast. The second bolt was in. After a good rest, I lowered off. Charlie climbed up to our high point, and so did Herb, but it was getting late, and we decided to go home and finish the route the following week.

The following week we were back and ready to climb. I volunteered to place bolt number three and began to climb, but I could not get to the second bolt. I kept falling off, and I just didn't have the steam to motor across the bulge. I was very frustrated when I lowered back down to Herb and Charlie. Herb took the gear. He climbed up and past bolt one to bolt two. He moved carefully and steadily across and commented about how hard it was so that I wouldn't feel so bad. I couldn't believe that I was unable to repeat the moves and felt like a real wimp. Herb placed the remainder of the bolts on the first pitch and put us up and slightly right of the water streak. I had to take tension on the rope to move to the second bolt as I went up to meet Charlie and Herb at the first belay. I was feeling awful now as I geared up to start pitch two.

We were under another bulge on the main face, and in order to stay with the water streak, it was necessary to move out left again and climb on the left side of a slight cleft in the face. Placing the first bolt for this pitch was not too bad. I returned, and Herb went out and put a bolt high up on the left side of the cleft, and then he came back in. I went out for bolt number three, slightly up and left of the cleft, where we could then begin to move back to the right. I felt like I should do more than my share since I had been so wimpy on the first pitch and offered to keep drilling.

About twelve or fifteen feet up and right from where I was perched, I could see what looked like a good foothold for a drilling stance. I moved across on smears and small edges to the spot. Unfortunately, the good foothold had dematerialized into a crappy, down-sloping smear, and I was now desperately far away from my last bolt and shaky. After a bit of discussion with Herb and Charlie – who were almost directly below me – I began to look for something else to stand on. I could see a possible foothold about ten feet above my head. I told Herb that I would go up and try it, and he reminded me that I was already looking at a thirty-foot fall from where I was. I rationalized that the climbing wasn't too bad and that the foothold seemed pretty good for drilling.

I began to climb on the smears and small pockets that characterize the upper pitches of Parker Bluff. When I got to the spot that would be my comfortable drilling stance, there was nothing there! Once again, I was trying to stand on a small, steeply sloping, crappy little nothing of a smear hold; I was going to die, and I knew it.

I looked down at Herb and Charlie, now some 35 or 40 feet below me. They huddled silently together at the anchors with their heads down as if they were praying. I looked down and left to my last bolt nearly 25 feet away. There was no way I could down-climb without peeling off the face. I had two of the fingers of my right hand on a minuscule edge, too small for hooking, and right by my face. My right toe was smearing on the nasty sloper while my left foot and left hand rested against the face on nothing. Somehow I was sticking to the rock, so I decided to try and drill. I began to pull on the tagline, and the heavy Bosch started to rattle up the face of the rock towards me. I would pull two feet of cord and chomp down with my teeth to prevent the line from slipping backward, pull two feet and chomp, pull two feet and chomp...Over and over again, I repeated this maneuver, and the drill slowly scraped its way up to me. As I pulled the cord, I could feel the sensation of something wedging between the tip of my right toe and the rock. I stopped pulling long enough to notice that the slack from the tag line was piling up on top of my right foot with one little piece wedged firmly between my shoe rubber and the rock. I was powerless to change the situation and just kept pulling up the Bosch. I hoped that I could just get the drill started and then place a hook over the bit shaft so that I could rest off of it.

After what seemed like an eon, I got the drill in my hand. I reached up and placed the tip of the bit against the rock, and squeezed the trigger. The drill made about two full revolutions, and I found myself reeling through space and screaming like a little girl at a Psycho screening. Time slowed to a crawl, and I could hear myself thinking as I fell towards Herb, Charlie, and earth:

"I wonder how long this will take? I better hold this stinking drill out away from me so I don't end up with it stuck in my leg!"

Suddenly I heard the sound of something skittering along the face of the rock and the sound of climbing gear clanging together. It sounded like someone was getting the wind knocked out of them. Zzzzzzsssssshh-hhaaa...Whump!!

As soon as I came to a stop, I could hear Herb and Charlie yelling at me.

"Are you okay?

"Patrick, are you okay?"

"My God, man, that was unbelievable!!"

"Are you okay?"

I righted myself and turned myself around so that I was facing the rock again. I started saying I was okay, but I hadn't assessed the damage yet. My left arm was still extended and holding the Bosch out away from my body. The arm felt numb, and the forearm ached terribly. I started to swing over to an area just below Herb's feet, and I handed Charlie the drill. My entire left arm, from the tip of my little finger to the tip of my elbow, was missing several layers of skin and dripping with blood. I was as high a kite on adrenaline, smiling, and happy to be alive.

"Wow, that was totally amazing!!!" I said.

We all started to breathe again, and each of us told the story of the fall from our own perspective. We figured that with rope stretch, it was about 50 feet. I came within a few feet of hitting Herb and Charlie until rope tension caused me to fly off towards our last bolt and away from them. We all regained our composure, and I decided to go up and try to drill again. Herb admonished me to keep it down to a reasonable distance away from the last bolt this time.

I climbed back up to the bolt above the cleft and then began to move right again above Herb and Charlie. This time, when I came to the first crappy smear, it didn't seem too bad for a stance. Compared to the stance I had when I fell, it now felt like a bivy ledge. I stood and drilled my bolt and then rested. I climbed and drilled two more before I went back down to Herb and Charlie. Herb took over for the rest of the pitch. He climbed flawlessly past my high point and placed the remaining few bolts of the second pitch for us. We all climbed the remainder of the pitch and gleefully rappelled off of the rock.

On the way down to the car, we began to discuss names for the route. Names like "Death Fall," "Nearer My God to Thee," "Welcome to Parker Bluff," and "Whipper Snapper" were discussed, but we couldn't agree on what to call it. Charlie finally came up with a solution. We would put all of the names we had thought of in a hat, and he would draw one out. As we sat at the cars in the waning sunlight, Charlie drew out the name Whipper Snapper.

Whipper Snapper. Photo: David Hickey

Whipper Snapper is rated 5.11c and follows the longest, most prominent water streak on the face of Parker Bluff. It turned out to be excellent climbing and well protected for a climb at that level. It also turned out to be a fond memory for me and another experience with Herb that I will always appreciate and never forget.

3

FATIMA AND THE QUIVERING THIGH
DOME ROCK

By Patrick Paul

One summer day in 1985, Herb Laeger, Greg Vernon, and I were doing perhaps the fourth or fifth ascent of Just Barely, a route that Herb, the irrepressible Ron Carson, and I had put up in the summer of '83. We were at the second belay, a vertical crack at the base of the prominent headwall of Dome Rock's southeast face, a total gear belay of four pieces linked together in an equal pull configuration with several spectra slings. The usual gear sort was happening, handing off of myriad equipage, quick-draws and slings and talking about the run-out pitch ahead when suddenly we were all dropping towards the ground some two hundred feet below. The top piece in our fine belay had popped and dropped us all about a foot and a half. We all nearly crapped our pants. We were all talking at once, "Whoa, what the hell, shit, God, what happened?" After we gained some composure, Greg announced he wasn't feeling it anymore and would rap off and head home. We fixed for a rappel and headed down.

I'm pretty sure it was my idea; at least I will take the credit for it. I had done just about every route at Dome Rock, and I could visualize a traverse in my mind's eye. I told Herb Laeger what I was thinking. "Sure, a girdle traverse of Dome Rock," Herb agreed. "Lots of places have a traverse route and why not Dome Rock?"

Herb and I agreed to use existing belay anchors at the top of each first pitch for pro and for anchors as we moved along. There were about 60 independent routes on the dome; we should find plenty of pro between natural features, protection bolts, and anchors. The route would start with ascending the Last Dihedral to its first belay and then traverse to the right.

The first traverse was on easy ground, but it soon became evident that the fall potential would be a lot greater than most routes on the dome. The distance between The Last Dihedral and Red Mushrooms was short, but the distance between Red Mushrooms and the first belay of Just Lovely, crossing over Skid Row, seemed a bit run out. We began to swing leads a hundred or so feet off the deck.

In our early days of climbing together, Ron Carson and I had gotten off route at The Needles. Ron kept saying as he belayed me. "Don't fall man; if you do, it's the big red smile for you." All I could imagine was a gruesome blood-streaked smiley face on the rock below if I flipped out and failed to make all the moves to an anchor. I made it, but Ron's visual was the real inspiration for staying on the rock.

Here were Herb and I on Dome Rock and looking at the big red smile. Every pitch had its easy but thought-provoking parts, and every pitch had its difficult, dicey, no pro, scary, don't make a wrong move or get in too deep part where a misstep could mean a nasty pendulum across a crystal band, over knobs and chicken-heads, while flailing and spinning out of control. Mind control was the order of the day.

Moving along past Just Barely, Pipe Dream, Carson-O-Genic, and Saucer Full of Secrets wasn't too bad. There seemed to be plenty of good features for the hands and feet, and there was even an occasional crack or bolt to catch some pro. The span between the top bolt on Saucer' and the corner on Arch Enemy was something else, though. I ended up leading this section, and I kept moving up higher and higher as I scuttled along, trying to find something for pro. Later in the decade, three more routes would go into this area, all rated 5.11 or harder, but now, it was just no man's land. It was in this section where I got almost terminal Elvis legs and my brain almost completely unraveled. I was sick to my stomach and almost crapping my pants. Every pore gave forth with moisture, and

I nearly exhausted my chalk bag, trying to stay dry before each "you're going to die now" move. The fixed pins on the Arch Enemy looked like excellent prospects from a thousand miles away, and after what seemed like a three-hour pitch, I set up a belay on the bolts at the second apex of the arch where more reasonable moves would get us to the dominant crystal bands on the dome.

We continued to move northward on the crystal bands that connected Arch Enemy, Satyr, Asteroid Belt, One Size Fits All, Between Nothingness and Eternity, and Tobin's Dihedral. It was on one of these short pitches that I found a "Thank God" protection point. As I was moving along the crystal band between established routes, clinging to the rock in a precarious set of sideways, balancing moves, my nose passed right in front of a worm-hole! A perfect ¾ inch diameter hole that went straight into the rock, like nothing I had ever seen on Dome Rock before or since. I stopped and contemplated how I might be able to use this hole to save my life. I tried a nut, but nothing would work or fit properly in the hole. Nuts were either too big to go in or too small to key in and stay. I tried a small cam, but I had nothing on my rack small enough to cam down and fit in. I found a small brass slider nut, which would fit in the hole, but like the other nuts, would not stay. I had to reduce the size of the hole and figured out that I could nest the ½ inch slider and a small stopper together for a perfectly solid piece. I was free to clip in and go for it to the next anchor with only a thirty or forty-foot pendulum to look at. It was great to have that piece.

The rest of the climb went mostly the same. We followed the crystal bands and used existing bolts, incipient cracks, knobs, and small bushes and trees for pro. The climbing got easier after Tobin's Dihedral, but there was never a moment without threat. Each pitch was amazing and filled with challenges for both the leader and the follower. It almost didn't matter if you were leading or following; if you blew it, you were going leave the big red smile and get hurt. I remembered an underground comic book called The Checkered Demon. It featured an exotic lady pirate character named Fatima, the captain of a renegade ship called the Quivering Thigh. It all seemed appropriate, the beauty and the terror. We named the ten-pitch traverse of Dome Rock, Fatima and the Quivering Thigh.

4

THE DANCE OF TOPO-USHA
HOMERS NOSE

By Richard Leversee

The Dream, July 10, 1977

It is really hard to believe that the dream was born so long ago, on a weed oiler somewhere between rows thirty-seven and thirty-eight of an orange grove near Exeter in the stifling heat of California's Central Valley. The temperature was ninety degrees in the shade, and the toxic weed oil was sizzling chemical burns into my already sweaty skin. It was still two long hours until lunch, and we were just making the turn into row thirty-eight when my head was raised by a wild sight. "Stop, dammit! What in the world is that? It can't be a rock." But the wildest thing about it was that being so steep; I knew it couldn't be anything but rock! The haze had cleared just enough to reveal a mammoth chunk of stone protruding from the Sierra crest like an enormous beach ball in the sand. This was Homers Nose. A chilling breeze ripped across the Central Valley.

That night I dug up all my old Alpine Journals and called Dave, "You've got to see this thing to believe it, and even then you might not. It looks like the whole bottom half overhangs and I don't think it's ever been climbed!" Dave, "Whoooa!"

The Research

In the next year and a half, I did my research, afraid to approach the monster just yet. I poured through all the old journals, guidebooks, and magazines I could get my hands on, checked into all the Central Valley climbing shops, and carefully and discreetly finagled any and all information out of all the climbers I could get a hold of. The guidebooks and magazines were encouraging; not a word about it, not even the mention of its existence! The wind was temporarily taken out of my sails in the Visalia climbing shop, "Homers Nose? Sure, I know a guy who's climbed it." So, following leads and referrals, I called up half of the population of Tulare County, with always the same reply, "No, I haven't climbed it, but so and so has," until finally, with all available sources exhausted, the verification remained unclaimed. "Dave, she's still a virgin!"

The big blow came while bouldering at Stanford with some Bay Area locals. Just what I had been afraid of all along, "Homers Nose? Oh, yeah. Beckey's been there." My heart sank, but I still dejectedly copied down the number anyway. "Hello, Fred? You don't know me, but..." "Oh, yeah, we went up there once, but the approach killed us. I don't know if the other guy went back or not. Why, are you thinking of climbing it?" "No, just curious," I lied. The dream was still alive!

"Dave, it must have been climbed. This is 1979, and besides, you can see the damned thing from Visalia!" I said depressingly. "Richard, have you talked to anyone who's climbed it?" asked Dave with wild excitement in his voice. "Well, no," I muttered. The dream was still very much alive! And so were the seeds of the first attempt sown.

The Attempt, November 17, 1979

So, with Dave unable to attend in November, Randy Powers and I started trudging up Salt Creek Ridge to what? A six-hundred-foot overhanging unclimbed dome which we hadn't even seen from closer than ten miles! (Our recon trip had been fogged out.) "Yeah, Randy, Beckey said that there's a huge chimney in the center of the face." "Oh, God, overhanging chimneys!" said Randy, adjusting the single rack of hexes on his shoulder. Finally, we had the first view of our objective, an utterly incredible sight! Even better than we had hoped. The whole lower half did overhang! There it sat, like a giant pumpkin, blank and solid, Absolutely awesome!

But after a day and a half in the fog, we rappelled off from two-hundred feet up and were stopped by a short overhanging blank section. We had to swing ourselves back into the anchors to retreat! Although the attempt had failed to produce a completed route, we now knew that this primo line up the center of the face was indeed virgin and that we would need hooks.

The Realization, August 2, 1980

"Hi, can I have my mail please?" Oh, no, the phone bill, and hmmm, what's this? A letter from Dave. Riiip. Dear Richard: Homers Nose...Let's do it! Signed Dave.

Homers Nose. Photo: Dave Obst

August 8, 1980

Then, with fifty-pound packs, two unsuspecting young climbers and one young sandbagger started up the "killer" approach. Five long, hard hours later, we arrived at the base of the route, thoroughly exhausted. The weather was perfectly clear and sunny this time, so after a much needed nap, John re-led the first pitch, ending on a small sloping shelf just above the crux free climbing, a short overhanging corner (5.10). The whole wall above overhung at one-hundred intimidating degrees! From the belay, a perfect A1 crack led up seventy feet to the previous high point where a faded blue sling fluttered free in the breezes. Here, twenty feet of overhanging hooking proceeded to sap my boldness. The bases of the hooks did not even touch the rock, but a copperhead and a number one stopper made it fairly sane (A3). The route was going! Above, fifty feet of unexpected, ugly 5.9 off-width led to a more welcome belay stance with the sun already setting. With cramping hands, we made two airy rappels back to planet Earth as we commonly know it. After a quick supper, we fell asleep exhausted, dreaming of first ascents and what might lie above tomorrow.

Dave Ohst ascends a fixed rope. Photo: Richard Leversee, Dave Ohst Collection

Richard Leversee near the top of Pitch 2, John Tuttle belays. Photo: Dave Ohst

D-Day, August 9, 1980

Shortly after dawn, three nervous spiders slowly began to jug up their lines into the sky, the last swinging wildly forty-five feet, free air into the void, before joining the others. From our perch, with views akin to the Shield Headwall, Dave led a short, thin traverse to the left and placed a bolt. Then, while terrifying and amazing both John and me, he cranked up a gripping 5.9/5.10 vertical section to where the angle eased off a bit. "Hey you guys we've got it in the bag!" he yelled. Our screams of elation echoed back. He quickly fired up the rest of the "Ohstest Chimney" to a huge bushy belay ledge. The last pitch was refreshingly easy and ended in a super belay cave just below the top. And just as intense as it had begun, so was it suddenly over. Homers Nose had been climbed!

John Tuttle, Richard Leversee, and Dave Ohst after the 1st Ascent of The Dance of Topo-Usha, Homers Nose. Photo: Dave Ohst Collection

"I just can't believe that it's only four pitches long," said John, bathing in the river that evening. But the most amazing aspect of the climb is the probability of it being a first ascent of a major Sierra dome. In a day and age when El Cap has been climbed thousands of times, and countless routes are being squeezed into every conceivable and inconceivable corner of the world, it is extremely rare to come across a jewel such as this.

Adventure is alive and well in California!

Homers Nose, "The Dance of Topo-Usha," IV5.10, A3

First Ascent: 08/09/1980, John Tuttle, Dave Ohst, Richard Leversee

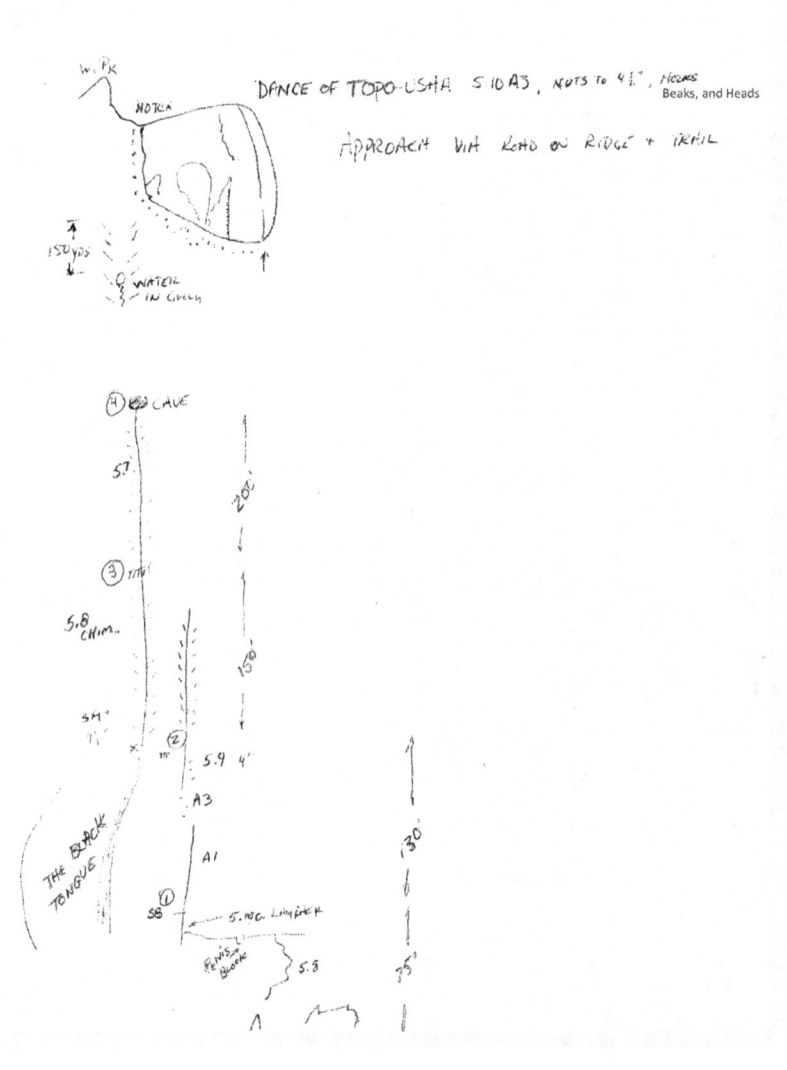

5

EL NIÑO

MORO ROCK, SEQUOIA NATIONAL PARK

By Brandon Thau

I had been looking at the smooth, overhanging east face of Moro Rock for years. During approaches to routes such as the South Face and Moro Oro, I'd been searching for a natural line up its blank headwall. While on a one-day ascent of Full Metal Jacket, Grant Gardner and I found a new line to climb and decided to make an attempt later in the year. Grant, Jody Pennycook, and I arrived at the Moro Rock parking lot after a day of classes at Cal Poly in San Luis Obispo. It was Veterans Day weekend in 1997, and we were taking four days off. Weather forecasters were talking about a phenomenon called "El Nino." During an El Nino event, warmer than average Pacific Ocean temperatures can lead to higher intensity precipitation over the west coast regions of the Americas. The excess precipitation has been known to bring floods and deep snowpacks. The forecast called for the first storm of the season to hit Monday night. We figured that three days would be plenty of time to climb the 1,200-foot route.

The next day we headed down the eastside gully with portaledges, big wall climbing gear, and ambition. The first pitch was my lead. It's an A2 variation of the first pitch of Full Metal Jacket (FMJ). It was the dirtiest pitch on the climb since it required scooping slimy mud out of the

Grant Gardener approaching the Great Half Moon, El Niño. Photo: Brandon Thau

crack to get good cam placements. Grant led the next pitch up the "Grey Half Moon." This "new wave" A3+ pitch has thin heading and nailing over the ramp that forms the second pitch of FMJ. At points on the pitch, Grant could have fallen and hit the sidewalk-like ramp. The difficulty and fall factor didn't seem to bother him, though. Grant was one of the strongest and most gifted aid climbers around. He went on to complete the first solo ascent of Reticent Wall (A5) on El Capitan before renowned climbers were able to claim it. Grant also established the first ascent of "Nightmare on California Street" (A4+), considered one of the most difficult aid routes on El Capitan. I was fortunate to be climbing with Grant since he was willing to lead the potentially dangerous pitches on our new route. The pitch ended at the "John De Aves," an abandoned bird nest atop a pillar with lots of bird poo. We set up a hanging camp here, right at the base of the bulging headwall.

We woke up Sunday morning with the sun rising over the Sierra crest. One of the great things about the east face of Moro is that no people or cars can be seen; only the High Sierra and the Kaweah River Valley are in view. The temperature was perfect as I started aiding the splitter crack up the overhanging face. "The Opiator" (A2+) pitch consisted of a 3/4 inch, straight-in crack that tapered down to beak piton size at the belay. It took a long time to lead the strenuous 110-degree over-hanging pitch. It wasn't until I was at the belay that I noticed the 100+ foot section above, that appeared blank from below, actually had a splitter

Grant Gardener on pitch 2, El Niño. Photo: Brandon Thau

Knifeblade/Beak crack running through it. I was definitely setting up the

belay here and handing the lead over to Grant. I drilled three 3/8 inch bolts, fixed the ropes, and started hauling from this extremely exposed belay. The belay was so overhanging that we were suspended away from the rock.

Grant started one of the best aid pitches anywhere. On the "Trust Your Pecker" pitch (A3), Grant placed all five of our bird beaks, back cleaned most of them, and placed them again. He placed a few small heads towards the top of the pitch and set up a belay underneath an overhang. This was our second hanging bivy. So far, we had placed no lead bolts or rivets.

Grant Gardner leads the "Trust Your Pecker" pitch on the 1st ascent of El Niño. Photo: Brandon Thau

Monday morning started with lots of high clouds moving in. We could tell that something big was headed our way. We still felt confident that we could top out by the end of the day. To make sure we were moving as fast as possible, I asked Grant to lead the next pitch. His free/aid lead zig-zagged until he gained one of the right angling cracks that comprise the upper east face of Moro. His lead took several hours, and the skies were getting darker. The fog was starting to move up the Kaweah River Valley far below. Grant finished his lead and fixed the lines. Jody's line hung right over the lip of an overhang. As with the last two pitches, she needed to be lowered out in order to ascend the fixed line. I lowered her out and let the rope go. She was on her own. After she had jugged 20 feet up the rope, there was a tearing sound. The rope's sheath had abraded and cut on a knob, and the sheath slid back about 2 feet, exposing the core of the rope. Jody was freaking out, and I thought I was about to watch someone die. Grant immediately rappelled down the tail of the haul line down to Jody, almost rappelling off the end due to panic. He quickly backed up Jody's line with an upside-down ascender below the cut area. After adding padding between the rock and the rope, he then had Jody switch over to the secure and intact haul line. She then jugged up to the safety of the belay station. We were all shaken by this experience. Our lives would have been much different if the rope had been fully cut.

When I arrived at the belay, it was starting to sprinkle. Quickly I grabbed the gear, ropes, and bolt kit and headed out onto the 6th lead. It was free climbing to the top, but on wet rock. The situation was starting to get serious. To reduce the risk, I placed two bolts on this 5.7 pitch that wouldn't be necessary in dry conditions. They were the first lead bolts of the route. By the time I had set up the belay, little streams of water had started to flow down the face. Grant and Jody followed the pitch with urgency.

Grant took the next lead, which continued on the right-leaning crack system. FMJ joined in at this point, so we felt some comfort knowing we were on an established route. About halfway up the pitch, it started to snow. Jody and I yelled at Grant to finish the pitch as we realized we were in deep trouble. Grant complained that he had lost feeling in his fingers and was having a hard time manipulating the ropes. Eventually, the ropes were fixed. Jody had been shaking for the last hour, and now she had the chance to get warm by jugging. We decided we needed to bivy, so Grant started to get a bolt ready for the portaledge. Suddenly Jody slid down the rope, as her ascenders were slipping on the icy rope. We couldn't believe it; even with teeth on the ascender cams, they weren't gripping the icy rope at all. Jody started to cry; this said a lot since most guys would have already been bawling. She used her hand to clear the snow and ice off the rope, then slid the ascender up and pressed the cam in with her thumb. There was still some slippage, but she managed to get to the anchor.

Brandon Thau leads a face pitch in the rain, hoping for a good bivy spot before the storm really hits. Photo: Grant Gardner, Brandon Thau Collection

Snow was collecting on ledges and was starting to slough off the rock; it became a blizzard. I started cleaning the pitch on ascenders and began to slide down the rope. I paused for a moment to rest and evaluate the situation. I told myself, "If you don't get up this rope, you will die." I used my numb hands to clear the snow and ice from the rope and moved slowly up the rope. I arrived at the belay to see Grant slumped on the ledge hypothermic. The portaledge anchor had not been setup up, and snow was piling up on our haulbags. Jody was huddling around Grant to keep warm. Immediately I started drilling a 1/4" bolt, hung a keyhole hanger on it, and setup up the double portaledge and fly. We scrambled into the hanging tent with our extra clothes and sleeping bags. We took off most of our clothes and tried to dry off. The waterproof fly trapped in most of the vapor and got our sleeping bags damp. None of us slept that night. We massaged our feet and hands to get feeling back in them. We had to beat the rain fly every ten minutes to knock off the snow collecting on it. We kept communicating with each other to make sure we weren't going hypothermic. I honestly didn't know if we were going to survive this ordeal. The traversing pitches and the big overhang below made rappelling off almost impossible. We had no other choice but to leave it for God to decide the outcome.

Brandon and Jody Pennycook following pitch 8 of El Niño during a break in the weather. Photo: Grant Gardner, Brandon Thau Collection

As morning approached, the rainfly became brighter. We sloughed off the snow and opened the fly. I saw one of the most spectacular views ever. The clouds had partially cleared, and everything in sight was encased in white. Floating ice crystals sparkled as they floated through the air. We quickly decided to make a run for the top. We gathered our critical gear and started climbing. We packed up the portaledge and haulbags and tied them to the ledge. We decided to leave them since they were now a liability. Within ten minutes of starting the pitch, the clouds obscured the sun, and the fog rolled in. Visibility was about 30 feet.

Luckily our climbing path was free of snow. However, it was running water, making climbing dangerous. We climbed the last two pitches as fast as we could. Once at the top, we were elated with joy — we had survived! We had enough energy to pose for a group picture. Shortly after topping out, it began to snow again. So, we started walking down the snowy stairs to the parking lot. About halfway down, I heard static from a radio. As I turned the corner, I startled a park ranger. He asked if my name was Brandon Thau. I said, "Yes, how did you know my name?" He responded that I had been listed as a missing person. He noted that my truck was in the parking lot and that the road was closed. He continued to say that the park service had contacted my parents to tell them of the situation. We walked back to the parking lot, where over a foot of snow had fallen. We got into my truck, put it into four-wheel drive, and headed home.

My parents were relieved to hear that I was safe, and I was relieved to be off the rock finally. A week later, we snowshoed up the closed road to

Moro Rock. More snow had fallen during the week. It was the first in a series of the El Nino storms of 1997. We rappelled two rope lengths off the top and retrieved our gear. Everything was soaked and weighed twice as much. Once again, we drove home, happy that our ordeal was over.

Happy to be Alive! Grant Gardner and Brandon Thau on the summit of El Niño, Moro Rock. Photo: Jody Pennycook, Brandon Thau Collection

6

THE FIN
EVERY DARK CLOUD HAS A SILVER LINING

By Patrick Paul

Y+ears ago, when I had only been seriously climbing for about six years, I was invited by my former roommate and mentor, Richard Leversee, to meet him and Eddie (E.C.) Joe, to explore the possibilities of a new route on the massive granite wing called "The Fin" that juts out from the northern base of the Castle Rock Spires in Sequoia National Park. Richard and I had been roommates in Camp Nelson for over a year and climbed together almost every weekend for nearly two years. Although he was ten years younger than me, he had a vast amount of climbing experience when I met him and was an excellent teacher and bold climber. He taught me to lead through many frightening and intense experiences on first ascents with purpose and gusto. Richard eventually moved away from Camp Nelson to go to college. I moved farther up the mountain to Ponderosa, where I was literally within walking distance of the Needles and Dome Rock. My life was composed of work, climbing, and more climbing every day and every weekend. After Richard had moved away, I heard from him only occasionally and only when high adventure was afoot.

The phone rang on a Monday evening. Richard made a few pleasantries and then began to unfurl his plan to go up to the Castle Rocks the following weekend in an attempt to put up a new route with Eddie Joe. Richard suggested that I be ready to meet him and Eddie at Hospital Rock in the Sequoia National Park next Friday evening. He also said I needed to be prepared for a major slog up steep slopes for hours and hours, carrying heavy packs in the heat through poison oak, fox-tail grass packed with ticks, and lots of rattlesnakes. It sounded just like many of the great adventures Richard and I had been on in the past. I was stoked. Without hesitation, I agreed to meet him, hung up the phone, and began excitedly packing gear for the trip.

Within an hour, the phone rang again, and it was Richard. He explained that when he called me earlier, he had not consulted with Eddie first about including me on the roster. After informing Eddie of his decision to call me, Eddie was not keen on the idea. Eddie didn't know me well, hadn't climbed with me, had only hung out with me a couple of times, and felt that I lacked the experience for a venture of this magnitude. Climbing at the Castle Rocks was serious business, and Eddie did not want to have his life in the hands of a novice. Richard reluctantly, and with some embarrassment, had to un-invite me. Richard apologized, and I accepted with great disappointment then hung up the phone.

As I lay in my bed that evening, I began to think about how disappointed I was. I was hurt that Eddie did not have any faith in me, and I was hurt that Richard had not gone to bat for me after taking the step to invite me. Then, an insidious idea began to creep into my head. My ego was bruised, and I wanted to do something dramatic to prove to Eddie that he was wrong.

By this time, I had already formed a climbing partnership with Ron Carson. Ron was strong and determined like Richard, and like Richard, he was younger than me by ten years. The only difference was that with Ron, I was the one with more experience. Ron had read about the first ascent of Sky Garden Wall that Richard and I had pulled off in the early spring of 1979. Sky Garden Wall was a formation in the Tule River canyon named by Richard because it was a literal vertical garden of dirt-filled cracks with small cactus and shrubbery of all kinds covering it from top to bottom. A reporter from the local Springville paper had hiked out to the grungy Sky Garden Wall with us, interviewed us, taken some pictures, and then said goodbye as we ascended the cliff above him.

In one day, Richard and I had finished a seven-hundred-foot ascent of the Silver Sword route, up the middle of Sky Garden. It was a grueling ascent up dirty cracks filled with dried mud, lichen and moss, shrubs, and small century plants with needle-sharp leaves. We made our way to the top of the cliff in one long, brutal day of climbing, cleaning, falling repeatedly, and scraping our way back up again. The sun was setting as we reached the top, and we were bruised, scratched, poked full of holes, and filthy from head to foot. We rappelled the cliff in the dark, illuminated by inferior army surplus headlamps that would not stay lit and flickered incessantly. At one point, we rappelled over an overhang to a ledge that had only one tiny cracked rock wedged in the back of the space we sat on. We were able to fix a pitiful last rappel using a single number seven stopper wedged in the tiny vertical

Patrick Paul and Richard Leversee as depicted in the Tule River Times at Sky Garden Wall, 1981. Photo: R. Baracco

crack formed by the split rock as an anchor. Since Richard was heavier than me, he went first to test the anchor. Minutes passed like hours in the dark, and I was startled as he screamed with joy when he rappelled off of the ends of the ropes and jumped down only a few feet to the ground. I couldn't keep my eyes off of that single stopper as he lowered himself down. There were no other ropes. If Richard managed to get himself killed on the rappel, then I would be stuck up here until I died of starvation or killed myself trying to climb down the overhanging cliff below me. The flimsy anchor didn't budge, didn't fray its cord, and thank God; it didn't pop out. After I was set to go, I turned my pathetic head-lamp off and lowered into the darkness. We were both so grateful to live to tell about the adventure.

Ron had read about the climb in The Tule River Times, got my number from the reporter, and called me up. I asked him if he wanted to do some first ascents. He wasn't sure what those were but said, "Yes!" We became climbing partners for the next seven years until Ron, with his strength and determination, surpassed me in ability and had to start climbing with much stronger climbers than me to do what he wanted to do.

I lay in my bed thinking of revenge. I decided to get up and call Ron. My plan was simple. We would take off work on Friday, meet up at Hospital Rock, head up early in the morning, and beat Richard and Eddie to The Fin. Ron had been up to the Castle Rocks once before as a young student in Tulare. His teacher, Charlie Knapp, had taken him hiking up the old, now abandoned and useless, trail from Paradise Creek. As I told him the story of being snubbed by Eddie and Richard, he just listened silently. When I finished talking, his only comment was that he had been up there before he was a climber and couldn't wait to get back. We were on, and I started packing again.

We met up at the agreed-upon time and place and proceeded to drive down the narrow road to Buckeye Flat Campground, where we would saddle ourselves with what seemed like a ton of climbing and camping gear and head across the Kaweah River to the old Paradise Peak Trail.

Richard had told me about The Fin before. He was up there once when he and another climbing partner had attempted a new route on the prow of the unusually slender granite dome that jutted northward from the main ridge of rock that made up the magnificent Castle Rocks. The Fin accommodated the shadow of the Castle Rock Spire every day like a massive white base plate for a gigantic sundial. From the mighty Kaweah River below, one can track the shadow of the spire as it moves across the face of the Fin in the high, burning sun of summer, an ancient thousand-foot-tall timepiece etched by the eons.

Richard was a teller of tall tales. He admired the lore and hyperbole of John Long and always colored his stories with rich bravado and humorous embellishment. Richard is a big guy, and so are his stories. I couldn't know if the reality would match the story he told, but following in his footsteps was always fun, sometimes dangerous, and always a great adventure.

While Ron and I worked our way along the trail, I relayed the description of the track as I could remember it from Richard's detailed recounting. "Follow the Paradise Peak Trail for a short distance past the point where two ridge lines intersected the trail and then turn left uphill steeply at the third." Immediately there was poison oak-- little immature knee-high bushes-- and ticks, dozens of ticks. The grassy, oak-strewn hill-side steepened sharply; we were challenged constantly to keep from brushing against the poison oak or losing our footing on slick, dry grass, and with each misstep, we had to stop, check each other for ticks and brush one or two from our legs. For more than two hours, Ron and I struggled up the grassy incline until we came to the faint trail, now almost indistinguishable, that used to be the easy way to the base of the majestic Castle Rocks. We made it through the worst part of the journey, and now all we had to do was follow the old trail as it meandered north-east and up to the gully below the Castles. We were sweating profusely, aching from head to foot from our heavy loads, feeling itchy and para-noid about ticks and poison oak. We were also grateful for having made it past the two rattlesnakes in the tall grass on our way up the clifflike hillside and excited to be here!

We moved along the trail, skirting below the forest apron underneath the massive granite spires of the Castles until we found "the second gully" below the spire, which happened to be marked by a tree that had fallen at eye level across our path. A right turn here took us up steeply through the forest until we arrived at some massive boulders wedged in amongst the trees directly below Castle Rock Spire. We spent the remainder of the afternoon procuring water from the creek, cleaning ourselves up, and assuring ourselves that we were not infested with ticks or covered in poison oak oils. We set to work digging out a comfortable camp under one of the huge boulders and getting all set up for a climbing adventure the following day. As late evening approached, we ventured up and across a hidden, well-shaded snowfield that fed the creek. We scram-bled to the base of The Fin and started looking around. We hiked up the gully between The Fin and the spire and then back to the north. As The Fin jutted northward, it got steeper, taller, and less featured. High up in the center of the face was an obvious dihedral that jutted out from the otherwise smooth wall. Near where we were standing was a small tree. It was a good starting point to draw a straight line up to the dihedral looming two-thirds of the way up the thousand-foot face. We scrambled up small corners, edges, and seams for about fifty or sixty feet until it looked like we would need gear to proceed safely. We downclimbed back to the tree and returned to our camp to rest and prepare for the next day.

Silver Lining. Photo: David Hickey

We embarked on our adventure again the following day, climbing up to our previous high point and surpassing it with gear. The climbing was relatively easy with occasional tricky moves of 5.9 or a little harder. As we looked up and the wall steepened before us, we could see that the wall bulged out some directly below our dihedral objective. This bulge became an intimidating obstacle as we moved higher and higher, and the ground got steeper and steeper. The rock before us and at our feet was yielding some pleasant surprises. If one looked far out ahead, the face looked menacingly blank, but as each step took us higher, a little hori-

zontal seam, upward-facing crack, or pocket would appear and offer a
place for protection or a good hand or foothold. We swung leads and
continued up cautiously. Each pitch continued to yield surprises. We
found little etched-out horizontal seams, small pockets, and short
vertical cracks that would accommodate a slider nut, a ball nut, a small
Tri-Cam, a TCU, or contrived nuts slung in opposition. It took a while to
figure out how to place pro that might arrest a fall, but the challenges of
placing were preferable to the cumbersome process of drilling bolts.
Both Ron and I preferred venturing a little farther to find a placement
over stopping to drill. We were lucky to find places that would suffice for
gear belays and only had to drill a couple of protection bolts and a couple
of bolted anchors. Our route had pretty magical climbing when you
consider that we were way the hell out there and only had a small bolt kit
to put up against a massive granite face.

After several pitches of good climbing on superb rock, we were
confronted with the bulge. It was now apparent that we were facing
some steep, blank, and extremely difficult, if not impossible, climbing if
we tried to continue straight ahead to the base of the dihedral objective.
I was leading, and it was time to make some decisions. Going left looked
very steep and hard, like the bulge. Going right might be more of the fun
and games we had gotten used to on this climb, but we couldn't tell. We
couldn't see anything to our immediate right that said, "come on over."
The ground in front of us still offered the best path, and I had to
continue up towards the bulge to see what might be revealed. The rock
was getting steep. The holds were thinning out, and the possibilities for
placing protection was becoming non-existent. I was running it out on
turf that was not encouraging at all. After several thin moves, I could see
to my right a trail of small diagonal seams and grooves flowing up at
about a 45-degree angle. A few moves to the right, and I was back on
solid featured granite, following a path to glory, headed towards a nice
left-facing corner about two pitches of diagonal climbing away. We would
avoid the bulge, though we were moving away from our dihedral; this
seemed like the most plausible course to take. We climbed this first long
diagonal pitch to a good ledge and put in a three-bolt anchor. It was
getting late, and we decided to rappel off, setting up two more anchors
on our way to the bottom.

The next day was Sunday, and we both had to be at work on Monday. We decided to retreat to the car and return in a week to finish the route. Richard and Eddie never came up that weekend, and we were denied the grinning glee of surprising them with our Castle Rocks coup.

Two weeks passed, and we geared up to return to The Fin. In the interim, I had told Herb Laeger about our adventure and asked him if he would like to come up and finish the route with us; he did. We all made the sweaty, tick, and poison oak-infested trudge back up to the little camp Ron and I had made, spent the night under the big boulder, and then climbed back to our high point the next day.

Herb led the long next pitch to the little rusty-colored left-facing corner, and we were set to try and get back to the base of the great dihedral that had been our target two weeks before. It was my turn to lead again, and I started up around a small roof, moving diagonally across and up towards the base of the dihedral. The character of the rock changed here, and I found myself moving over small edges and smears. The traditional seams and pockets we had become accustomed to had not appeared. I managed on thin terrain for some way and placed a bolt. Scanning the landscape out ahead didn't produce any prospects for easier, more

A climber approaches the great dihedral on Silver Lining. Photo: David Hickey

featured ground. I proceeded on, still focusing on the base of the dihedral as my objective. But moving was painfully slow as I searched for tiny hand and footholds in the blank face. Herb and Ron were both coaching me from below to find some protection. "You better get something in pretty soon, man" After what seemed like miles of unprotected, shaky climbing, I arrived at a decent spot to drill another bolt. I was looking at a nasty pendulum fall if I didn't get something in the rock and calm down. When the bolt was in, I clipped in and moved on to the base of the dihedral and set up a belay to bring Ron and Herb up.

The weather had changed as we climbed from sunny and clear to cloudy, cold, and threatening. Puffy dark clouds with beautiful white fringes hung over our heads as we scoped out the dihedral above and contemplated the next pitch. It looked like we had at least two more long pitches to get to the top, and the late afternoon was darkening with ominous clouds. We once again opted to lower off and finish the route the next day. We needed to do two sketchy diagonal rappels to get back to our three-bolt anchor on the ledge. The first rappel was very tenuous over a smooth slab back to the rusty corner. The second rappel was easier to the triple anchor, but one still risked a long pendulum fall if there were any mistakes in footing. The rappels took a long time, and it was getting dark as we pulled our ropes down to set up for the final straight shot to the ground.

Silver Lining. Photo: David Hickey

Physics played a nasty trick on us while we attempted to retrieve our rappel ropes. We watched an overhand knot tie itself into the end of the rope as the rope rolled and tumbled its way back up to the anchor slings. We witnessed the knot appear at the end of the rope like a magician's sleight of hand and watched in frustration as the knot hung up in the rappel sling, out of reach above us. We pulled and pulled to no avail. It was stuck. One of us would have to climb back up in the dark to get it. We put our headlamps on. I looked at Herb and Ron; they looked at each other and then at me and started to laugh. I didn't own an actual headlamp and had contrived one for myself by taking a bicycle inner tube, cutting a section out to slip a small flashlight into, with the ends of the rubber tube stapled and taped together to form a band. When I put it on, it was so tight it pulled my eyelids wide open, making me look like some crazed barn owl. I turned the flashlight on and couldn't get it adjusted to illuminate anything directly in front of me. It firmly stayed plastered to the side of my head with the beam pointing to the left.

I told Ron and Herb that I would climb up to retrieve the stuck rope if Herb would let me use his headlamp for the journey. He agreed without hesitation, and I proceeded into the dark, following the uncooperative rappel rope back to the corner. Once there, I anchored in, pulled up the rope I had returned on, and set up another rappel. It was freaky. Here I was out in the dark, alone on the side of a thousand-foot wall in the high Sierra. I saw the light of Ron's headlamp far off in the distance below me. I realized that if I made one small mistake, it might cost the lives of all three of us. They were down there alone too and without ropes, clipped into three tiny bolts in the middle of a broad granite face in the wilderness. I imagined that if I failed to get back to them, they would be stuck there for eternity. I carefully rappelled to them; we successfully retrieved the ropes, and finished our rappel to the bottom, and descended back to camp, where we were surprised to find Ron's old teacher and mentor, Charlie Knapp, waiting for us with a warming fire.

The following day we discussed our options for the time we had left in the weekend. We had noticed another highly featured line farther up the wall to the south of our route, which we now called Silver Lining, after the beautiful black and white laced clouds that had dogged us all afternoon the previous day. We discussed that it would be good to get to the top of The Fin by an easier route and set up a rappel route. An established rappel route would facilitate an easy escape after finishing our climb or for other climbers who may paint on this magnificent canvas in the future.

We said goodbye to Charlie and proceeded up the gully between The Fin and Castle Rock Spire, where a short bit of awkward climbing got us to the point where the long narrow summit ridge of The Fin joined the mountain. It's so narrow in one spot that one feels like straddling a saddle and scooting along for several yards, looking down hundreds of feet on both sides, rather than balancing on the thing like a high wire artist.

We moved north along the ridge to a spot near the top of Silver Lining and slung a manzanita bush to rappel. We finished the rap route next to and near where we had journeyed up the face the previous day. In the morning, on our way up the gully, we scoped out other lines up the broad face of The Fin. After rappelling, we moved back up gully to a point almost directly across from the spire. We began climbing up a natural line of small corners and seams in a pretty direct route to the top. This climb was much easier than Silver Lining, and we moved quickly, swinging leads on mostly 5.7 ground with an occasional move of 5.9. With good belays and protection, we were at the summit ridge by the early evening. Ron suggested we name the route for his friend and mentor, Charlie Knapp. Our rappel route facilitated a retreat back to our camp. We headed home the following day with a plan to return on the coming July 4th weekend to finish Silver Lining.

The Independence Day weekend arrived, and our group assembled with the addition of one new member, Corrina Peterson, a Ridgecrest climber whom Herb and I had met while climbing with Greg Vernon at Owens Ridge. We were excited to go back up to the Castle Rocks to finish Silver Lining and possibly do another route, but none of us looked forward with anything but dread to the grueling trudge up the mountain from the Buckeye Flat Campground. I proposed a new logistical plan for getting to The Fin. We would leave a vehicle at Buckeye Flat Campground, drive to Atwell Mill in Mineral King, hike up the easy Paradise Peak trail and then follow the connecting ridge out to the Castle Rocks. After completing our work, it would be easy to hike down to our car at Buckeye, grab a Pizza in Three Rivers, and retrieve our second vehicle in comfort.

We deposited our escape vehicle, drove to Atwell Mill, hiked the Paradise Peak trail up through a beautiful Sequoia grove, and turned right at the appropriate spot to follow the contours out to the Castle Rocks. It was a beautiful hike. We couldn't help but stop frequently and marvel at the incredible rock formation we were on top of. I named the topmost spire Sleeping Beauty's Castle, and we all noted lines we would like to explore in the future. Beautiful white clouds drifted toward us from the San Joaquin Valley, and they seemed to be at eye level.

By mid-day, we were navigating our way through manzanita and tall brush, working our way towards where we thought The Fin must connect to the main ridge of the Castles, and beginning to get cold as the clouds started swirling in around us. In a very short time, we were immersed in a wet, chilling fog and had to feel our way along the tops of the massive slabs of granite that make up the western edge of the Castles. The spires we marveled at a few minutes earlier were gone. Manzanita reached out to snag us from a dense mist as we carefully felt our way along in zero visibility. A whiteout.

For the rest of the afternoon and evening, we felt our way through the brush and trees prodding our way between wet slabs of rock and moving along the cliffside until we came to a crevasse. We were lost on a treelined ramp but were aware of the steep terrain to our left, vertical mossy rock on our right, and an abyss in front of us. We could see only a few feet in any direction, and it was getting dark. I wanted to move forward and considered rappelling into the chasm before us. How far down did this thing go? Herb picked up a big rock and tossed it. After a long wait, we finally heard it shatter far below. We set up camp and spent a dismally dreary night in the wetness. We were still in damp fog in the morning as we packed up our camp to plod down through the steep forest to our left.

Patrick Paul on Silver Lining. Photo: Ron Carson

In a short time, the clouds rose above us, and we could see that we were in a steep forest heading down towards the old Castle Rocks Trail. We came to the top of a gigantic slab and could see Moro Rock across the Kaweah Canyon. We were way west of where we wanted to be. We sat down to rest at this viewpoint and tried to figure out which way might be best to go. After a moment or two of talking, a deep rumbling sound came from our right, and we began to shift back and forth. Five inches to the left, five inches to the right, and repeat. It was bizarre! The whole body of the Sierra was being shifted back and forth with us on top of it by an earthquake whose epicenter was the Mammoth Lakes. It all just as suddenly stopped, and we could hear rock falling from the west side of the spire and its adjacent cliffs. After we got done with our "Wows" and "Oh my Gods," and looking around to make sure a tree wasn't going to fall on us, Ron said, "Wouldn't it be weird to be climbing when that happened? Like having your hand in a crack and watching the crack just pinch down on your hand or something." The image was terrifying.

We decided to abandon any further effort to get to Silver Lining and finish. We were tired, we were still far away from our objective, and none of us wanted to be in a place where we could be killed by rockfall if there was another earthquake or a big aftershock. Down we went to our car at Atwell Mill.

Time went by. I didn't return to finish the first ascent of Silver Lining. I got married and did other things with my new climbing partner, Kelly.

The year after our last attempt, Ron, Herb, and his wife, Eve, returned and finished Silver Lining. I would go back many years later with Greg Smith and repeat the complete route. It was beautiful, but that damn approach was worse. More snakes, ticks, and poison oak than ever, and the trail was more overgrown and harder to find. Horrible!

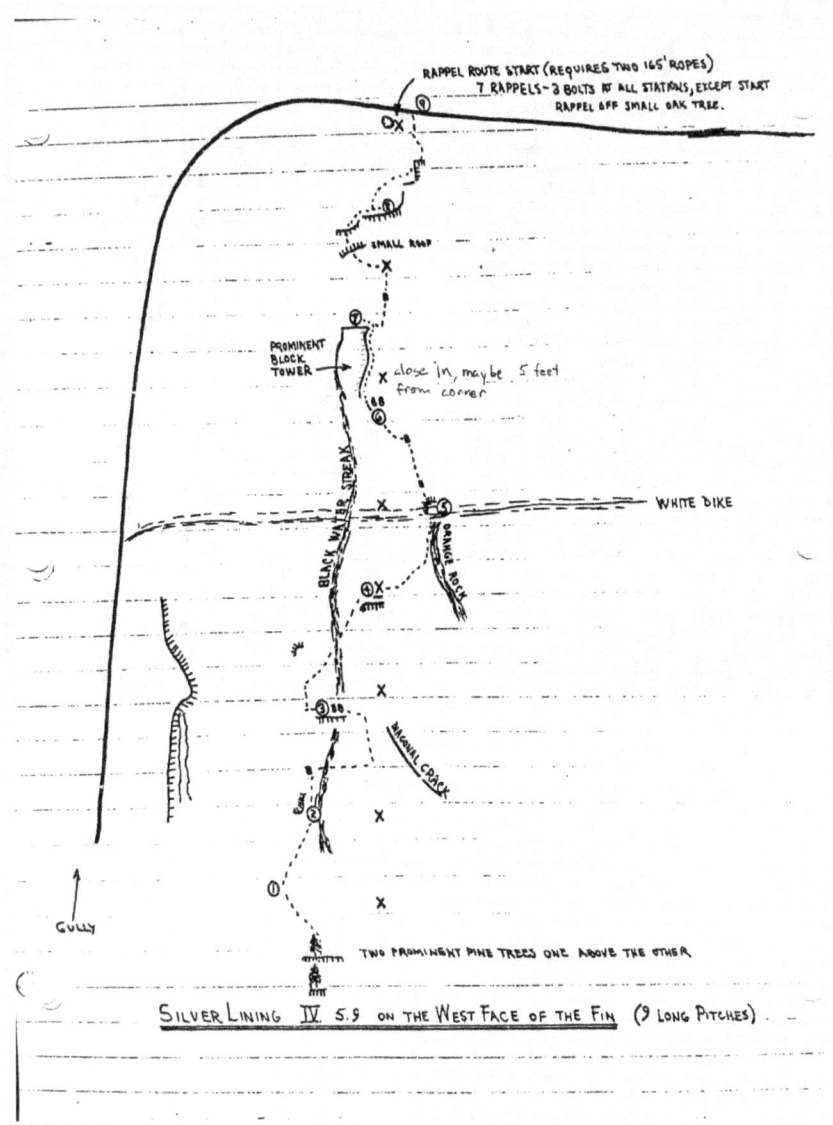

7

THE GORGE OF DESPAIR

KINGS CANYON NATIONAL PARK

By Kristian Solem

"For wild and rugged grandeur, the Kings River region of the Sierra Nevada has no peer. A mighty panorama, beginning at the wandering streams, sweeping up the terrifying gorges past jagged spires, and culminating in towering granite peaks presents itself to the adventurer.

It is indeed an awe-inspiring sight to break out of the pine forest onto the rim of Tehipite Valley and gaze across at the opposite mountain wall, fantastically cut up into multiple flying turrets soaring in the blue haze. The great river, four thousand feet below, sends its dull roar echoing about the valley." — Hervey Voge, *A Climber's Guide to the Sierra*, 1954

Hervey Voge sets a fine example of how climbers tend to romanticize the mountains, the spires, the great walls of stone. These places draw us to adventure like moths to a flame. And drawn I was when I first heard of a wild and remote place called the Gorge of Despair.

I was chatting with my friend Richard Whitney, a climber and mountain man from California. He asked me if I had ever heard of the Gorge of Despair.

"No. Have you been there?"

"I don't think many people have."

"But you know where it is?"

"The Kings River region of the Sierra. It's a remote hanging canyon which, at its bottom, drops off for about 2,000 feet into the middle fork of the Kings River. Word is there's a lot of great rock climbing in there."

When Richard said remote, that stood for something.

From Afar

1994

Richard had sown the seed, but fourteen years would pass before Guy Keesee and I stood looking down into the great gorge as we descended from the crest of Harrington Pass. One thing was for sure: we had earned this view. Our packs, full of food, sleeping bags, a small tent, and climbing gear, weighed in at 80 pounds. We'd just carried them up a gain of about 6,300 feet in ten miles. Finally, we reached the pass at an elevation of 10,640 feet above the sea.

Mount Harrington. Photo: Guy Keesee

Harrington Pass is a saddle offering passage over the Monarch

Divide, a high crest of land that separates the south and the middle forks of the Kings River. To the west of the pass is Mount Harrington, to the east the slightly higher but less impressive Hogback.

A peak is said to have prominence when its summit stands well above its surroundings, thus offering a great view. Mount Harrington is just such a peak, and before starting our descent into the gorge, we had to climb it simply because it was there. The summit route is an easy but exposed rock climb, a quick scramble; climb up, look around, and climb down. Then it was time to shoulder our loads one more time and head down into the gorge, losing 2,000 feet of hard-won elevation in two miles.

Guy and I each carried one non-essential item. He brought an SLR camera and a bunch of film, a couple of extra pounds, but well worth it. I took a D trumpet, a horn about half the size and weight of a standard trumpet. It was worth every ounce. Certainly, the Gorge of Despair had never heard the trumpet solos from Mahler's Fifth Symphony, the brilliant high solos from Bach, or the beautiful slow movement of Haydn's trumpet concerto. Sending out the sound of my trumpet to peal off the rock walls and echo about the place was as much fun as I have ever had playing music. Climbing, the thing that had lured me away from a career in music, brought me to this extraordinary experience I could never have imagined.

When you cross the pass, you commit yourself to true wilderness. Only a faint path along the side of a small lake at the top of the gorge gives evidence of human passage. Taking in the view of the vast surrounding forests and mountains, you will not see a single structure or trace of civilization. In the dark of night, you will not see a single light. The only sounds are the breeze in the trees and the rushing waters of the creek as it races down through the gorge on its way to a fantastic cascade, falling thousands of feet to join the Kings River.

When we were planning this trip, Guy and I pored over maps and the rare guidebook or two with some mention of the area. A well-respected climber, Steve Roper, produced a Sierra guidebook in 1976. He mentions the Gorge of Despair as having "a steep, arduous approach; while only twelve miles in length, a vertical rise of 6,300 feet is involved in crossing the Monarch Divide[1]."

"Only twelve miles…" The words of a hardman.

We learned that there are granite formations that are a rock climber's dream. Using the words of Hervey Voge, these towers are referred to as turrets: The Cobra Turret, The Comandante and Corporale Turrets, The Silver Turret...

The Silver Turret. Photo: Guy Keesee

As we hiked down into the gorge, the summit of a granite formation peeked over the crest of a ridge. As we headed downhill, it grew. Then it grew some more. At last, after teasing us for so long, it showed itself. So, this was the Silver Turret.

I was utterly unprepared for what I saw. The east face, which presented itself to us, had to be 1,000 feet tall. The left two-thirds of the wall featured dozens of overhangs, one after another, separated by sections of steep slabs. The right third of the wall was a sheer, nearly blank face. The corrugated left side and the clean vertical wall on the right met, forming a shallow corner of about forty degrees. This feature, the union of the two faces, was the only natural line for a climb on the entire wall. And what a climb it would be, a grand prize indeed.

We hiked down and camped at the base. I assumed that we would start climbing the next morning, but I sensed my partner's reluctance.

"Guy, we're here. It's a once in a lifetime deal."

"Kris, we can't do this." He can speak with emphasis in a unique way. I've never quite figured it out, but when he's sure of himself, or a point needs to be made, there it is, and there it was right then.

"Think about it. Do you want to get stuck halfway up this thing with no way to get down? Forget it."

Eventually, I had to concede that we were not prepared to commit to such a big climb. We were under-equipped.

"I promise I'll come back with you next year. We'll bring what we need, we'll get it done."

I was sure as hell going to hold him to his word.

"Hey Kris, do you see that crack about 2/3's of the way up the steep side of The Cobra?"

"Yeah…" It was barely visible. While I was moping around, Guy had been looking for an opportunity.

"We're gonna walk over there and check it out." There was that emphasis once again. Apparently, we had a plan.

We broke camp and set about crossing the gorge, down to the stream and up the other side. It looked like a nice hike. We had no idea what we were getting into.

During my formative years as a climber, I spent a lot of time in New York State's Adirondack Mountains. These mountains are not tall, the highest being Mount Marcy at 5,344 feet, but they are harsh. While the fearsome winter conditions intimidate the toughest of mountaineers, the summer poses its own set of challenges. One of them is struggling through nearly impenetrable thickets of bushes and small trees, all the while moving over rocks, streams, logs, hornet's nests, and so forth. This business is called bushwhacking, and it has been known to break the spirit of all but the most intrepid hikers and climbers. When Guy and I began our traverse of the gorge, this vile activity was the furthest thing from my mind, but when we arrived at the creek, we were confronted with a wide, dense, entangled hedge of alder ten to fifteen feet tall. We began to fight our way across.

About halfway through, I decided I was going to die there. I was stuck and could not move. My pack, all eighty pounds of it, was hopelessly hung up, but I couldn't do anything about it because the rest of me was hung up as well. The stream, swollen with snowmelt from the high country, raced under my feet. What an ignominious way to go.

Our disappearance would be a mystery. A search party would find evidence of our camp, but they would never think to look for us here. Sooner or later, our decomposed remains would end up in the creek. A bit at a time, we'd ride down the gorge, over the precipice, and down into the rapids of the mighty Kings River. Eventually, we'd end up fertilizing farmland in California's central valley.

The view from the summit of the Silver Turret. Photo: Guy Keesee

The Cobra is the formation in the center. Prow of Cobra follows the sunny slab and ridgeline to the top. The steep south face is in the shade.
Below are Comandante and Corporale Turrets. Fascination Point is seen in the low left corner.
Beyond, across the chasm of the Kings River, is the wilderness of Blue Canyon, one of the furthest places from a drivable road in the lower 48 states.

After several bouts of violent thrashing and swearing like a drunk sailor, I emerged from the cursed alder. Guy had taken a course parallel to mine and suffered equally. Thrashed, we staggered uphill and camped under the very toe of the Cobra. We were under the start of a climb called Prow of Cobra. It probably hadn't been climbed since its first ascent in 1979 by a pair of climbers not burdened with a reluctance for adventure, Gary Valle and Greg Bender.

Looking up at the long slab of beautiful granite, we decided to do this climb before heading up under the south face to inspect the crack Guy had spied from across the gorge. We ate some food and sacked out early. Tomorrow was going to be a big day.

In the morning, we woke up to a large pile of bear crap right in front of our tent. Welcome to the Gorge of Despair.

The climb was outstanding. Hervey Voge's words — "wild and rugged grandeur" — were well-chosen indeed. From the summit, we looked down into an abyss of 4,000 feet, an uninterrupted drop down to the river. Even for seasoned climbers, this sight was mind-numbing.

Rappelling off the Cobra Comandante Turret lies behind. In the distance, across the canyon, stands the massive Tehipite Dome. Photo: Guy Keesee

Having finished the main course, we made our descent, walked down-hill a short distance, and climbed the Comandante Turret for dessert.

Most climbers just go climbing. By this, I mean they go to established climbing areas and do established climbs. But every established climb began with a first ascent, a trip into the unknown with no sure outcome. Some climbers lust for this brand of excitement, and you could count on Guy and me to be among them. It was time to inspect the Cobra's steep south face and check out the crack we had come so far to see. That morning we broke camp and headed uphill.

We studied the face of rock as we hiked uphill. Then, there it was. If a climb this beautiful were anywhere near a road, its first ascent would have been done more than a half-century ago, and it would have been climbed countless times since. But it was ours, a plum ripe for the picking.

There were about fifty feet of vertical face climbing to reach the bottom of the crack. I took some small steel hooks, a hand drill, a hammer, and a few bolts. I climbed up some easy moves at the start. Then the climbing got harder. This is where I placed my first bolt to protect the first hard moves.

I set one of my hooks on an edge on the rock. It held my weight while I used the hand drill and hammer to chisel a 5/16" diameter, 1½" deep hole in the rock, tiresome and time-consuming work. Then I hammered in the bolt. I clipped a carabiner to the newly placed bolt, clipped my rope through the 'biner, and climbed up higher.

When I was a sufficient distance above the first bolt, I found an edge, set my hook, and placed a second. I repeated the process one more time and was within reach of the crack.

When I had the third bolt in, I lowered back to the ground and pulled down the ropes. To count the climb as finished, I had to lead it free without using aid (hanging on my hooks, a bolt, or the rope). It was getting to be late afternoon, and my arms were exhausted. We would finish the climb tomorrow.

I woke sore and tired. We were running out of food. But on this last day, if I could suck it up, this climb just might get done. The first fifty feet were hard. Then hopefully, it would be in the bag. I was in no hurry to get started.

We ate a meager breakfast of sardines, jerky, and pemmican, with good coffee. I played my trumpet for a while and did some stretching. At about noon, I was ready to go.

Despite being tired to the bone, I climbed the face in good style. Then came the crack. It was stunning; perfect moderate climbing for 100 feet. I reached a nice spot to belay, drilled two bolts for an anchor, and Guy came up. One more beautiful pitch led to the top.

Guy named our route "From Afar." We offered a grade of 5.11c.

Kristian Solem hanging from a small hook on an edge, drilling the hole for the third bolt. Photo: Guy Keesee

Kristian Solem leading From Afar. Photo: Guy Keesee

My Knee!

1995

The cowboy looked at me in disbelief. My lycra tights were striped in a random pattern of black, white, red, and blue. I still smelled of the scotch I drank too much of the night before, back in Los Angeles. Our packs weighed in at 100 pounds; we brought enough climbing gear to attempt the Silver Turret's impressive east face. This time we'd engaged the services of the Kings Canyon Pack Outfit. The cowboy would ride his horse, leading a mule carrying our packs.

The horse and mule could carry our loads up to Grizzly Lake or as far as we could get by three o'clock, whichever came first. I worked off my hangover as we hiked up the steep trail to meet the cowboy, who took a different route from the pack station. He was surprised to find us waiting at the junction where his trail joined ours. He was even more surprised when we moved fast and made Grizzly Lake well before his turnaround time. From there, the terrain was too rocky for the horse and mule. We had to shoulder our loads, carry them up another thousand feet of elevation to Harrington Pass, and then down to set up camp at the base of the Silver Turret. The 100-pound pack on my 140-pound frame was taking a toll on me. I rested every chance I could get, sitting on a boulder or a log. Looking ahead, I'd pick my next objective, stagger over to it, and rest. But I didn't dare take my pack off for fear that I wouldn't be able to raise it again.

The wall we were here to climb loomed above. It would have been intimidating enough if it were near a road and had already been climbed a few times. But if anything were to go wrong out here, we would be entirely on our own. This is what climbing in the Gorge of Despair was all about. Today you can carry a small device and call via satellite for rescue. The helicopter will come. In 1994 we were in the game 100 percent.

The next morning I could barely walk. Guy was obviously made of tougher stock than I. We took the day off.

After our rest day, it was time to climb. I still felt like rubber, but there was no putting it off.

Guy led first, trailing double ropes up toward where we expected to find our route, the meeting of the highly featured wall on the left with the blank vertical face on the right. But as would happen time and time again, the rock forced us out to the left of our planned route. Since Guy had no choice but to end the first pitch to the left of the corner, I had to take the second pitch up through a series of steep slabs, punctuated by flaps and overhangs.

Guy followed my lead quickly, and soon enough, two pitches were in the bag. What came next looked crazy. Would this be a showstopper? We decided I'd have a go at leading it. I started climbing.

So far, we had placed six bolts, one to protect the leader at a tricky spot on the first pitch, two for an anchor at the top of that pitch, and three on the second pitch to protect the leader. This made for hard work and slow going. I didn't want to take the time to place another one here. Guy was skeptical.

I climbed up onto a blade of rock that stuck out of the wall like a diving board. The exposure was insane. Looking down into the Gorge of Despair and further down into the Kings River canyon, there were thousands of feet of air beneath my shoes. I moved up, came to a nice crack where I set some gear to protect myself and made a couple more moves up towards the crux. I felt tired and shaky, and the climbing was hard. I fell.

I'd fallen about 10 feet before Guy's belay could arrest my fall. When I stopped, hanging on the ropes, I had one leg on each side of the narrow diving board, precariously close to an excruciating injury. I climbed back up and placed a bolt a few moves below where I fell. There'd be no straddling the diving board now. With the bolt in, I came down to the belay and rested. It was getting late. We rappelled back to the ground. Tomorrow we could climb fast to this high point and keep on going. By mid-morning, we were looking up at the obstacle I had to surmount.

I climbed out, unwillingly, onto the diving board which had so nearly castrated me the day before. Standing there, looking up, I studied the problem. When I climbed up and clipped the bolt, I'd be face to face with one of the countless overhangs which defined the left two-thirds of the wall. The only handholds were a thin upside-down lip at the very back of the overhang. With my hands palms up, I'd have to cling to the tiny holds with my fingertips, leaning back far enough to press my feet into the nearly featureless face under the overhang. This was unlike any undercling I'd ever seen.

Moving across to the right, I would constantly have to adapt. The art of it would be to have a relaxed, fluid, lower body with smooth footwork, all the while leaning back and fiercely holding onto the minimal undercling staring me in the face. Pulling this off looked desperate — delicacy and power all at once.

Years later, the great British climber Leo Houlding summed up this kind of moment; "Now is when I have to relax, like I've never relaxed before."

I closed my eyes and took a series of deep breaths.

Climbers talk about being in the bubble. Nothing else exists except for that which is directly in front of you. It's a state of total concentration.

At that moment, in my bubble, I had all the time in the world to make these moves.

As a climber, I had always enjoyed a dancelike style of movement, but this problem wasn't about looking pretty. Success would only come with power and determination. It was time to get ugly.

I launched into the athletic sequence of moves traversing back right to the corner. Once past the difficulties, I raced up easier rock to a nice ledge and drilled two bolts for an anchor. I was pleased with myself and optimistic about the outcome of our adventure.

Now it was Guy's turn. Keeping him on a close belay, I pulled up the ropes as he climbed. Suddenly they went tight. Guy had come off and was hanging on them. It was no big deal, the moves were desperate, and he fell. He would figure them out soon enough. But time went by, and nothing changed; he just hung there, not moving. I thought I heard him yell something, but I couldn't make it out. Something was wrong. Then I heard it: "My Kneeee!"

As he fought his way across the undercling, he got his leg twisted into a weird angle. When he fell, he wrenched it in all the wrong ways. We had no way to know it at the time, but he had a severe meniscus tear. With the help of the rope, he climbed the rest of the pitch on one leg.

When I saw his knee, my heart sank. He had a serious injury. The knee was swelling fast, and it was locked; he couldn't flex it. I could see that he was in real pain. To make matters worse, our climbing route didn't come up from directly below. Rather, we had followed a long arching line. Even without Guy's injury, rappelling down the way we came up would be difficult at best. We had to go straight down. I'd have to rappel to the end of the ropes and arrange an anchor, probably bolts. Guy would be on his own as he set himself up for the rappel and came down to join me. Then we'd retrieve the ropes and rappel again. Maybe the second rappel would reach the base of the wall.

Down I went. This place was creeping me out. Being on the climbing route was one thing; it made sense to be there. But here, cold in the shade, alone and in trouble, lowering myself like a spider on its web — it was nuts. This was not a place for humans. At the end of my rope, I placed two bolts. At least the work warmed me up. Soon enough, Guy joined me. The two of us hung, like meat, on the vertical wall with no ledge to stand on. It was time to pull the ropes and do the second rappel.

I started pulling down the red rope. It came easily. The end of the blue rope was going up. Shortly we'd have them back and rappel to the ground. Then, as if things weren't already bad enough, the ropes jammed. The spirits of the gorge were trifling with us. Their message was clear: "If you can get out of this fix you can leave."

I pulled on the red cord with all my might. Nothing. Guy put his back into it too. Again, nothing. Our ropes appeared to be hopelessly jammed. But on what? It didn't matter.

I had one option. I had to ascend the red rope, a nightmare scenario. The end of the blue rope was about twenty feet above us. Once I was up there, with my weight on both ropes, I would be safe. I could go on up and fix the problem. But what if my body weight pulled the ropes loose before I had both? If I were almost up to the blue rope when they came free, I'd fall forty feet before the red rope, its end still attached to the anchor, would catch me. This fall would be a factor of two, the most energy a climbing fall can generate. Either the prussic knot attaching me to the rope would break, sending me to my death, or I'd be injured by the force of the fall. I thought about the two of us up there, Guy with his injury and me, hanging 20 feet below, with a broken back. Of course, there was a possibility that the jam would not come entirely free, thus creating enough friction to slow my fall, a long shot for sure. Those sorts of things happen on slabs. Our wall was vertical.

I began setting up the rig. I was going to use a technique practiced by any climber worth their salt, expressly for an emergency such as ours. Two knots, prussics, would enable me to move up the rope like an inch-worm. It was time to unclip from the anchor and start going up. I felt like I was going to puke. I was cold, tired, and scared. I wasn't thinking straight. Then it hit me. There was one last thing to try before I played my game of Russian roulette with the ropes. I kept myself attached to the anchor with a slack cord. I was going to need some room to move.

Standing in the pair of loops used for going up the rope, I started jumping in place. With the springy stretch of the 160 feet of thin rope—

one of the doubles--above me, I was able to get a good rhythm going, almost like being on a trampoline. Soon I was generating some real force. I felt it move an inch or two, then it cut loose, not a slow slide to freedom but rather in an instant. Bam! I swung hard into the wall, the ropes were ours, and we lived to tell the tale—sort of. There was no one to tell the tale to until my injured partner was rescued, and I was the rescuer. Or so I thought.

Guy spent the next day with his knee packed in snow. I wandered about. My mood was dark. This place where I had felt so at home, so free and happy, turned gloomy and oppressive. I was ill at ease. How the hell were we going to get out?

When I got up the next morning, planning to sort out our options, Guy was sitting on a log with his leg wrapped in his sleeping pad. He had it cinched down tight with compression straps. He stood up.

"I can walk with this."

"How far?"

"Back to the car. What other choice do I have?"

I filled my pack with as much of our gear as I could carry. I cached some of the heavier items, the hammer, drill, bolts, etc., possibly setting the stage for my return. Guy's job was to walk out, if possible. He carried only his camera in his otherwise empty pack.

I brought up the rear as Guy walked stiff-legged up to Harrington Pass, a trailless gain of 2,000 feet in two miles. I followed as he crossed the pass and headed down toward Grizzly Lake, through a rugged boulder field about a half-mile across. Many of these granite boulders were the size of a refrigerator; some were bigger. He couldn't bend his leg, but he found a way over or around each new obstacle. Eventually, we were at the spot where the cowboy had dropped us off. Nine miles to go.

We got back to the car after dark. Guy had just walked twelve miles non-stop, from deep in the Gorge of Despair up and over a high pass and down 6,300 feet in nine miles to the trailhead, all with a severely injured knee. I've never, before or since, been prouder of a climbing partner. He barfed and passed out. I undid my pack straps and let it fall to the ground with a resounding thud, pulled a few warm beers out of the trunk, and relaxed. It was over, or so I thought.

Coffee the next morning never tasted so good.

"So, Kris, what do you want to do now?"

"What kind of a question is that? We're getting you back to LA to get that knee looked at."

"This is vacation time. I'll get my knee fixed on sick time."

"Good god man, I think that hike cost you some brain cells."

"Seriously, I don't want to go home yet. Let's go to The Needles."

"The Needles? Are you nuts?"

"You'll pick up climbing partners no problem. I'll have breakfast at the Ponderosa, hang out on the front porch 'till they open the bar, and spend the afternoon chatting with Red."

The Ponderosa is the only establishment within twenty miles of The Needles; three rooms to rent, a restaurant, bar, cold beer, and basic camping supplies. Red was the bartender back then, and he was one hell of a lot of fun to chat it up with.

So that's what we did for the better part of a week.

DESPAIRADOES

1997

For the next two years, a day didn't pass without the Silver Turret crossing my mind, even if only for a moment. I broke the idea to Guy about going in again. I told him I wanted to bring a third climber, Chelsea Griffie. In the summer of 1997, we were on our way. I was laser-focused on getting this job done, and Chelsea was a big asset to our team. She was a strong, ambitious climber who immersed herself in the sport. Among many things, she went on to become the first African American woman to climb El Capitan, Yosemite's rite of passage. We were good friends, and our climbing relationship was solid.

There's not a lot to say about the approach hike. It was becoming routine, and soon enough, we were back at our camp under the Silver Turret's east face. We sorted gear. Blast-off was first thing in the morning. A little later, over food, Guy spoke up.

"You two should just go up and do this thing. If the three of us go up, it won't happen."

I was quiet. Part of my mind told me this was the right call. But climbing partnerships are serious business. Guy was here with us, and his knee was good.

"I dunno Guy, the way I see it you're part of the team."

"You two need to go up and do this. I'll climb the south ridge and meet you on top. I'll bring the camera. We'll party." He was sincere, a trusted friend with no BS. The decision was made.

There is a major feature on this wall. Guy called it the Gorilla Face. It's a remarkable profile, like something you might find on the face of a coin minted in the land of Planet of the Apes.

I expected it to offer up some hard climbing, at least I hoped so. If the climb had two difficult pitches down low and went to the top easily from there, it would hardly be a classic. As it turned out, I got what I was looking for.

Our goal was to climb the wall from bottom to top with no falls, no hanging on the rope, no backtracking to try a hard section again. When the time came to turn my back on the Silver Turret and walk out of the Gorge of Despair, it had to be with an unquestionable free ascent of this route. No asterisks, as climbers say. Nothing less would do.

There's a climb in Yosemite called Astroman. When it was first done, it was a test piece. Today it's considered a "must do" for any serious Yosemite climber. Erik Eriksson invited me to do it with him. I was honored, thrilled, and terrified. I wasn't terrified by the climb. I was afraid I wouldn't measure up to Erik's exacting standards. We swung leads, meaning I would lead a pitch and Erik the next, and so forth. As it happened, the demanding "endurance corner" fell to me. Nearly finished, confident that I had it in the bag, I missed a small foothold. I made the move even more strenuous than it already was and fell. Our ascent was tainted. I praised the Lord when Erik fell off a hard move higher up. At least now we were even. I led the last pitch. It's the only pitch on the climb, out of ten, that's on less than perfect granite and is dangerous. I'll never forget leading that pitch, feeling good while knowing the risk, all the while enjoying the smell of the pine trees such a short distance above. Many climbers, dare I say most, would have walked away from our ascent saying they had done Astroman, but not Erik and me.

I sat in silence, taking in the unreal view across Yosemite Valley to Half Dome. Erik spoke first.

"Can you come back next week and try it again?"

I knew exactly what he meant, but I didn't answer fast enough.

"You're not satisfied, are you?"

We came back and did it.

This was the standard I was setting for myself on this remote back-country climb. As our little fire died down, I asked Chelsea if she wanted to swing leads, assuming she would. She declined, saying, "This baby is yours. If one of us is gonna screw it up it's going to be you."

Alright then. This baby was mine.

Red Danskin tights? Check. Nikon sunglasses? Check. Booting up to get on the biggest wall in the Gorge of Despair? Priceless. Photo: Guy Keesee

The next morning, we were off. I'd been living for this day for two years. I needed to relax "like I'd never relaxed before." We climbed fast, and soon we were past the old high point, from where Guy and I had rappelled two years before. We were stapled to the vertical wall by two bolts, confronted by the Gorilla Face.

A perfect thin crack split the gorilla's nose, ending at its brow. From there, it looked like I could hand traverse left, out from under the brow, and climb around the end to finish. I looked Chelsea in the eyes, steeled myself, and set forth.

I climbed across to the thin crack. I was like a fly on the gorilla's nose. The crack varied between a quarter and a half-inch wide, marginal at best for fingertips. About two-thirds of the way to the brow, just when I thought I had it, I got a little impatient with a tiny foothold and fell. Hanging from my gear, I sized up the moves and finished the pitch. These were, by far, the most challenging moves on the climb. I set two bolts for an anchor, Chelsea came up, and we rappelled to the ground. A momentary lapse of concentration and the attempt was spoiled.

We took a rest day. Our effort on the following day would be my last chance. One fall, and it would be game over.

When the time came, I was surprised to find myself calm and relaxed. By mid-day, we were up at the gorilla's face.

"Well Chelsea, this is it. Now or never."

"You have this. It's a piece of cake for you."

I was hyper-alert. There would be no lapses of concentration this time. I climbed across and up to the thin crack. It was time for perfect execution. Nothing less would do.

I was moving well, and to conserve energy, I placed minimal protection. Then, there it was, that nasty little foothold I slipped off last time. As I stepped up and smeared the toe of my shoe on it, I whispered under my breath.

"C'mon you little bugger, don't let me down now." I was in the bubble. As I'd become accustomed to over two decades of climbing, my sense of the passage of time slowed. This one moment had been four years in the making. I conjured weightlessness as I pressed my toe down on the tiny crystal sticking out from the rock and began to stand up on it. "That's it, stand up straight." Just out of reach, the crack offered up its first good slot for fingers, an opening about three-quarters of an inch wide. The straighter up I stood, the less secure my foot was. Three inches. "Jesus, just stand up on it." Then it was two inches; then one, then my fingers were in the slot. It was over. There was nothing left but easy climbing to the top. As promised, Guy met us on the summit. We partied and took pictures as the sun sank into the San Joaquin Valley fog in the west.

The summit. Photo: Guy Keesee

Four years, three trips in, the first ascent of From Afar, one serious injury, a harrowing epic descent, one hardcore self-rescue, one clean lead, and it was done. We named the climb Despairadoes and offered a grade of 5.12.

Despairadoes The undercling starts the third pitch. Pitch 5 climbs the Gorilla Face. The arrow marks the line of our escape rappels after Guy's injury in 1995. Photo: Guy Keesee

8

IN THE NICHE OF TIME

TEHIPITE DOME

By E.C. Joe

Saturday Night Special

One of the enjoyable aspects of working in a mountain shop was interacting with customers and hearing about their adventures. I got to know Ron Felton through his frequent visits to Sunrise Mountaineering. It was easy talking about technical climbing hardware with him, as he was familiar with construction and repairing cars. Ron had a candid view of the world, and I enjoyed hearing about his climbing exploits around Calaveras Dome near Lake Tahoe. After a few conversations, it soon became apparent that Ron's head for the game would enable some shared adventures.

Ron was eager to see different climbing areas, so I invited Ron and his buddies to tag-a-along on an outing to Chimney Rocks in Sequoia. Even though I would be pretty busy instructing a climbing course that weekend, I promised Ron that we could get together and climb during my free time Saturday evening.

While most of the group was retired about camp, we got busy racking up. I had scoped out a new face climbing route on the Crystal Wall, named for its mysterious geodes that populate several face climbs there on otherwise uniquely "bubbly" granite. Daylight was long gone. However, Ron, Jim Wright, and I headed out by headlamp, hoping to eventually climb the route by the light of the full moon. Unfortunately, the moonlight eluded us during our whole journey up the rock, but that didn't slow us down. Each of us took a turn climbing up through new territory with no bolt kit. This was a challenge to our anchoring skills, as we were forced to utilize the rock's convoluted and knobby surface to wedge protection in-between. In any other situation, venue, or in different company, this type of activity could have resulted in a major epic. Instead, our frolic in the dark, "Saturday Night Special," set the stage for Ron and I to forge new climbs together on grander rock.

> *It's a Saturday Night Special,*
> *Got Cams of Blue and Gold,*
> *Ain't Good for Nuthin,'*
> *Runout 60 Feet on the Rope*

A grander rock future ended up being not too distant. I had recently finished a new route on Voodoo Dome at the Needles called "Cross-bones."[1] and while on that climb, I spotted yet another project to start on. Ron agreed to join me for this new line with little persuasion — a fairly direct route up the South Face of Voodoo Dome. We packed up Ron's weathered orange Dodge van for the voyage. Ron had van camping down, with just enough creature comforts one would need for hanging out, including a set of homemade stools and table, a welcome alternative to sitting inside the van. Both of us were excited to do the new route and set up basecamp near Needlerock Creek alongside the road below the dome.

Sorting gear for a known route is easy. Sorting gear for a first ascent is much less so. It's a guessing game. To provide adequate protection for our endeavor, one set of micro, wired nuts and Stoppers was always a good start. At least half of the route appeared to have climbable cracks, so a double set of cams was in order, from tiny fingertip size cracks to three inches wide. We tossed in one four-inch cam and the smallest three Tri-Cams to round things out for the unexpected wide crack and odd, shallow finger pockets. No one wants to be begging for the cam or nut that was left behind. One lead rope, a lightweight, 5.5 mm haul line, ten shoulder-length slings, eight quickdraws, twenty carabiners, a bolt kit, and a hammer were added to the pile as well. A couple of windbreakers, light microfleece pullovers, fleece gloves, hats, and headlamps, considered standard equipment at the Needles, were not to be forgotten. Along with all the gear, there were four liters of water, Vitalyte®, and "wall munchies" like energy bars. The difficult part was to organize the gear into two medium backpacks, then the next day, carry it all uphill for close to an hour to the rock.

After the gear sort, we needed to have some dinner and get some rest. Ron conjured up a one-pot stew with some fixins on the side. There was plenty to go around, so much that we should have invited people for dinner! Sure that we would need as much energy as possible for the next day's climb, I was intent on finishing off the stew, which I did to Ron's surprise. Even though there was the absence of a warm campfire, it didn't stop us from weaving some entertaining tales for each other. The finale of the evening was Ron's animated description of a climb that had him falling backward over one of the homemade stools, disappearing in a cloud of dust over the edge of the road!

The new route, "Voodoo Chil (Child)"[2] went smoothly the next day. After which, Ron and I became regular climbing partners. This was an easy link since we shared a passion for new routes, and an increasing trust partly developed on Voodoo Dome. The stage was set for more new route adventures.

Ron Felton on Hetch Hetchy Dome.
Photo: E.C. Joe

Pioneering new rock climbs had become "my thing" early in my climbing experience. Climbing new routes at "roadside" crags became as simple as "Lather, Rinse, Repeat." However, pioneering a new climb in remote areas on a large wall was never as clear-cut. In particular, big wall climbing in the backcountry had never been popular in the Sierra compared to exclusive free climbing routes. Traveling to sights unseen normally involved careful planning and logistics. Planning for a remote big wall complicated this exponentially with the need to carry arcane tools like pitons, heads, hooks, hammer, and a portable water supply for days. I enjoyed any sort of backcountry climbing, but climbing backcountry big walls brought on a higher level of commitment, spontaneity, and adventure. Or perhaps, is that when experience, risk, boldness, stupidity collide?

Tehipite Valley. Photo: E.C. Joe

"Tehi... How do you pronounce that?"

Tehipite Valley is a uniquely beautiful place where the Middle Fork of the Kings River flows. As a result of ancient glacial action, it's a deep gorge with extensive granite walls, forested floor, with an emerald green river snaking its way from east to west. Tehipite Valley rivals Yosemite Valley in many ways; however, Tehipite Valley's remote and relatively untouched nature made it most appealing to me. It was a place frozen in time, raw and primal. The lack of human visitation there was substantiated during my attempts to recruit interest in Tehipite. The typical response was, "Whaa? Tehi — How do you pronounce that? WHERE is that?!" Furthermore, to suggest hiking any considerable distance to do a big wall climb that one couldn't park their vehicle below was counter-intuitive to them. Unfettered, I still wanted to climb Tehipite Dome, noted as "the largest granite dome in the Sierra Nevada."[3]

The Middle Fork of the Kings River, Tehipite Valley. Photo: E.C. Joe

Tehipite Dome is deep in the Sierra backcountry and stands in mute testimony to the few pioneers who first established its routes. When compared to other Sierra walls, Tehipite Dome stands alone. One guidebook listed two major technical routes found on the immense south face: one in 1963 by Fred Beckey, Herb Swedlund, Ken Weeks, and John Ahern, and the second, the first grade VI in the Sierra backcountry was done in 1970 by Chuck Kroger, Curt Chadwick, and Norm Weeden.[4] At the time, there were few backcountry climbs in the Sierra of similar length or grade like those and were seldom repeated. The remote nature of climbing in the backcountry requires a climber to truly step up their game and to be prepared for some punishment to take on such adventures.

What the guidebook couldn't convey was how visually intimidating it was in person. Imagine: nearly three Empire State Buildings stacked on top of each other, proudly standing there with nothing else to rival it. During my first trips, I respectfully resigned myself to exploring the valley, visiting waterfalls, petrographs, and swimming in the Kings River's spectacular crystal clear emerald green pools. Meanwhile, I scoured the walls of Tehipite for any viable route on which to climb. It was an immense piece of stone that appeared to lack any apparent weaknesses to piece together a climbing route. After viewing the wall at different times of the day and from various vantage points, I eventually discovered a fairly continuous crack system that could harbor a route. It was thin and steep.

I knew the route that I had chosen to climb on Tehipite Dome would be the best line. Having hiked out to Tehipite Valley twice and then on a third opportunity, bailing at the last minute, it was difficult committing to a trip to climb Tehipite again. Planning, logistics, and partner selection all needed to be in perfect alignment. The two visits in 1991 and 1995 ended up as reconnaissance trips as a result of imperfect alignment. Miscalculating exactly how many water bottles to bring was like forgetting the rope, and if you don't have the proper hardware, it won't matter how many water bottles you brought. My last bailout caused a rift between Richard Leversee, my longtime backcountry climbing partner, and me. Once, I jokingly told him that our shared accomplishments had made us like the "Lennon and McCartney of the Sierra." Richard and I had, at that time, climbed the first ascents of nearly all of the most coveted and longest technical big wall routes in the Sierra backcountry. The rift developed into an ungentlemanly competition to climb Tehipite. The race was on.

Ron was keen on joining me on the project; however, we figured it would be good to recruit a third person to help schlep loads of gear. Ron's friend, Guy Zielski, agreed to help us with our task. Ron and I would have to share the leads because Guy had limited lead experience, but Guy could undoubtedly help by carrying a load and hauling bags on the wall. We planned to take up to two weeks for the project, if necessary. This is not the team I had envisioned. I really would have liked Richard to join us, but he had made separate plans for Tehipite. Once I got word of his timeline, I set mine earlier, determined to win the race.

Going for Broke

The trail from Wishon Reservoir was deserted. The wilderness ranger station, the last outpost out in Crown Valley, was closed for the season. We spent a day and a half on the approach, the extra half-day due to Guy's knee giving out from the serious schlepping. Ron and I shared most of Guy's load, and I gave him some major painkillers to ease his grief. Once in Tehipite Valley, we had some welcome, cooling rain for the next two and a half days while we camped at a small site next to Crown Creek.

Ron caught some trout with some line and a lure fastened to the end of a trekking pole. I didn't have much luck with that method. The one thing that I did attract was a curious water snake while standing on a tiny island fishing. I was petrified as the dark-colored snake slithered onto my foot. Luckily, the snake went away as quickly as it came. I lost interest in fishing after that. We ate pretty well, using foil for cooking the fish on a wood fire, especially with the rice mix that we combined with some home-dried veggies. Voila! — a one-pot stew for our only pot. We took full advantage of the pleasures of having hot food because once we were on the wall, we would only have cold "wall food."

During the rainy period, we moved our loads of gear up the enormous talus slope that led up to the base of the wall. It was unstable, like a house of cards stacked with huge boulders. We periodically hid from the rain in caves formed in the talus. At the base of the wall, we cached enough food, water, and bivouac gear for a one-night stay. Then we scrambled above five hundred feet of third and fourth class terrain to the start of our intended route, stashing almost all of our gear there. The start was located just left of the

Ron Felton showing his cooking chops as Guy Zielsky looks on. Photo: E.C. Joe

1970 Kroger Route and at the left side of a prominent pyramid formation. Afterward, we fixed ropes and descended back down to find a bivy site for the night at the base of the wall.

The best site to bivy was the only place that wasn't on a major slope, but it was far from perfect, as it was strewn with rocks and debris. Guy was about to voice his concern about the site's quality when Ron and I, without a word spoken, whipped into action. Our work was so intense and quick that Guy stood there astonished. When the dust cleared, a haven for three, now reasonably flat, appeared complete with a natural fireplace to warm our feet. We settled into our bivy sacks and watched the next wave of the storm coming in from the South. Guy had a Walkman® with a radio that worked well from our vantage point. The weather forecast was for clear skies ahead.

We were up before first light the following day and left the comfort of our bivy, and ascended back to the start of the climb. It was difficult for me to wrap my head around the view. The wall above overhung so radically; we could see our intended route for at least 800 feet! Ron climbed a pitch to the left up some wet and slimy shelves to a small tree ledge to keep us out of the path of potential rockfall. Ron took the second lead as well to make up for the poor-quality approach pitch. Ron nailed up and right on a thin ramp, then tension-traversed to a prominent arête to the right, which marked the main feature of our intended route. There he intercepted the crack system that we hoped would lead us to the base of a huge pillar, hundreds of feet up. Out of our sight, around the corner of the arête, Ron fell onto a sling lassoed around a tooth of granite. He remained tenacious as he led into the night hours using all twelve of our "Beak" pitons in the process. Beaks or "Peckers" are pitons for insipid cracks. These car key-sized pitons look like a nautical toy anchor with one hook removed. In practice, it's hammered into a seam, where the remaining hook (blade) chops its way into the rock like a hatchet into a stump. If lucky, the blade will hook in a full inch or so; if not, the blade only needs to penetrate a minute fraction of that to be usable. In either instance, it's esoteric and scary. The crack he had followed eventually disappeared, leaving him with a wild hook traverse to a belay on a sloping ledge a full rope length out.

I cleaned the pitch by headlamp. The pitch overhung and leaned to the right, making it difficult to clean. The process seemed to take forever in the dark. The rope and my headlamp were my only guides. Wielding my hammer was my only relief. Upon arriving at the belay, I found Ron hypothermic and barely responsive. I laid over him to warm him up and gave him a shell garment. He was soon able to join the action again. It wasn't too long after we got the haulbags stuck in the only tree out on the cliff. It was epic untangling the jam by headlamp. Exhausted, we squeezed out a bivy back at a "ledge" below the tree.

The ledge turned out to be a four-foot-wide by three-foot deep by two-foot thick boulder wedged precariously at the base of the tree. Our butts rested on a small lip of rock that was part of the wall and rested our feet on the boulder. Sitting closely together, side by side, we prepared for the night. We speculated about the difficulty of the climbing above and how we "easily" burned 12 hours of daylight like it was nothing. We realized that a long journey lay ahead if we were only going to complete a pitch or so per day. Alarmed, we started the rationing of our supplies that night.

"Our water supply was calculated by using an old bullshit Yosemite standard of "1.5 quarts of water per person, per day," that we increased to 2+ quarts per person...To conserve our precious water supply, we used a filter to fill our bottles for the night from a pocket we scraped out below a scum-filled seepage."

On El Capitan, in Yosemite Valley, canned food is standard fare; durable containers that include plenty of water with the contents. Humping a week's worth of canned food to the base of El Capitan from the meadow was no task compared to staging for a big wall 20 miles into the wilderness. To save weight, we had packed military surplus Meals Ready to Eat, or "MREs." Each was intended to be an individual "field ration," stripped down to the essential meal requirement for one of America's Finest Fighting Force for a day. The entrée itself came in a "soft can" (foil pouch) that we would split three ways, then we supplemented that with a variety of trail food and whatever else was included in the MRE. Ron joked that the government made MREs so salty and with so little fiber on purpose, so a soldier would have no choice but to be mad and ready to kill from constipation caused by eating them. No jokes aside, in some military circles, MREs have been used in "Dietary Manipulation" in conjunction with interrogating prisoners of war and are known as "Three Lies for the Price of One...it's not a Meal, it's not Ready, and you can't Eat it."[5] We had only brought 8 gallons of water with us, supposedly enough for 5-days on the wall. Our water supply was calculated by using an old bullshit Yosemite standard of "1.5 quarts of water per person, per day," that we increased to 2+ quarts per person. On past walls I'd done, this did seem reasonable without swilling. To conserve our precious water supply, we used a filter to fill our bottles for the night from a pocket we scraped out below a scum-filled seepage. Sleeping was not particularly easy. I suppose I slept some since I remember being woken to Guy and Ron cursing me for snoring.

Ron and Guy swelter in the Hot Pocket. Photo: E.C. Joe

Before dawn, we moved to the sloping ledge above. The weather had changed radically. The previous days of cool weather were gone. We were amidst a heatwave that placed us in an even more difficult situation with our limited water supply. Above the belay, I led a steep crack on aid to a difficult off-width/chimney. I yelled back occasionally to answer the cries of discomfort and impatience from my partners. The belay ledge below was a saucer-shaped feature where Ron and Guy were the main microwave entrée! Little did they know or care that I was dealing with my own hell of slithering, stemming, runout, and trying to be careful not to fall. Nearing the top of the pitch, in a partially loose wide section, a briefcase-shaped block of granite fell into my lap. In the backcountry, an overhanging wall is never the right place for a crisis. Stay calm. I warned the guys. It sounded as if they could give a shit. Lock-off the legs. Lift the block and put it...back. Stay! I found a crack that only a small Alien Cam would fit in for protection. I used it not only for myself but also to protect Ron & Guy by keeping the rope from flossing the block out. I gladly left that spot. Eliminating the apparent dangers, I reached an easy ramp that led to a mausoleum-like alcove with a ledge behind a prominent colossal pillar.

An Omen

The best feature of the "Mausoleum" was that it was in the shade. We were now in the belly of the beast, deep inside Tehipite Dome. This bizarre shelter of stone was a welcome relief from the intense sun that had beat us down so badly. This break allowed us to gain back some morale. In the narrow causeway of our living quarters, we joked around, lounged, and slept. While exploring our surroundings, we noticed that a peregrine falcon was frequenting the area. To be able to witness the activity of these masters of the air was a treat. The peregrine's cries lifted our spirit. I have been told

The Mausoleum. Photo: E.C. Joe

that in Native American lore, when hawks appear, that it's a good omen for a traveler.

We had another airborne visitor that day. A small, single-engine airplane circled above the dome. I suspected that it was Richard checking on our progress. (Later, I found that he was.) We attempted to wave through a small open space, but we were probably so dwarfed by our surroundings be noticed.

Ron Felton on the Roof Traverse. Photo: E.C. Joe

The climbing to the top of the pillar proved extremely difficult; Ron climbed mixed free and aid above our haven. Then Ron traversed left to the main arête by nailing left underneath a long, impressive horizontal roof for nearly 100 feet. Ron and I got quite a show when Guy and the haulbags swung out from the ledge behind the pillar. Guy didn't enjoy the show as much as we did, "What in the hell did you get me into, you motherfucker! When I get off of this thing, I'm going to kick your ass!" Cleaning the pitch was challenging. Traveling horizontally, I risked popping out pieces of gear and taking falls as though on lead. Fortunately, that was the exception and not the rule. We had worked our way back onto the arête, totally exposed and physically committed.

The next lead was spectacular climbing up a headwall with a steep thin crack system near the arête. It was reminiscent of the upper headwall on the "Shield" of El Capitan I had climbed in 1980, a vast expanse of rock, split by a solitary crack. Even though we had been diligent in starting climbing well before dawn, the short autumn days always left us pushing into the dark hours of the night. We were climbing nearly full 60-meter pitches that involved time-consuming, difficult aid, burning up daylight as I had never imagined. Regardless of years of experience, I still had one speed on this kind of stuff, not particularly fast, but steady. I was only about halfway out on the lead when I heard that neither of them could stay awake to belay me. I reached a spot where I had intended to place a bolt, drilled it, then orchestrated some pieces together to safely return to the belay and rappelled down the haul line fixed to my high point while Guy belayed me on the lead rope. When I got level with the belay, I was at least twenty feet out in space from the wall! Ron then reeled me in with the end of the haul line.

We should have thought to fix a line to get back down to the comfort of the mausoleum. The wall was too steep and the mausoleum too far to the side to return without it. Hindsight is 20/20. Right? Guy and I hung in single-point hammocks while Ron hung in a boson's seat. We passed around our rations of food and water for the night. Afterward, the battle ensued to get

Guy and Ron at the Roof Bivy. Photo: E.C. Joe

comfortable and to keep the chill of the night out. None of us won our battles. I was glad to have left the discomfort of the bivy in the dark hours before dawn to resume the lead.

The headwall crack was stunning and required a variety of tiny nuts, copperhead placements, small cams, and pitons. The crack ended, and I drilled a short bolt and bat hook ladder to a tiny belay stance near the arête. The position here was exposed, some 800 feet above our starting point, and the steepness was surreal, but the reality was confirmed each time Guy and the haulbags launched into space to ascend his rope to the belay. Guy had only climbed on a handful of small crags. This was his first big wall, and he got a virtual "Berlitz" course on the basic rules of big wall climbing and the safe use of ascenders at the base of the climb.

Guy Zielski launches into space. Photo: E.C. Joe

The Sea of Granite

On the wall above, the features that we had hoped were usable cracks turned out to be mere ripples in the golden granite. Fortunately, we were now at the top of the overhanging part of the wall. Now, there was just vertical blank rock! Our reference was a crumpled 11 by 17 inch photograph of Tehipite that I had taken on a previous trip. And while it may not have been accurate to judge for usable cracks, it was great for figuring where we were in a sea of granite. We had passed the point of no return after the third pitch. There was a blank wall ahead with no cracks. What we had to do next has been an anathema to some climbers for decades — drill, bat hook, rivet, and bolt our way up the wall.

Guy Zielsky cashing in his rewards air miles. Photo: Ron Felton

Warren Harding had admitted to "inventing" the "Bat Hook," a tool for efficiently climbing through expanses of blank rock, which he devised for the first ascent of South Face of Half Dome. The Bat Hook was a modified Chouinard Climbing Equipment "Cliff Hanger" with the sides of the business-end ground down to insert tightly into a shallow, 1/4" deep, 1/4" diameter hole drilled with a hand-held percussion drill. Once set, a climber could attach a ladder made of nylon webbing (etrier) to it and advance up the rock face. Harding's one-time climbing partner, Dean Caldwell, "improved" on the concept by introducing the flathead aluminum rivet to insert permanently into a hole with a tiny wire loop "hanger" from which an etrier could be hung.[6] The whole idea was to reduce the fifteen to twenty minutes it took to hand drill a hole for a full bolt, 1.25" deep, to five minutes.[7] Even though many "purists" have decried this method, other climbers embraced it in order to connect intermittent crack systems. And in doing so, some of the wildest and most difficult big wall rock climbs were established that never would have otherwise existed. Indeed, all of us wanted to climb rocks via their natural features and not drill our way up them because drilling is way too much work. Bat hooking in itself can be dicey, especially if you prescribe to "The Harding Method" of using eight or ten bat hooks or rivets in a row before placing a sound bolt for protection.[8] It takes "big boy pants" to do that.

Ron went out onto the blank, golden wall above, where he boldly bat hooked, riveted, bolted, and beaked his way just short of a good crack system, a full rope length out. This pitch was "out there." If Ron had fallen would have meant taking a huge one, most likely ripping out all the hooks, rivets, and beaks and undoubtedly landing on the large spike of granite next to the belay stance. Again, the pitch consumed most of our daylight. After cleaning the pitch, Ron and I rappelled down to bivy at the start of the pitch. The high jinx of a full hanging bivouac was always the same; thrashing about to get comfortable, being on guard not to drop anything, making sure to stay tied in, and trying not to piss on the ropes or each other. Restless nights were the norm, but after a few days, we'd be guaranteed sleep from sheer exhaustion.

The next day arrived, and we were wearing thin, psychologically and physically. Ron grew impatient with the time in which I was moving on lead, and arguments arose. He failed to realize that his leads weren't breaking any speed records either. We were losing it due to the lack of sleep, water, and heat exhaustion. Committed to climbing Tehipite Dome, each of us cursed the mention of being defeated. Besides, it was impossible to retreat from this beast. It was too overhanging. We needed to climb to survive. Dehydrated and hungry, we entertained our fantasies with a ration of Gummie Life Savers instead of water.

The next lead was mixed. The climbing included some welcome hand cracks and then aid up an acutely angled corner, o.k., a groove. The nailing and nutting was awkward and time-consuming. The end of the lead was a full mantle onto the belay stance. What made it terrifying was that the rope drag was terrible. Choices: fight the rope drag or pull up a bunch of slack before each move. Each had a similar risk, both with potentially ugly consequences; falling or falling further. I pulled up enough slack to make the move and made it — then lost my balance. Luckily, I recovered to keep myself from falling off backward off of the mantle. I was at least ten feet out from my last piece of protection with probably an additional two full arm lengths of slack rope. That would have been a long fall. I yelled down to announce that the angle eased off some and that we might get to free climb and make better time.

It seemed like we were moving in slow motion. After nailing a short section above, Ron downclimbed a diagonal ramp down and right to a ledge at the base of a huge corner. It was great to reach a place that we could stand or sit again. The only problem was that the ledge, the "Sierra Sahara," was sheltered from any breeze whatsoever, which allowed the sun to continue its daily ritual of roasting us. It was a major effort to do anything without coming close to passing out. While waiting for Ron to finish free climbing the next pitch, I lay in the shade of a tiny bush in hopes of getting cooler. Hauling the bags across the lower-angled terrain negated any energy and time saved by free climbing. It was exhausting. Low-angled hauling sucks!

Ron Felton in the sea of granite. Photo: E.C. Joe

The following lead appeared easy, although, with every few moves, I felt that I was going to pass out. I tried to hyperventilate to cool myself down. The crew complained about me being too slow. I told them the truth that I was doing the best I could. My so-called easy lead up the enormous left-facing corner started to look improbable. I plugged in a good cam and followed a natural feature out left to a straight-in crack system. I thought that a bolt would have been good there, but I was too exhausted to spend the time. So, I cranked off some irreversible moves to a spot that I thought would take protection. It didn't. I looked back to assess my situation.

I was about 40 feet up and left from that good cam. The left-facing corner loomed below with my name on it. What I was standing on was not a good stance for anything. I faced falling and slamming into the corner. So, I moved on. I was able to get something in finally, and I was spent. I resorted to the "French Free" method to conserve my overall strength, a combination of free climbing, pulling-up or resting on anchors, aid climbing, or whatever worked. The lead sadly did not get us to the terrace that we know exists up there, somewhere. The significant progress we had made was difficult to appreciate since surviving was the only thing we collectively thought about. The priority was to reach the terrace above to find the spring that supposedly existed there. We hadn't made it yet.

Ron led through as darkness greeted us again. Guy was really out of it. When Ron finished his lead, I told Guy to immediately ascend on my rope while I dealt with the haulbags and the anchor. I gave him the end of my rope, checked his knot, and sent him off. Then, as I started to muscle the bags around, I realized that I had not tied myself into Guy's rope during the trade. There I was 2,000 feet off the deck, unroped on a sloping ramp, holding on to my etriers with one hand! I was too far gone to act like it was a big deal, and I tied myself back in. This occurrence was a harsh reminder to double-check everything, especially when at wit's end.

The three long, difficult free pitches finally got us to the terrace that divided the lower wall from the upper dome. That night we split the last of our water, a third of a quart, and the little food that remained. Then, as if choreographed, we all licked the jelly off of our MRE crackers and pondered eating them for only a brief moment. Finding them too dry to chew, we then tossed them into the abyss. Ron and I then ventured across the ledge. The spring on the ledge was only a seepage. However, there was enough to dampen a T-shirt in which to cool our brows down.

To Die For?

The morning of our sixth day on the wall and the tenth day out from the trailhead we discussed our predicament with temperaments still edgy. A total breakdown between Ron, Guy, and myself was imminent. Then we were startled by a peregrine falcon perched next to us on a bush! The mood changed, and we decided that it was best to stay together and planned to escape by following the terrace into the woods until we reached some water. We would have to worry about the upper half of the dome some other time. Mysteriously, we were directed to a minuscule source of water by the peregrine falcon's cry and flight path over the spot, enough to stave off our dehydration. A good omen, indeed! Later, we found a creek northwest of the dome where we could make camp. We had just enough cookable trail food to feed ourselves for the two days of walking out to the trailhead.

Alive to Climb Another Day

E.C Joe follows a difficult face pitch on the upper dome. Photo: Ron Felton, E.C. Joe Collection

By mid-October, Ron, Guy, and I returned. We hiked eighteen miles in one day back to the same creek that we had camped at after our retreat. Our spirits were high as we traversed back down to the route's high point—the continuation on the upper dome aligned with our route on the lower wall. I led to the left, out onto a prominent arête. Ron cruised up a classic, difficult steep face pitch to a blocky ledge below a steep headwall. We were fresh, and it seemed like we had all but forgotten the suffering and conflict that we had endured during our last visit.

On the headwall, I followed straight thin cracks up through two major horizontal crack bands. This allowed me to tension traverse left to a diagonal ramp that ended at a belay just below a prominent right-facing corner/chimney. The climbing was difficult. The pitches were long and on excellent rock. Ron led up an awkward step up to the left and then right, followed by some difficult moves up a chimney to a belay at the intersection of a wide crack that led up and left.

We hoped that this crack would give us a direct line to the summit.

The wide section proved grueling for me but opened up to intricate mixed free and aid moves. This gave us access to a ledge just left of another but much easier wide crack. This lead was short, only about eighty feet. I headed right a few moves to an enjoyable left-facing corner. The day seemed much less eventful than any of the days on the lower wall, and the climbing was almost entirely free. We had to be efficient because we faced even shorter daylight hours now. We were going to finish it. We committed to climb the remainder of the route in a day and brought no bivy gear, and carried just enough food and water for the day. We had no intention of backing down or staying another night on the rock and preferred to climb through the dark.

*E.C. Joe near the summit of Tehipite Dome. Photo: Ron Felton, E.C.
Joe Collection*

Our headlamps barely broke through autumn darkness. As the terrain rounded, we expected to arrive near the summit, but our headlamps had created a mirage of an unreachable horizon. After four more long pitches of easy, runout face climbing, we unroped at blocky ledges well below the true summit and continued to the top via an awkward scramble. There, we partook in a tribal rite of signing the summit register, then sat quietly and viewed the stars and witnessed the deafening silence of the wilderness night. The crisp autumn air had a message; that winter was nigh. We had completed our journey In the Niche of Time.

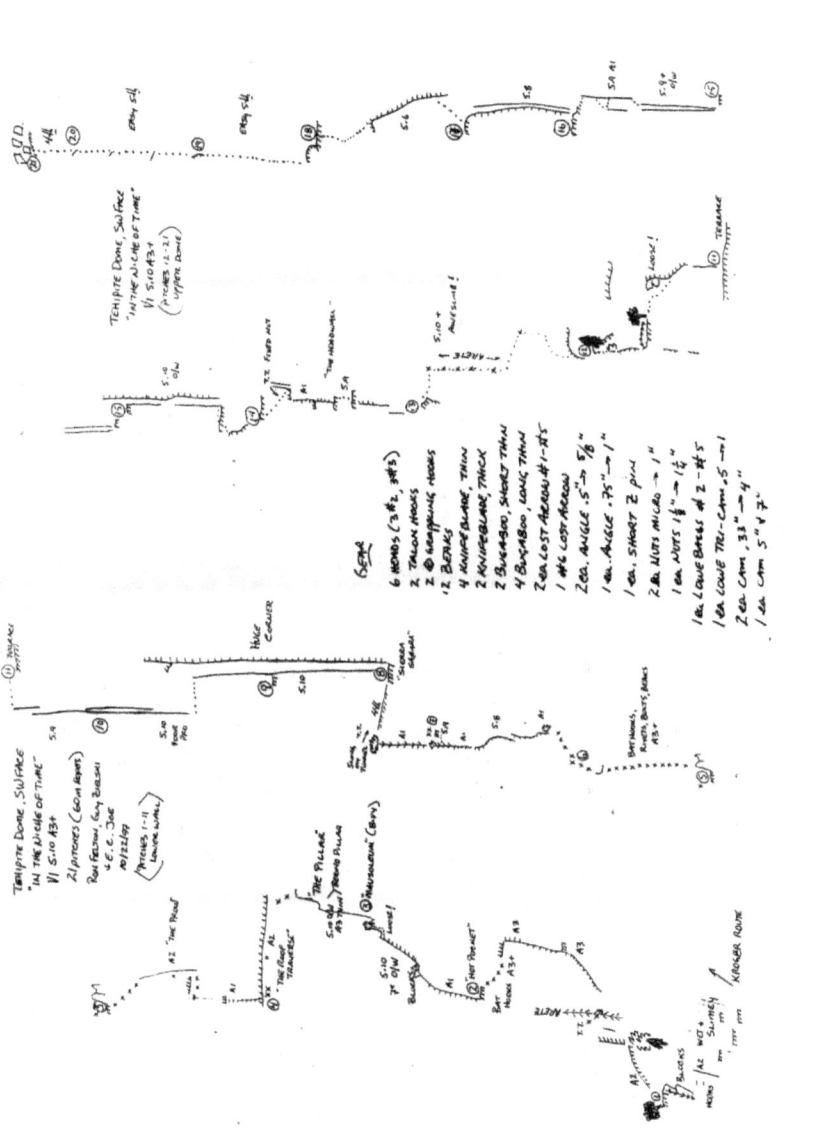

TEMPITE DOME, SOUTH FACE
"IN THE NICHE OF TIME"
VI 5.10 A3+

21 PITCHES (4600 ROPES)

RON FREEMAN, GUY BERLOW
J.E.C. JONE
10/22/99

(PITCHES 1-11
LOWER WALL)

TEMPITE DOME, SOUTH FACE
"IN THE NICHE OF TIME"
VI 5.10 A3+
(PITCHES 12-21
UPPER DOME)

GEAR

6 HORNS (3 #2, 3 #3)
2 TALON HOOKS
2 HARPOON HOOKS
12 BEAKS
4 KNIFEBLADE, THIN
2 KNIFEBLADE, THICK
2 BUGABOO, SHORT THIN
4 BUGABOO, LONG THIN
2 EA LOST ARROW #1-#5
1 #6 LOST ARROW
2 EA. ANGLE .5" → 5/8"
1 EA. ANGLE .75" → 1"
1 EA. SHORT 2 pin
2 EA. NUTS MICRO → 1"
1 EA. NUTS 1¼" → 1½"
1 EA. LOWE BALLS #1-2 —#5
1 EA. LOWE TRI-CAM —5 —1
2 EA. CAM .33" — 4"
1 EA. CAM 5" V 7"

SECTION III

PAYING IT FORWARD

"Service To Others Is The Rent You Pay For Your Room Here On Earth."
— *Muhammad Ali*

1

THE SOUTHERN SIERRA CLIMBERS' ASSOCIATION

By E.C. Joe & Patrick Paul

More and more climbers and other outdoor enthusiasts sought the unique and limited wilderness of the Southern Sierra beyond the early '80s. The influx of these new travelers brought attention to environmental impacts and safety issues at the more popular destinations; trail finding impacts, erosion, lack of sanitary facilities, litter, and legacy fixed anchors. The Southern Sierra is a widespread area with no central climbing "scene," making it difficult to achieve a critical mass of persons interested in addressing those impacts.

Whereas the then newly formed Access Fund had been active around the country, on a local level, their reach seemed distant. Fortunately, a small group of dedicated climbers interested in preserving the climbing environment, educating climbers, and working with land managers to continue having full access to climbing areas established the non-profit Southern Sierra Climbers' Association in 1997. In doing so, the SSCA developed a working relationship with the Access Fund and the American Safe Climbing Association to maintain access to Southern Sierra climbing areas while fostering our partnerships with land managers.

The members of the SSCA selflessly gave back to the climbing community and helped to preserve the climbing environment for years to follow. Unfortunately, the SSCA's life was short-lived, disbanding in 2006. Nonetheless, SSCA's short run was long on accomplishments:

SSCA Accomplishments:

- Developed a partnership with the USDA Forest Service and the Access Fund to provide a permanent toilet at the Needles of California
- Provided and maintained a stokes litter and first responder kit at The Needles of California
- Worked with the Buck Rock Foundation and the USDA Forest Service to retread the stairs, repair the plumbing, and restore the handrail at The Needles fire lookout
- Provided portable potties at Dome Rock (currently not funded by the USDA/FS)
- Placed "Please Do Not Throw Rocks" signs at Dome Rock to help keep climbers safe
- Worked with the American Safe Climbing Association to replace bolts at The Needles, Fresno Dome, Courtright Reservoir, Dome Rock, Chimney Rocks, and many other climbing areas in the southern Sierra
- Worked with the USDA Forest Service & Sequoia National Park in Peregrine Falcon surveys and management
- Worked the Sequoia National Park Service in conducting two large scale cleanups at Moro Rock, in Sequoia National Park
- Worked in partnership with the Buck Rock Foundation and the USDA Forest Service doing maintenance work at Buck Rock
- Built or maintained climber's trails at Dome Rock, Hermit Spire, Trilogy rock, Bald Eagle Peak, and other areas to reduce adverse impacts on the terrain

No - 'Not a bust. SSCA members working with Rangers at Moro Rock in Sequoia National Park to clean up litter, including items discarded by tourists that ended up along the base of the rock. Photo: René Ardesch Collection

2

THE PEREGRINE FALCON SURVEY OF THE SIERRA NEVADA, THE '90S

By Lee Aulman

D uring the mid-1960s, raptor biologists and falconers noted a steep population decline of the American peregrine falcon (Falco peregrinus anatum) across most North America. It was determined that the species was extinct east of the Mississippi River. A few pairs of peregrines were still occupying the cliffs in Colorado. There were only two known pairs in California, one on El Capitan in Yosemite Valley and one on Morro Rock in Morro Bay. Eventually, the precipitous population decline was correlated with organochlorine pesticide contamination, particularly DDT (dichloro-diphenyl-trichloroethane), which resulted in severe eggshell thinning and reproductive failure.

The rapid decline of the American peregrine falcon generated an impressive human effort to save the species from extinction in North America. The peregrine became the most studied animal by scientists since the confirmed decline during the early 1960s, with the environmental toxicological aspects most emphasized. High levels of DDT and other chlorinated hydrocarbon residues were found in peregrine eggs and the remains from dead adults. It was now confirmed: that these types of long-lived contaminants biomagnified in various species, particularly ones high on the food chain, the apex predators like peregrines.

The Peregrines' Champions, Lee Aulman, Yvon Chouinard, and Shawn
Hayes below the Lompoc Skull, 2021. Photo: Malinda Chouinard

Widespread studies began with numerous species, including eagles, pelicans, ocean-dwelling predators like orcas, sharks, and sea lions. All samples showed significant storage of various combinations of these pollutants in the fatty tissues and livers of the aforementioned species. Subsequent research confirmed a similar effect with humans with some serious caveats. DDT and the other toxic compounds (polychlorinated biphenyls "PCBs," dieldrin, dioxins, etc.) were found in controlled laboratory experiments to be carcinogenic and, in some cases, mutagenic and teratogenic. The threat to human health concerns led to the banning of all of these poisons in the United States during the early 1980s. It is quite ironic that the world's fastest and fiercest bird poisoned by man-made chemicals led to the discovery of the health threat to humanity. As our friend Galen Rowell said, "...the peregrine falcon became our mine canary for mother earth."

Multiple wildlife agencies, raptor biologists, falconers, and climbers began the effort of saving peregrines from extinction. Yvon Chouinard was one of the first climbers to conduct cliff surveys to hopefully find surviving nests or collect eggshell samples for toxicological analysis. Yosemite climbers made it possible for us to have captive-bred young peregrines in the North American face of El Capitan. These individuals included Rob Roy Ramey III, Kurt Stotzenberg, John Yablonski, Walt Shipley, Jim Elias, Jim Bridwell, and others. Captive breeding facilities were established using legally acquired peregrines prior to the species listing as endangered from very generous falconers. One facility was located in Colorado and the west coast version, the Santa Cruz Predatory Bird Research Group (SCPBRG) at the University of California at Santa Cruz. I began work for SCPBRG in 1985 to perform the necessary peregrine nest climbing, mainly on the unconsolidated coastal and Channel Islands cliffs. Our management area also included much of the northern interior of California. As young captive peregrines were released back into the wild, the population began to increase and later bred on their own successfully due to the banning of DDT and the other long-lived organochlorine poisons. My work also included the high priority California Condor project with 14 individuals in the wild and bald eagle research. Both species were negatively affected by organochlorines, as well.

When my time at Santa Cruz was up, I moved on to other wildlife projects. In 1991, I was selected by Steve Anderson, a biologist for the Hume Lake Ranger District, to survey the length of the Sierra Nevada Mountain range from the El Dorado National Forest to the Sequoia National Forest to the south. This area included areas within the Kings and Sequoia National Parks, and the survey became a collaborative effort between agencies through park representative Harold Werner. The first objective was to perform a helicopter survey of priority cliff systems and monoliths, like Balloon Dome. In the early eighties, a survey by peregrine experts had found no peregrine confirmations, only eagles and red-tailed hawks.

During the helicopter survey, I observed one adult peregrine high on the south face of Tehipite Dome, situated in Kings Canyon National Park along the Middle Fork of the Kings River, and eventually assessed the cliffs with nesting potential in the Sierra forests. Being based at the Hume Lake Ranger District, I enacted ground surveys that focused on the most desirable sites.

The field notes of peregrine researcher John "Zak" Ball noted "... climbers being 'bombed'..." at the Needles of the Sequoia National Forest by peregrines. I'm sure many climbers have encountered adult peregrines, called the "fiercest and fastest bird," while near the nest cliffs. As I, on occasion, have been whacked by these highly territorial and aggressive nest defenders during the earlier reintroduction activities.

Upon arriving at the vintage Needles Lookout, the fire lookout, Margee Kelly, told me what she thought was a smaller red-tailed hawk chasing away larger ones to the east. As I observed from the tower, I saw one of the "smaller red-tails" land on one of the large Needles formations. It was an adult peregrine! Afterward, I located the nest site and heard at least two hungry and screaming young and observed the adults bringing in avian prey for feeding. It is during this time when the adults attain their highest degree of territorial ferocity. The note from the climber's report to the prior researcher had helped lead me to them.

Donnell Reservoir was the next survey. The 1980 survey noted a lack of ledges on the massive granite face above the reservoir, but I saw plenty of large ledges suitable for peregrines during the helicopter check. After much humping through rough terrain, I located a nest with one young on a ledge fairly high-up, on a vertical wall, and above the lake. I already knew that peregrines and climbers were of the same habitat, with different agendas and goals.

Upon my return from the office, I was put in touch with Eddie Joe, whom I heard from some of the Yosemite climbers. He was a well-known climber in the Southern Sierra. Eddie, during a conversation, told me he thought peregrines were at Moro Rock in Sequoia National Park and seemed to be very interested in the falcons' situation. I explained that they were slowly recovering from the population crash and that some nests still had man-made contaminant problems. I also stated that the goal would be to collect nest contents (eggshell fragments, etc.) for toxicological analysis.

A friend who essentially became my climbing partner on the Big Sur, Galen Rowell, was also interested in helping with the Sierra birds, time allowing. Nest entries would only occur after any peregrine young fledged, or if the adults have abandoned the nests after rearing young or, in the event of a reproductive failure.

I had heard from Pacific Gas & Electric (PG&E) officials that peregrines had been observed at Calaveras Dome by climbers from Hammer Dome across the valley. I located them near the dome on a smaller cliff and confirmed three young peregrines being produced.

Fuller Buttes, Balloon Dome, Sunset Point in the Sierra National Forest, and Tehipite Dome had breeding peregrines. A noted climber, Richard Leversee, reported to Eddie that at Patterson Bluffs in the Sierra NF, he had seen peregrines on the west end and prairie falcons on the east. It was past the breeding season, so I didn't follow up with those observations. They were back in the Sierra! I monitored all of the nests for successful fledges of any young and for nest failure, twice each.

Now was the time to see if we could recover nest contents, especially for evidence of eggshell thinning and soft tissue for the toxicologists I had long worked with. The first nest to be entered was on the south face above Donnell Reservoir. The terrain of the sheer granite cliffs of the Sierra would perhaps require a different strategy to recover samples than I had used on the loose cliffs of the California coast. This strategy would require more skilled climbers than myself, me being a loose rock and rappel guy. Access to these nests may not be from the top, but climbing to nests via sheer cliffs from below.

A biologist from the Summit Ranger District, Kathy Burnett, had arranged to get me into the Donnell nest with two excellent free climbers, Ed Noringer and Garth Allen. Kathy, Ed, Garth, and I accessed the wall at Donnell Lake via boat. Ed and Garth climbed up the vertical wall with precision and fixed a rope for me to ascend, which I did fairly rapidly. The ledge was exposed and windblown. Unfortunately, the nest had very little collective evidence to be recovered. The positive part was that the peregrines had fledged a young. I thanked Ed and Garth and headed for the next objective: Moro Rock.

There I was to rendezvous with climber Eddie Joe and fellow climbers Dave Hickey and Rene Ardesch. We took the stairs to the top and proceeded, down climbing to the south-end. We negotiated our way down to a ledge above from the nest cave. The guys set up for Eddie to rappel down, then traverse across the vertical face to get into the nest. Eddie recovered three beautifully pigmented peregrine eggs intact that the adults had abandoned after forty-five days of incubation, well past the average thirty-two days.

We got out of there, and at a shady spot, I began checking the eggs for dents; all of us were very interested in the state of the egg condition. The first egg I held was extremely lightweight, the next an egg with a tiny dent was seemingly normal, and the third with a moderate weight.

This was a very important peregrine nest salvage because of the results we received from the toxicologists at the Long Marine Laboratory in Santa Cruz. One egg died early in incubation with a small embryo, another of the young died halfway through the period, and the third at

Abandoned Peregrine Eggs in an Aerie, Moro Rock, Sequoia National Park. Photo: E.C. Joe

the end. The analysis showed very high levels of hexachlorobenzene (HCB), a toxic seed fumigant, the very toxic polychlorinated PCBs, and very low levels of DDT, hence the relative good eggshell condition.

A subsequent survey to the east face of Moro Rock and another to Chimney Rock on the shared border of Sequoia National Park and Forest with Eddie and John Mottashed had similar results.

The eminent scientists stated the only way for those contaminants to be present in peregrine eggs had to have been due to the atmospheric movement of the toxins into Sequoia Park from the wind and heat from the

Central San Joaquin Valley. This was a significant scientific discovery, and these climbers made it happen.

The next effort would be to get to the Needles nest site, where the adult peregrines had fledged two young. Eddie and Roy Swafford met me at the magnificent Needles, where we headed for the north side of the Witch and Necromancer Needles to a rappel station in an attempt to locate the nest. Eddie went down first and said something like, "You're not going to believe this..."

We all went into a cave-like shaft system, well inside the rock, where we saw ringtail tracks and an area enough for someone to live in. Eddie found an exit chute leading down to where we rappelled down and encountered another chute system. It was surreal, going back into the formation and similar to the first, but a little more precarious because in this chute was a large, sharp cylindrical granite flake at the top of the descending exit, barely sitting there, looked at Roy and Eddie and said,

"This almost is a scene out of the *'Raiders of the Lost Arc.'*" They agreed. We got down to the bottom without being able to intercept the nest. Empty-handed but enlightened by the experience, we all had to ascend our fixed ropes and hike out.

Returning the next week with Eddie and David Hickey, Eddie then ascended to a belay point across from an old raven's nest that the peregrines had taken over; just one crack system over from where our previous attempt ended the weekend prior. Eddie had to lower down, pendulum on the rope, and climb up to the nest site. Nest remains contained a dead peregrine young that was probably out-competed for food by its siblings, some fragments and prey remains. The samples revealed a low DDT level and other contaminants, a good sign for these magnificent birds.

A final trip to the Needles to watch the healthy flying young falcons included Eddie Joe, Galen Rowell, Brian Allison, Michael Sewell, Ron Felton, and myself. Galen and Michael focused on photographing the birds. We immensely enjoyed the day with Eddie and Galen cajoling about climbing with Ron before they free climbed a wicked-looking route, Igor Unchained.

Ron Felton, E.C. Joe, Lee Aulman, and Galen Rowell observing peregrines at the Needles. Photo: Brian Allison, E.C. Joe Collection

I am forever grateful to all the exceptional climbers who dedicated their time, offered their skill and enthusiasm to make a difference in this critical and successful Sierra peregrine survey of 1991-95.

3
———

THE NORMALIZATION OF DEVIANCE

By E.C. Joe

The normalization of deviance is defined as: *"The gradual process through which unacceptable practice or standards become acceptable. As the deviant behavior is repeated without catastrophic results, it becomes the social norm for the organization."* — Dr. Diane Vaughan, The Challenger Launch Decision

W
e were nearly done with the climb. Dave Dobby and I were on a nice comfy ledge, securely tied to a small pine tree some sixty feet below the summit of Fairview Dome. Fairview Dome is one of the largest granite domes in Tuolumne Meadows of Yosemite National Park high country at an elevation of 9,435 feet. The "Regular Route," with close to 1,000 feet of moderate climbing, is wonderfully situated with stunning views of the Sierra. A frequent customer at Sunrise Mountaineering, Dave had asked me to lead him and his business associate Richard up this route. I had previously accompanied them to "Gemini Cracks" on Hammer Dome near Lake Tahoe. They felt comfortable after that successful excursion, now they wanted to do something longer and more challenging. The morning started out typical for the high Sierra with crystal clear skies and crisp cold air. Dave was belaying his friend Richard up to our niche, less than

100 feet from the summit. Meanwhile, I gazed across the horizon and became concerned.

It was unusual for thunderheads to start building in the early morning in August, and the clouds evolved exponentially fast. The clouds, thunder, and lightning quickly engulfed the dome. I instructed Dave to tie off Richard's belay rope. Richard wasn't too happy about it, but I told Richard to hunker down the best that he could on the open slab, as a lightning strike was imminent. Dave and I attempted to minimize our body contact with the rock, which meant one butt cheek each, and our heels. The deafening sound of each lightning strike moved ever closer. Terrified, I curled up in a fetal position, with my mind crying for the sound to stop.

BOOM!! Dave and I went airborne! We were thrown violently upwards and to the end of our rope securements like junkyard dogs on a mission. I felt as if someone had slammed one butt cheek with a baseball bat for a home run. And as quickly as we had taken flight, like rag dolls, we plopped back onto the ledge. Immediately, a massive hail storm ensued.

The hailstorm receded in minutes to scattered rays of sunshine, and what remained was an eerie calm with three soaked climbers, three chalk bags half full of hail, all attached to a little lone pine tree near the top of the dome.

I yelled at Dave, "Are you O.K.!!" Dave had a blank stare towards the meadows and didn't respond until my third try.

"Uh, uh, yeah..." Dave stuttered.

I peered down the slab, "Richard!"

"I'm O.K., what's going on up there?" Richard, fortunately, had not shared our experience.

Richard got no reply as my forearms and hands involuntarily curled up like unfurled fern fronds. It was extremely painful to straighten them and when I did so, they would immediately curl back up. I was worried that I might not be able to lead he rest of the way to the summit and told Dave that he might have to lead. If things already weren't stressful enough, Dave looked at me like, "...Obi-Wan Kenobi. You're my only hope." After the sideshow, I made sure that Dave was good to belay Richard the rest of the way. We gathered our collective spirits once together at our beloved tree. I lead up the final sixty feet, fearful of breaching the slab to the summit area expecting another lightning strike. Thankfully, all was calm and was able to guide us all to the top safely. The Force was strong with us that day!

I had been a climbing instructor, on occasion as a climbing guide, and had various jobs related to climbing for decades. This vocation had all started by chance, as I never had a clue about teaching. Faced with an absence of climbing prospects once I had "the climbing bug," I became adept at utilizing unwitting acquaintances for partners as a resource. As a result, I learned to "stack the deck" to ensure our survival by performing quick, but thorough technical instruction detailed enough to foster a "safe" partner. Word must have got around, as the owner of the local climbing shop in Bakersfield, Dick Banner enticed me to share my knowledge; teach in trade for gear. Ultimately, I was the unwitting one. Reflecting back, I never would have done it unless my heart wasn't in it, even though teaching wasn't a natural thing for me. However, my passion for climbing helped me to get it right.

Rock climbing instruction and guiding never became a full-time gig for me, and I must give mucho kudos to those who did so. Being in the fold entails so much more than leading a climb, placing anchors, holding a client's rope, topping out, and calling it day at the office. A guide must constantly "shape-shift" their relationship with their client besides being their competent rock guide. This included at the appropriate time, being a best friend, coach, drill sergeant, wise old sage, comedian, therapist; like an empathetic bartender, at the ready for stories of life's challenges, besides assuring the client's safety. The guide must be as natural at his skills as breathing. The complex tasks of guiding overshadow the romantic visions of the quintessential mountain guide, with the wind at their back, on a summit gazing at the sunset, and living out their passion in the outdoors. The reality is that its serious work to strive for the best experience and safety for the client. Keeping an impeccable reputation in this type of work as any job is important, because that reputation defines who we are.

Climbers are often called upon to do various "climbing related" work, sometimes foreign to climbing itself, except for the technical aspects. Rigging anchors for peregrine surveys, installing artificial climbing walls, securing aviary nets, investigating climbing tragedies, and negotiating with land managers are only a few of the odd jobs I participated in. In the mid-'80s I relocated to Northern California, and by chance, I created a niche for myself in the East San Francisco Bay Area. I developed experiential climbing excursions for youth, various levels of adult climbing instruction programs which included Bay Area Senior Girl Scout climbing excursions. Later, I became a Climbing Merit Badge Counselor, which led me to develop a climbing instructor certification program for adult leaders and senior scouts of the San Francisco Bay Area Council of the Boy Scouts of America.

During my youth, I had been part of the scouting program and loved it. As an adult, participating as a contractor for the scouting climbing program presented some unique challenges to my ideals and values. Trish Ferenz of the council approached me to work as a volunteer on their rock climbing program. Trish was an enthusiastic advocate for the program. Strangely, Trish seemed to be the only one with a pulse, amongst a bunch of men labeled as scout executives dressed in scout uniforms wandering the halls of the San Leandro SFBAC office. She tasked me with the role to help the council initiate their indoor rock climbing gym program and implement a certification course for adult and senior scouts for outdoor climbing activities.

The national scout office had certification guidelines for ropes courses but at the time, they had no criteria specific for climbing. I had been certified to run top rope, and guide rock climbs through the rigorous American Mountain Guide Association program, as well as having had years of climbing experience to back it up. My task was to integrate the national scouting protocols with the "standard of care" in the climbing world. Ropes courses typically are conducted on manmade structures, while the climbing venues are outside. The standards, in my opinion, would have to weigh towards AMGA standards. My ultimate challenge was to get (almost entirely) non-climbing adults to appreciate the hazards of running a climbing event, use the gear properly, and run an event safely. These were things that take guides years to master. I was about to put these people through what would be akin to a Berlitz course. Was this a crazy idea? Was this even possible?

About a year earlier, I had a skeptic after my merit badge presentation at Rancho Los Mochos Scout camp near Livermore. A parent scoffed as he stood with his hands at his hips, "What's all 'this'? These boys aren't training to be 'expert' climbers? Do they really need to know all 'this stuff'?"

E.C. Joe demonstrates to the scouts how to tie-in. Photo: Joe Metz, E.C. Joe Collection

I stood my ground, "No, they aren't training to be experts. However, if they don't learn this stuff correctly now, if they ever choose go out on their own, the chances of them getting injured or killed will be much less. Kids learn by example. Besides, much of this stuff is in the merit badge requirements." The parent replied, "...that what the kids did on their own time was not his problem." Geez...

I had gone into uncharted waters. Looking back, I get it. The outdoor endeavors in scouting, like camping, hiking, or whatever, aren't half as technical as roped rock climbing. This parent was just oblivious to how much could go wrong in comparison to a campout. Eventually, I figured that this guy was an exception to the rule as all of the other parents at the presentation had grasped the importance of it all and thanked me. Nonetheless, there were still dark waters ahead.

It was the evening of the very first Rock Climbing Instructor Certification Course for the SFBAC. The course consisted of several meetings over four days; one weekday evening in the classroom, an entire weekend outside, and one full weekend day outdoors for a written (multiple choice) test, followed by a practical final exam. Each subsequent meeting was designed to build upon the skills a candidate had learned in the previous sessions. The majority of the candidates enlisted in the program had little or no experience with climbing. My approach was to start from scratch, no matter how much experience any person in the course had. If a candidate had relevant skills, I would utilize them as a resource to assist with those who were lacking. Besides, scouting was about working as a team, right?

Before the course, I was informed by John Maxfield, a scout executive for the SFBAC, to expect Ben Hodges, the "official" climbing instructor for the council's Camp Wente near Willits, CA to be attending. Ben was also affiliated with a troop in Oakland, and John expressed how much the kids loved him. John wanted Ben to receive the certification to continue with the camp program before the summer. Ben introduced himself and insisted that he be referred to as "The Rock." This comment was so ridiculous I ignored it.

There were ten candidates in attendance. During the classroom exercise, I had set the rules for the course. First, show-up on time, because of the extensive amount of material to be covered. I expressed that I would start on time and late-comers would not be accommodated to catch up. Everyone would have to be "all-in" to learn the skills and to run a climbing event on their own safely. One candidate lamented on the four-day commitment, expressing that it was too long and that he had made plans on one of the scheduled days of the course. He asked for the option to take the course a section at a time and finish later. When that would have been, I had no idea. The four day course, which I had previously vetted with a group of experienced scouters and climbers would not work if it was split-up, due to its immersive nature. I refused the request since the course schedule had been posted when he signed up. I had to tell him to drop out or change his plans. He decided to change his plans.

The curriculum was extensive, including a basic introduction to ropes, webbing, knots, carabiners, their proper applications for climbing, and a lesson on belaying. Of course, there were the typical hiccups with tying knots and properly belaying, but curiously, Ben, a climbing instructor, had more difficulty performing these skills than the newbies did. By the end of the first evening, everyone was exhausted, not by the curriculum, but by Ben's incessant interruptions of eye-rolling stories on random topics that he was a pilot, mountaineer, sharpshooter, and how he had risen from the ranks in the military, retiring as a "full bird colonel." Ben seemed a friendly enough person, so everyone indulged him politely; however, I knew all of our thoughts were in concert with, "PLEASE STOP!"

I locked up our meeting room, the Sunrise shop, and as we exited through the climbing gym, we passed under a large poster of Yosemite's El Capitan with all of the currently established routes overlaid on it. Ben stopped to gaze at it.

"Here's the route I did!" Ben says to get my attention, and I turn back around.

Ben scrolled a finger over the longest route on the map most of us know as "The Wall of the Early Morning Light."

"Yeah, I led a battalion of special forces up this, 'led the whole way and set the ropes, they ascended the ropes behind me with full packs, guns and ammo — and we did it in a day," looking at me as if for some confirmation. I wanted to shut this guy down, badly, but instead I humored him. He's the council's guy. Right? At the time, I knew the route had yet to be climbed in a day with two people, but a battalion of soldiers in one day? Plus, I had done the 19th ascent of the route in the early '80s, and it took three of us seven days.

"Really? That's cool, man." Who IS this guy? I asked myself, Is this a *test?*

I turned and walked away toward the exit; then, I heard Ben tell one of the other candidates, "We did it entirely at night when the campers were all sleeping and slipped out of sight before dawn. Nobody even knew we were there." Wow...

Who was this guy? According to the adult Scouters, the scouts loved Ben, maybe because he presented himself as bigger than life. He was a man, on in his years. Ben had a deep voice with a commanding tone. He could bark out orders to the scouts like a drill sergeant, and the kids would fall in line. Of all the comments from the adult Scouters, one recollection stood out from Ron Hermanson. Ben had introduced himself as "The Rock" at the Ironworks climbing gym in Berkeley. Ben had been accompanying his troop to the venue but had deserted them, offering to belay Ron on a climb. Unbeknownst to Ron, a gym staff member policing the area had raced over to back up Ben's belay while Ron's wellbeing quite literally hung in the balance. Ben had not been certified by the gym to belay anyone! The staff member gently scolded Ron to enlist an experienced belayer in the future. Afterward, over beer and pizza, Ben expanded on his background to Ron by boasting that he was retired from the military, was a pilot and that he had to "stand down my flying for a while," so that he could teach the scouts about rock climbing safety that summer at Camp Wente, near Willits. Ron reflected that he was glad that he hadn't fallen and learned that just because someone is wearing a harness and gear doesn't necessarily mean they know what to do with it.

Prior to the outdoor portion of the course, the council requested Ron Hermanson, and I check the anchors at the Camp Wente climbing area. We made a marathon one-day road trip from the Bay Area to Willits and back; the anchors were fine. During our visit, by chance, we saw Ben in action. Ben was running about back and forth from the base of the rock to the top, all of the time shouting orders at two scouts climbing. Ben was at the top with two other inexperienced scouts on the ground belaying the climbers, unsupervised. In addition to this, both belay ropes had enough slack in them that if there had been a fall, either climber would have hit the ground. The climbers were noticeably scared to fall and perhaps their will to survive got them to the top. Ben greeted them at the top and untied them at the riskiest location, at the edge of the climbing face. In most top rope settings, a climber is to remain secured to the rope until they're lowered back safely to the ground. After these tense observations, Ben rappelled off of the top, bounding out from the rock and from side to side wildly, looking towards Ron and I and yelled, "I'm working the rock!"

Ron and I were concerned as Ben's performance was not of a competent rock climbing instructor, especially one running a camp rock climbing program. It felt almost criminal not to intervene, but this was Ben's gig designated by the council. Instead of bucking the scouting hierarchy and their motives, maybe having Ben take the course and pass certification would change things.

The weekend of the outdoor segment of the course arrived. After parking, we schlepped ropes and gear up to Rock City Park in Mt.

Diablo State Park. That Saturday, we covered "non-destructive" anchors, natural and artificial, how to choose and place them for top roping a climb. Candidates worked in pairs, and by the end of the day, after much practice, they set up a mock top rope site and rappel on their own, including all of the staging elements on the ground. This dynamic made for an interesting learning experience vs. leaving each person to figure things out independently. I called it "anchoring by committee."

To ensure that each candidate knew all of their knots, I made sure that any rope or webbing used had to be tied on the spot. Ben had proudly brought some old webbing slings to use with pre-tied grapevine and water knots. All of the knots had extremely short tails exiting the knots; so short the ends could enter into the knot and untie when heavily weighted. The grapevine knot is not customarily used in webbing for our application because it was difficult to check for correctness and it was too easy for newbies to tie incorrectly. The water knot was the acceptable knot to use with at least six-inch tails. I told Ben that he could use them, but he would need to re-tie them correctly, but he was unable to do so. I requested that Ron take him aside for a remedial lesson on the water knot before we started up. Otherwise, the day was a good one, with only the common issues of learning new skills.

At the end of an outing, I commonly debriefed the small staff I worked with. This "group hug" served to alert each other to the day's close calls, hiccups in teaching methods, potential trouble spots, or life-threatening situations. All of us were in agreement to keep a close eye on Ben, as he would rely on his partner to "carry" him by allowing them to do all of the technical work of setting anchors and tying knots. Ben's skills appeared foreign to him even though he had been a working climbing instructor. Foreign to us was Ben's endless blather of stories. He shared with us that he owned a Hummer, a helicopter (curiously mentioned as one flew overhead), and a Soviet MiG-21 that he was working on while stored in his backyard in Oakland. Ben recounted a fantastical life. This guy was the Forrest Gump. I had never encountered anyone like this, and I didn't have the credentials to delve into his psyche. I had a job to do.

That Sunday morning, Ben was a no-show. As indicated, we departed without him on schedule. Out of breath and apologetic, Ben scurried to the course site an hour late. Somehow, not one of his many vehicles could start, and he had to finagle a ride from someone. I allowed him to stay, but put him on notice that whatever he had missed would be on him to figure out. This was a busy day where the instruction had begun at the parking lot. I discussed how to safely manage a group of scouts from point "a," the parking lot, to point "b," the climbing site; the verbal rules set forth about following instructions, recognizing hazards (like poison oak, rattlesnakes, or unsafe terrain), my expectations of them, make sure to enact the BSA "Buddy" rule, and have an adult or someone you can trust, walk last behind the group.

Once at the site, each candidate set up a top rope and rappel event from scratch. Each iteration of our top rope sites became visual tools for everyone to discuss and learn from various perspectives to set anchors. Each candidate had to explain to the group why they constructed their anchors in the manner they did and how it was supposed to work. Afterward, they had an opportunity to manage the site; each candidate took a turn as the climbing instructor as their peers played the roles of inexperienced "scouts." My staff also participated, as I served as the "referee" by watching how safely the candidate/instructor would set up and manage the activity. Before commencing a scenario, the scout participants would randomly select a note of instructions indicating their role. The roles ranged from nothing special to goofing up a knot, carabiner, belay, not securing their harness properly, freaking out, to wandering off-site. Each role had been realistically drawn from situations I had encountered from working with climbing groups. I would stop the activity at any point if an "unsafe act" was committed where a potential injury or a threat to life was imminent. Any participant could commit an unsafe act. It was the instructor's responsibility not to commit any unsafe act themselves and to be vigilant for any missteps of the scouts and take action accordingly. What could go wrong?

Unlike camping, a climbing activity with inexperienced persons has many working parts that need to be in concert to prevent injury or death: ropes, knots, anchors, a variety of technical gear, and live participants. It's crucial that the climbing instructor keep watchful eyes on their flock, lest a belayer's brake hand go astray, a knot strand goes the wrong way, a helmet buckle dangles undone, or not doubling back your webbing harness through the buckle. Ultimately, the instructor must be mindful to stacking the deck in their favor. The top rope site scenarios were developed to help the candidates become aware of this, remain in control, and not get overwhelmed.

There was adequate time to practice and have a group discussion to build confidence. Each candidate was given a verbal list of items they needed to practice or be mindful of for managing a group of scouts. As Ron and I had witnessed at Camp Wente, Ben was his own enemy by shouting confusing instructions, chaotically running back and forth from the base of the rock to the top, and being unable to recognize hazardous situations like an unfinished knot, or too much slack in a belay rope — all unsafe acts. Ben merely disregarded all proper management skills, like staying posted at the base, where it was easier to assist the unskilled belayers and climbers. His performance was in stark contrast to his peers, who had followed instructions and had no unsafe acts. Nonetheless, the session ended with all candidates' finals set for the next weekend.

The written test was a mere rehash of terms, procedures, and policies visited during their training. Everyone got through that. The practical exam was much more difficult, as it was a performance test of each instructor in real-time. I took great satisfaction in watching each candidate run their climbing and rappel activities from "car to car" safely. And then there was Ben. Ben's modus operandi continued to be at the top of the rock to "direct" the activity. In his haste to be in that position, he had failed to finish tying the scout into the belay rope and failed to double-check it before leaving. From the top, Ben instructed the scout to climb up while being belayed by another scout. At the moment the climber stepped onto the rock, I had to halt the final as a failure. If the climber had placed their full weight on the rope, the rope would have slipped through the harness, resulting in a fall to the ground. The fact that Ben had failed took a moment to settle in. Then Ben began pleading for a second chance, "... I gotta have this!" I told him that, "I will have to speak to John Maxfield, but for now, we're done. You have a lot of practicing to do."

I went to see John at the scout center in San Leandro, where I got a somewhat cold reception, especially since he had already heard that Ben had not passed. John adamantly told me how Ben had been such a long-time asset to his troop and the council, that he was already working as Camp Wente's climbing instructor, and that he expected Ben to pass. I was candid and expressed my concerns about Ben and that I did not think he could ever pass certification. Frustrated, I felt the pressure of a "good ol' boy" system. I felt it was unethical and unsafe to reward a person to a position that they were incompetent and unqualified for. John clearly wanted Ben to pass based on loyalty, and as a member in good standing. Welcome to the corporate world, Ed.

"O.K., I'll schedule another final for him," I told John, but I never heard from Ben for months.

Eventually, in December of that year, Ben showed up at my job at Sunrise Mountain Sports, "I'm ready. I need this. I need this certification so I can work the rock with the kids next season. I gotta get it done this year."

Seriously, Ben chose to meet on Sunday, December the 31st, 2000. I agreed. Before the event, I had to secure the participation of some certified BSA climbing instructors and a few of my trusted staff, who were gracious enough to assist with the scenario on New Year's Eve. Fortunately, there were no winter storms that weekend. Unfortunately, Ben failed once again, with him oblivious to a harness not being secured on a scout, bumbling around with his knots, and running about. Ben pleaded with me to pass him, to give him another chance, and that he *had* to have this. It had been over six months since the original final exam and here we were. He hadn't improved or performed any differently. Ben had obviously never practiced.

"How long do you think I can practice before I can try again?" Ben asked.

At this point, I felt as if I had been sold a bill of goods. I laid out the truth, "You already had six months to get ready for this. Ben, you could practice this stuff 24/7 for the next six months and I don't think you can ever pass this certification. We're talking about the safety of other peoples' kids here. You're not meant to do this." Frustrated, I called Ben out on the stories that I knew weren't true, including the El Capitan tale, that they did not fool me and that I did not appreciate any of it. Ben's lack of self-awareness and living behind his facade of stories was a sad thing to witness. It was clear to me that Ben had mental health issues. I believe that Ben had fun with the kids on the rock, trying to live a romantic vision of the mountain guide. Fortunately, nobody was injured or killed while he was in charge. Begrudgingly, the scout executive backed my recommendation not to certify Ben as a BSA Climbing Instructor.

Instead, scout executive, John Maxfield rewarded Ben by placing him in charge of the — Camp Wente Rifle Range...Lightning *does* strike the same place twice!

4

VOODOO CHILI

By Randy Steele

I t was a typical sweltering San Joaquin Valley summer day in 1995. We had spent a long, boring four hour drive through the valley from Manteca. My dad and I were east of Porterville on the winding, twisting Highway 190. Eventually, we passed the Ponderosa, a "Deliverance" era mountain boy grill and bar, the only establishment we'd seen in about an hour. A short while later, we saw a lonely sign that read "Dome Rock," our camp spot for the weekend. I had grown up in Oregon, Lakeport, and Ukiah, among other places, where I had been called an "Asian Redneck," because of my accent while looking Asian and being O.K. with mixing guns and liquor. When I saw Eddie, "EC" Joe for the first time, even I was thrown for a loop; another Asian in this place, one that everybody knew, one who knew his way around this place, one who was a local legend. He was kind of a small guy with a mustache, black, curled hair, and a sly-looking grin all packaged in a social being complemented with a wealth of knowledge about climbing in the Kern area. Eddie Joe knew this place, and he had the first ascents to prove it: Romantic Warrior, Imaginary Voyage, and the classic White Punks on Dope. He even co-wrote the first Kern River climbing guide! But he didn't talk about that sort of thing; he didn't self-promote or condescend;

he was a nice guy, down to earth, like, "...if you fall, you might die, no big deal, dude. Rock on in the great gig in the sky, I'll see you there." We had come to this place to climb, and we had met the right person in Eddie Joe.

Saturday morning arrived, and the Eastern, orange-like sun lit up a silhouette of spires and domes to the north called the "Needles." This is where Eddie Joe cut his teeth as a climber. They looked so far away, the Needles, but you could still see the streaked-black, emerald-green, and canary-yellow formations against the indigo-blue sky. These formations were vivid and brilliant; if you don't believe me, just look at the cover of Moser's Needles guide. There was an eeriness, too, because we knew we were in the middle of nowhere. Eddie Joe and I were probably the only Asians within a hundred-mile radius: he's got curly hair, is he even Asian? You know, if you mashed an ankle out here on a ledge or ground fall, you would be in a lot of pain for a long, long time. That was the beauty of the Needles; they were remote, primitive, eerie, beautiful, so anti-Yosemite.

We had to change our focus away from the eeriness, as we were to participate in a sponsored technical rock climbing course to learn about lead climbing. We climbed with the protection of a top rope at Trilogy Rock, then practiced lead climbing on top rope while at Parker Bluff and Dome Rock; we practiced setting gear and setting anchors. I watched as two of our classmates practiced setting up a "hanging" belay anchor 3 feet off the deck. Wow, three whole feet of exposure! They started complaining and squawking at each other, just the sort of stuff we didn't want to hear.

Dad's recent divorce and the squawking of civilization were a couple of things we went to the Needles to escape from. So, we set up our belay, three pieces minimum, says Eddie Joe, and we settle into our "hanging belay," a whopping 3 feet off the ground. We could feel the exposure; yeah, we felt like a couple of idiots. Afterward, the students were supposed to positively critique each other's anchor set-up, and the gals said, "You can't just use 3 pieces! They're not equalized! That top piece looks loose! Blah, Blah, Blah!" We put our weight onto our creation to test it out. The top piece, a small nut, stays put, but alas, we experienced the dreaded CARABINER SHIFT, and our asses dropped an inch. Immediately, one of the gals chided, "SEE!"

Well, enter Ron Felton, the care-free guide, Eddie Joe's apprentice, the Yin to Eddie Joe's Yang. He trundled over in a cloud of dust, saying, "Fuck it! That fucker ain't goin' nowhere!" Ron grabbed the top piece, pulled down hard on it, then stood in the sling attached to the nut and said, "Fuck it! It makes a great fuckin' foothold, too!"

It was a long day. Dad and I were in need of some comfort food and to fuel up for the next day. As we pulled the Stagg Chili, hot dogs, and buns out of the ice chest, we overheard the guides talking about taking the students out on their first multi-pitch "trad" (traditional) routes. One guide and his girlfriend would climb Warlock Needle; good times, I'm sure. In addition to Warlock, I overheard Demon, Witch, Sorcerer, Wizard, and Voodoo, all the names of the massive yellow-black-green formations that make up the Needles. The talk settled on Voodoo Dome. "Great!" I thought that's an omen that just adds to the eeriness and mystique. One team would climb the classic White Punks on Dope, 5.8+. However, we somehow got cast on a climb called Voodoo Child, or "Voodoo Chil'," Eddie Joe corrects us that it's only 5.9+ and he's sure we can handle it, so the two teams would accompany Eddie Joe and Ron on these routes.

"I'll take Phil and Randy," Eddie Joe says.

Sweet! It's like the journey to destroy the Death Star, and we would get to fly with Red Leader. Cool! I knew I could handle a 5.8+ and that White Punks on Dope was a classic. According to the Needles guide, *"White Punks on Dope, thought by some to be the best moderate route in the Southern Sierra."* But what about this Voodoo Chil', a 5.9+ that measures a mere 900 feet? That didn't sound like a classic, and it definitely didn't sound like a moderate. We had climbed Jorgie's Crack, a 60 foot, 5.10a hand crack at the Pinnacles near Hollister, and that was on our first day climbing. Now, six months later, our best was still in the 5.10 range. Jorgie's Crack, at 60 feet, felt sustained, so were we prepared for 900 feet of 5.9+? Were we being short-changed out of a classic? Were we about to be sandbagged by a local legend? Does anybody care? Meanwhile, the six cans of Stagg Chili, the 12 hot dogs, and the 12 buns were calling, and we knew we needed the carbohydrates and fuel for the climb. Anxiously, we ate our last supper.

It was Sunday morning, and the two teams were hiking up towards Voodoo Dome from Needlerock Creek. I was afraid but somewhat ener-gized, bursting with carbohydrates from last night's chili feed. Dad and I didn't want to disappoint our guides with a weak performance. After a mile or so of steep bushwhacking, we found ourselves at the base of Voodoo Dome. We roped up, and I felt a new, nervous energy taking over. Eddie Joe glided effortlessly up the first-hand crack pitch in about 5 minutes; he wasn't alarmingly fast, just methodical and sure. When he placed pro, it was like second nature, as if he had never stopped to place any at all. Observing his style, I was sure he didn't even need it; he did the first ascent, after all. I was next. The climbing appeared to be nothing too complex, I thought; it's just an average hand crack. I wasn't nearly as fluid as Eddie Joe, and I took twice as long with about twice as much sketch. Phil followed, and we all found ourselves at a hanging belay, a first for Phil and I. So there we were, 150 feet off the deck, with three people (at a grand total of about 500 pounds including gear), hanging off about three pieces of expertly placed gear. Eddie Joe coyly assured us, "A1, 'bomber,' trust it." What's wrong with these people?!

Complicating our situation, Phil farted; not just a regular fart, but one of those 5-second, "wetter-than-a-whale" farts. Urgently, Eddie belayed Phil down over to the "safety" of a nearby manzanita-covered ledge. Yesterday, our guides had told us never to untie while on route; however, Phil *had* to untie to drop a wet, brown pile of...Well, it was every bit of disgusting, but Eddie Joe and I had to laugh. The next few pitches were nothing short of incredible finger and hand cracks interspersed with stems and high-steps over roofs. The climbing was definitely 5.9+, but I had almost wished it had been 5.10a just to be able to say we did it, even though the 5.9+ was quite hard enough.

Above, Phil and I engaged in a full-on "fart war," blasting the belay with one fart after another. It sounded like the scene in Blazing Saddles where all the Rednecks farted around the campfire while eating a big pot of beans; same shit. Once more, Phil asked for the toilet paper while he was at a prominent ledge below us. I tied the roll to the rope for a TP belay; there's a picture of it somewhere. Damn, Phil... Eddie and I laughed.

To make things worse, the second half of the climb was face climbing. Phil and I weren't used to face climbing. Eddie Joe effortlessly climbed about 160 feet and clipped about a half-a-dozen bolts in a typical Needles runout. Phil and I floundered and sketched, as we didn't have the security of any muscle-friendly cracks. We finally reached the last pitch, and I was to go last. I knew there was a traverse somewhere, but Phil had unclipped all the gear. I wondered where the route went; it couldn't be any harder than 5.9+, right? It felt like 5.10+! Great...I was a rookie climber wearing a backpack, I was off-route, 900 feet off the deck, and I was about to take my first fall of the day. Oh, and since Eddie Joe used double 8.5 mm ropes to lead, that meant I was on a *thin* rope, one that he assured us would withstand a top rope fall. Above, dad told Eddie Joe that he had cleaned all the gear at the traverse and that I might be in for a swing if I fell. Eddie Joe calmly said, "He'll be alright, he's a good climber."

They probably said a hell of a lot more than that because I couldn't move for at least 5 minutes, affixed to some hopeless tiny knobs 900 feet up. FUCK! A fall, a scream, a pair of soiled underwear. Dad said, "There he goes!" My first real fall was maybe 5 feet with a little swing; then, the rope caught me. When I topped out, I shook Eddie Joe's hand. Eddie Joe and Phil laughed. We relaxed, listened to the wind, took in the thousands of green trees, the granite domes, and the ribbon blue Kern River below from the superior vantage point atop the summit of Voodoo Dome.

Somewhere, somebody else wasn't having such a great time. It was Ron, who was about to reach a belay ledge just below the summit. He had run out of rope trying to reach the belay ledge and had begun to yell at his party down below. "Unhook the belay! Simul-climb! Fuck! Fuckers!" He was miles above his last bolt and maybe 15 feet below the ledge, telling two rookies to unclip and simul-climb so he could reach the belay ledge below the final pitch. There was no place to set up a belay, and I don't think Ron was about to downclimb 150 feet. Just the day before, our guides were lecturing us to "NEVER UNTIE FROM THE BELAY! NEVER!" Ron was sweating, yelling, ranting, cussing---"Fuck!" Eventually, one of his students unclipped from the anchor and climbed up enough to enable Ron to reach the security of the ledge. A half-hour later, his group topped out. Not more than a minute later, his job done, Ron smoked a fat joint. Relieved, he said, "By the way, what was that smell down there?" We explained that Phil had some digestion problems. Ron let loose, "You fuckers! You guys shit all over the place, didn't you?! What about the chimney?"

By that time, our laughter said it all. We still laugh just thinking about it. I've also heard the term "flatulence poker" thrown around on the Internet. We agree that Ron was the first to fold. It was a hilarious finish to a great day.

Come to find out; we did the 2nd ascent of Voodoo Chil', which I am especially proud to have been part of. Nothing in my climbing world will ever compare to that first multi-pitch climb. Even though it's years later, the memories are vital and vivid due to the extremely rich experience. The company and camaraderie of the whole entourage will never be forgotten by Phil and I. Eddie "EC" Joe, "Thank You!" — Steele.

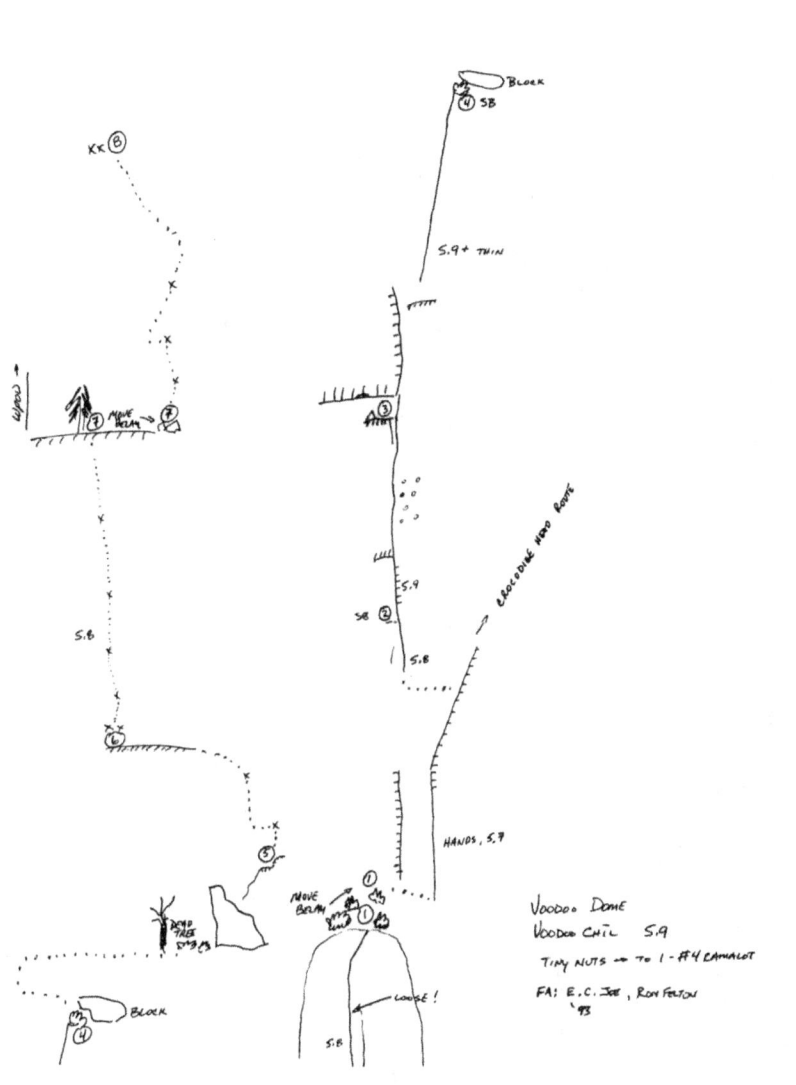

Block
④ SB

5.9+ THIN

⑤

KK ⑧

↑
CHINU

MOVE
BELAY ⑦ ⑦

⑤

CROCODILE KRO ROPE

5.8

5.9

SB ②

5.8

©

③

HANDS, 5.7

MOVE
BELAY ①
①

DEAD
TREE
5"9 ©

Block

LOOSE!

④ Block

5.8

VOODOO DOME
VOODOO CHIL 5.9
TINY NUTS ⇝ TO 1-#4 CAMALOT
FA: E.C. JOE , RON FELTON
'93

5

REQUIEM FOR THE LOOKOUT

By Linda Adams, Kathy Allison, and Patrick Paul

For over 100 years, fire lookouts have been a mainstay in fire suppression and forest management in the United States. Strategically placed fire lookouts and the people who work in them have performed the crucial service of early fire detection, operated as vital communications liaisons, and in many cases, tourist information centers and tourist destinations. Some fire lookout personnel, such as those dedicated people who have worked at The Needles and Buck Rock lookouts, have even served uniquely as invaluable USDA Forest Service ambassadors and spokespersons.

For almost three-quarters of a century, the Needles fire lookout had been one of the premier representatives of all that is positive and good about public land management. Built by the Civilian Conservation Corps in 1937-1938, The Needles was quite possibly the most impressively situated fire tower perched as it is on one of several granite needle-like domes rising up from the depths of the Kern Canyon. Since 1938, The Needles fire cab has served the public interest, helped to suppress catastrophic fires, been a vital communications link for foresters, been a spectacular tourist destination for multiple generations and has played an important role in the natural and climbing history of the Southern Sierra.

The history of The Needles fire lookout is well known among members of the Forest Service. It would be rare to find a forester in Southern and Central California who hadn't been to The Needles or heard of it. The unique location of The Needles fire cab placed high on one of the most spectacular rock formations in America set it apart as a "must see," must visit, must experience piece of public architecture and history. Recognized for its world-class climbing, the Needles has long been a popular destination for adventurers from all over the world.

The Needles fire cab was not just a fire lookout. And it was more than a popular tourist destination. The two and one-half mile scenic hike for more than a few generations of outdoor enthusiasts was a legacy experience. Many generations of children had their first outdoor experience hiking out to visit "that little gray castle in the sky." Today, many older people recall the formative experience while trailing behind their parents, immersed, wide-eyed, in the wonder of that magical place, climbing the stairs, stepping onto the catwalk atop the highest point of the Needles rock formation. There they could partake of the astounding view that might otherwise only be had by raptors, ringtail cats, and few daredevil rock climbers. Making a yearly pilgrimage to the Needles had become a tradition for many. Like John Muir, wishing to pass the experience on to future generations, many lovers of the breathtaking beauty of the outdoors brought their children and grandchildren to the Needles year after year. It would be difficult to match such a formative experience. So many times have people made the journey to the Needles, spirits elevated and soaring like the peregrine falcons that dive and lord over the rocks and souls embraced by this unique experience unlike any other.

Many of the old lookouts have been abandoned or replaced by technology that can do as good a job at fire detection as any human being. Many of the old lookouts have been perched on high, obscure, and mundane overlooks that, although functional in their day, were not spectacular or breathtaking to those who seldom visited them. Very few fire lookouts have been worthy of the word of mouth reputation, magazine articles, newspaper articles, or the television coverage the Needles had garnered over the decades. The Needles had captured the attention of many and fueled the imaginations of all who have been there, seen it, or read about it.

An antenna and web-cam could do a good enough job of detecting fires. But an antenna and a web-cam could never provide the ambassadorship, the public relations, the character building, the history talk, or the awakening of the love of the outdoors that the old Needles fire lookout had done with a pleasant representative; there each summer day to tell stories, show people what was out there, and help them reflect on the awesome majesty within their view.

Margie Kelly. Photo: René Ardesch

Over twenty years of living and working at her spectacular, solitary post in an antique fourteen-foot square cabin, perched atop the 1,000-

foot granite pinnacle named Magician, had written Margee Kelly into history as one of the longest working fire lookouts on the Sequoia National Forest. Margee first came from Colorado to the Needles Lookout in 1988, a record-breaking fire season for those years.

About her trek up to her new home that year, Margee says, "The first time I climbed the stairs, I would have been on my hands and knees had I not come up with my boss." The Needles was the most remote of the Sequoia lookouts. A 2-1/2 mile hike along a shady, forested trail and then a climb up almost 200 stairs, suspended in mid-air-spanning from pinnacle to pinnacle, were required to reach the lookout at 8,245 feet elevation. Yes, that was a long way back down for groceries, a shower, the outhouse, or a beer with friends after work. The helicopter brought propane and water, but Margee would mountain bike the 2-1/2 miles out the trail and back for a shower and laundry, hauling her groceries in a backpack. Between hiking the trail and climbing the stairs to her home in the sky, she stayed in shape.

Since her initiation at the Needles in 1988, Margee had overcome her acrophobia by becoming a skilled rock climber. She had also earned a reputation among the international rock climbing community at the Needles for baking chocolate chip cookies on Sunday. Margee's propane-powered bakery was at the high point on the bright granite pinnacles, powdered with sulfur lichen, that distinguish the Needles.

Spooky Book, Margee's black cat, was named for climbing routes by Herb and Eve Laeger, rock climbers who put up many first ascents in the 1970s and 1980s. Spooky kept Margee company for many years in her home among the spires of the Needles named Witch, Warlock, Wizard, Charlatan, Sorcerer, and Voodoo. But the Needles was not always a magically peaceful place of black cats and cookies, with telescopic views of rock climbers, giant sequoia trees, and Mt. Whitney. Margee had stories of lightning strikes around her lookout more impressive than any 4th of July fireworks. "The brightest light you've ever seen; the loudest crack-boom you've ever heard. A jolt of adrenaline to your heart, followed by a little shakiness afterward. From the lookout, storms were… well…supernatural." And lightning meant lightning fires - Margee had reported as many as 80 and as few as three fires in a season. Between fires, she kept up maintenance as needed — painter, window washer, and handyman for her exposed 1938 wood cabin. She was host to thousands of visitors each summer, making Needles one of the Sequoia's most visited lookouts.

Fire Lookouts like Margee are an increasingly rare breed who keep the historic traditions of living and working out in the forest and sharing those traditions with their visitors. In our age of replacing people with technology, the 100-year old lookout traditions breathe the fresh air of real people in historic places into our increasingly virtual reality. Lots of family and friends had come to visit the Lady of the Needles over the years. Included are her grandsons Kyle and Alee, who was carried up in a backpack when he was only one year old. Besides people who regularly visit the Needles every year, there were also Jim and Margaret. This pair of seldom seen peregrine falcons had come to accept Margee as part of the aerie environment. Margee told how hysterical it was one year to watch their three floppy-winged young fledglings learn to fly. And how awesome it was when the black and white, missile-like raptors dove at 90 mph to pluck prey out of the sky. Another mostly friendly visit was while Margee was on her mountain bike, accidentally getting between a momma bear and her three cubs, "She looked me in the eye and snorted! Eventually, finally as I stood frozen, big momma just walked away."

Margee said that in addition to the rock climbers and bike rides, lightning shows, and wild encounters, her 20+ years at her solitary post in the sky had heightened her senses. Minuscule changes in the landscape, like a distant rock slab that fell in the night, a subtle change in humidity or wind direction, the flapping of Margaret's wings as she positioned for a dive into the Kern Canyon — were all pleasures Margee may not have noticed without her life as one of the longest working fire lookouts on the Sequoia National Forest. "How much better could it get?" says Margee - Spring, 2008.

July 29, 2011: "Porterville. Needles. Emergency Traffic. The roof of the lookout is on fire and I need immediate assistance." With those words, Margee Kelly called in the most important smoke report of her career.

An ember from the woodstove landed on the original 1938 shake roof of The Needles Fire Lookout, sparking a fire that quickly spread along the roof and eventually into the attic. Grabbing the fire extinguisher, Margee fought to put the fire out, even climbing up on a ladder placed on the catwalk in an attempt to get closer to the blaze.

Sequoia Forest Helicopter 522 launched from the Peppermint Helibase in a matter of minutes, dropping several buckets of water on the structure in what Margee calls "a heroic effort to save the lookout." Unfortunately, their efforts were in vain.

Margee and her two grandchildren, who were visiting her at the time, escaped without injury and stood helpless as they watched their beloved tower succumb to the fire. Twenty-four years of Margee's accumulated treasures went up in flame — collections of photos, memorabilia, newspaper clippings, first edition author-autographed books, a recently refurbished telescope, pottery, and so much more perished in the fire.

It is not surprising that there had been an overwhelming outpouring of concern for Margee as well as questions about the future of The Needles Lookout. Despite substantial public outcry supporting the restoration of the lookout, the Forest Service currently does not plan to re-build the lookout, a daunting task given current health and safety regulations, codes, red-tape, and location.

The Needles Lookout, Sunset. Photo: E.C. Joe

The Needles had provided more than anyone expected. The taxpayers who paid for the lookout generations ago had no idea that they were creating a living museum, a goodwill ambassador's post, a comfort station, a nature preserve, a climber's Mecca, and a shrine to the workers of the CCC and WPA of the Great Depression. The Needles was, and still could be a great taxpayer investment. The Needles Lookout must be restored for those who have come to love it, for those who want to see their tax dollars spent on meaningful endeavors that reinforce and support real American values, and for future generations of people who deserve to share in the unique experience that previous generations were so lucky to have.

Editor's Note: *This article was merged, edited, and published with the permission of the authors Linda Adams, Kathy Allison, Patrick Paul, and the Forest Fire Lookout Association from the Buck Rock Foundation website,* buck-rock.org, *and from the article, "Sequoia Lookout Achieves Milestone," written by the 1976 Needles Lookout, Linda Adams. FFLA Newsletter, Vol. 19, No. 2.* Spring 2008, p. 7.

SECTION IV

VIGNETTES

Jon Allen takes a morning celebratory Dragon Dance in the Canebrake. Photo: E.C. Joe

"Where Have I Known You Before?"
— Neville Potter

1

THE PURVEYOR OF SELFLESSNESS

By E.C. Joe

In my mind's eye, I can see him standing there behind that rustic wooden log counter in Bigfoot Mountaineering. Dick Banner was always upbeat and quick to tell a joke. You could talk to him about anything, or any subject, as many of us did. Dick had a background in aeronautical engineering for NASA and had worked on projects like the XB-70 supersonic strategic bomber. Dick retired from that life and bought himself the mountain shop. He was an avid outdoor enthusiast, but Dick was more of a people enthusiast; he loved interacting with people; the shop was just his lure. Here was a man with the biggest hearts, quick to give, never expecting to receive anything in return, and always interested and caring in everyone's endeavors. This man had such an enthusiasm for life. For me, Dick Banner was even more than this.

Dick was my biggest supporter. I would often spend my spare time hanging out at the shop. At some point, he encouraged me to teach. I don't remember which was first, the climbing courses or cross-country skiing, but I remember how difficult it was and how Dick helped me be more comfortable teaching and with myself. Even though I felt like a complete fool the evenings I taught those initial classes, Dick would attempt to brighten my thoughts by saying, "You did great!" He helped me with organizing myself to implement those courses and navigate the clients. After getting the kinks out, we had a win-win-win situation for Bigfoot, its customers, and myself. There would never have been outdoor courses in the area at that time if not for Dick's foresight. Decades have passed since that first class I instructed for Dick. Since then, I have worked on my own as a climbing instructor and guide. Ironically, I managed a mountain shop and shared my passion for the outdoors with others, just as Dick had. The teaching skills I had developed back then allowed me to become a Department of Transportation Trainer and a DMV Commercial License Examiner. I am thankful to Dick for having a vision about me that I could not fathom for myself at the time.

Dick loved the mountains, and the shop allowed him to share that with others. He once suggested that the accomplishments that I and others had done on the rocks should be documented and shared. He recommended that I put together a rock climbing guide to the Kern Slabs near Kernville, CA. Dick gracefully financed the venture and the first climbing guide to the Kern Slabs and was a great success. Dick's vision didn't stop there, as he was instrumental in helping Richard Leversee and I publish the first-ever rock climbing guide to the entire Kern Canyon. Dick was worthy of having written the Forward for that unique book.

I can remember my surprise when Dick showed up at Scodie Spire, a remote granite crag in the high desert of the South Fork of the Kern River drainage with a big, "Hi!" Dick just made a day of it and came up to lend us support, bring us extra water, and check out what mischief we had been up to. Once, he dedicated his off time to help me create several "torture" devices that I would train on; I had never seen him more animated!

Dick constantly displayed his generous support and belief in everyone's outdoor adventures. He organized some of the greatest "slide show-with-a-dinner" events, where renowned outdoor adventurists would visit to share and inspire us. Through these events, Dick brought the whole outdoor community together. Even the warring factions of the community made peace at these events because Dick was the common denominator. He was the glue.

Everybody loved Dick Banner. Richard Duer Banner 1930 - 2005

Richard "Dick" Banner. Photo: Jane Banner Collection

2

SERENDIPITY

By E. C. Joe

The view of our objective from Cecil Lake was as elusive as the route description in the book *Fifty Classic Climbs of North America*. The Southeast Face of Clyde Minaret is the tallest of over a dozen jagged, granite peaks of what is known as the Ritter Range of the Sierra Nevada, California. The Minarets, for climbers, evoke a feeling of the Alps, albeit on a "Mini-Me" scale, but with similar risks. Knocking-off routes from this book was an obsession for some. Others took a more casual approach to the list and only climbed them if the opportunity arose. I preferred the more casual approach to the "50 Classics," even though my personal philosophy to climbing was anything but casual. Climbing in a world full of rocks with no routes on them took priority over established routes.

Roland Burkert and I both knew that nothing was certain when you venture out into the wilderness, especially climbing rocks. Perhaps, that aspect may be the underlying allure of climbing for some of us. Sometimes there's success, and more times than we want to admit, we get shut down. There's never a foregone conclusion.

As climber Warren Harding put it after the first ascent of El Capitan in Yosemite Valley, "... it was not at all clear to me who was the conqueror and who was the conquered. I do recall that El Cap seemed to be in much better condition than I was."

Roland had been a competent climbing partner for many an adventure. It was important for partners to have the right temperament, not only for getting along with each other but more for getting along with each other when shit goes down when you're cold, hungry, or tired. In addition, it helps to be adept technically, have good mountain sense, and have enough resolve not to freak out. Those things can carry more weight than one's climbing ability. We depended on each other in ways more complex than to merely hold on to a rope. Who else was going to be there to have your back? Roland was damn near "the perfect partner." Roland and I climbed routes over a diverse selection of venues, from the Kern River Canyon to the big walls of Yosemite.

"I like that when we go climbing it's hardly ever in the same place," Roland remarked.

I cannot recall how Roland and I met. I figure that it was around 1976 and very likely at Bigfoot Mountaineering in Bakersfield. If I was not working or climbing, I was there. I was, by proxy, Bakersfield's resident climbing "bum" of sorts. Roland's demeanor always was polite, spoke succinctly, and had the skill to extinguish any bad situation.

The guy loved to dance. On more than one occasion, while en route to or from a climbing trip, Roland would insist on stopping at a random roadhouse, like on a Friday night. Yes, I said roadhouse, like in the movie. A neon sign adorned the outside of the rustic building. Inside, the walls were painted a dark color, and like most dive bars, the place probably looked like shit in the daylight. A country band was loud and on cue; the place was packed.

We had an unusually large climbing group that night. There were six of us. Typically, it'd be only the two of us. Yep. There we were, at "Don's Crossroads." Well, while Roland was busy out on the dance floor with the ladies, the rest of us sat at our makeshift table/pool table downing brews. We had to have appeared out of place; our clothes were a bit "off," but the LONG HAIR! Roland sported a curly perm that was not outrageous for the time, but as a joke, he would wear this t-shirt emblazoned on the front in all caps with, "NO I AM NOT JOHN TRAVOLTA."

The band's set was over, and radio music got piped through the house speakers. Roland retreated to his seat by my side at our place against the back wall of the joint. We were all having a good time when a man came through the entrance; ball cap, plaid shirt, jeans, and cowboy boots. The guy clearly was not steady on his feet, as he most likely had partied before his arrival. As the door closed behind him, he surveyed the venue, looking like the Terminator searching for Sarah Conner. During his scan, he somehow locked onto his target. Roland. Trouble headed our way. The guy staggered, somewhat directly to the pool table, and stood across the table from Roland.

"I...dooon't liiiike thaaaa waaay youuuu looook!"

I was coiled and ready to respond with a long neck bottle to the side of his head. I thought about how bad it could get. Then, Roland rose from his seat and outstretched his right hand towards him, "Hi, my name is Roland, and let me introduce you to ALL of my friends (slowly naming all five of us)."

Roland's play was brilliant, as this guy never expected a handshake or a polite response. The guy swayed as he looked back and forth at the group, then turned around, headed for the exit, and went outside.

"We gotta go," I told Roland and the guys.

On the way out, we witnessed the same guy trying to pick a fight out in the parking lot. Nothing like a good fist to face discussion!

Climbs can turn for better or worse in a moment like that, too. There's uncertainty. However, who is to say a turn for the worse might be for the better?

The Minarets. Photo: E.C. Joe

We were highly accustomed to climbing on most granite. However, Clyde Minaret was unique from what we were used to, as the rock was excessively fractured horizontally, making for difficult route finding. Paired with the sketchy route description, we got lost. We had planned for a long, one-day ascent and descent. There was no time for wandering; the days were awfully short in October. However, there was no shame in retreat, especially for our logistical error in planning. With only a single rope, we would have to make twice as many rappels as if we had brought a second line. That proved to be tricky, as once you double the number of anchors required, it can quickly devour the rack of gear.

Once back at the base of the rock, we packed our tools to prepare to descend the probably 75-yard pyramid of snow to the talus, then forest to our camp. The sun had turned the surface slushy and slick from the firm and crunchy texture on our early morning approach. Roland and I eschewed ice axes to go light. Instead, we planned to each use a single long piton as crude old-school ice daggers to steady ourselves on the slope.

Before I knew it, without any tool in hand, Roland said, "This seems OK, I'm going for it."

Going for it, he did. Roland launched, accelerating like he had been shot out of a cannon down the icy slope. He was out of control and unable to arrest the fall. I stood there at the top of the slope, helpless. When Roland reached the talus field at the bottom, he slammed into a Volkswagen Beetle-sized boulder straight-on, deflecting off to the side like a rag doll. There he laid motionless.

"ARE YOU OK?!!"

There was no reply. I thought, "FUCK, I gotta get down there!" I had my tool and stabbed the slope and kicked what steps into the slush that I could, a method that would take forever, it seemed. Then, I slipped. Off I went! I tried to arrest the best I could, digging the piton in along with my elbows and toes. I was still moving too fast, and hitting any undulation would toss me from facing the slope to facing out. It was a high-speed struggle to have some semblance of control. Towards the bottom, I was facing out and was headed right for Roland. I could see that he was conscious. I reached the talus, moving so fast, I felt like I skimmed over all the rocks without touching them. Somehow, I was able to safely plant my feet, which immediately brought me from Mach 1 to 0 mph and into a standing position directly in front of Roland. We looked at each other in disbelief. I asked him if he was OK.

"I hurt my ankle," which, from what I just witnessed, seemed like a radical understatement.

We made it "safely" back to our camp. Roland was doing better but bruised. Good thing, no broken bones. Retiring to a hot freeze-dried dinner and into our sleeping bags and bivy sacks for the night was an only temporary respite.

Rain...I'm talking RAIN! That night it was pouring down hard, so hard that the surrounding area was flooding. It was incessant. We both sensed that this storm was NOT an ordinary event.

At sometime after midnight, I said, "I think we need to get outta here."

"But we shall continue with style."
— Anderl Meier, The Eiger Sanction. Photo: E.C. Joe

By headlamp, we were on the move. Tiny rivulets we had stepped across during our hike in were now ten feet wide. The flow wasn't too fast, so I went for it. It was at least thigh deep. Shit! That was pretty scary. Roland followed. It rained the whole way out to the trailhead and into the daylight hours. Later, I had heard that a nearby trail bridge had washed out from the deluge.

Back at Roland's truck, we put some dry clothes on, gorged on whatever food we could find, and basked in the warmth of the sun inside the truck cab. Soon we were barreling down Hwy 395 towards home, silent and mesmerized by the hum of the engine and the long stretch of road ahead. Intuitively, Roland and I looked at each other, in an exchange of grins like the cat that ate a canary, but only for a moment, as we returned our gaze to the road, then broke into hysterical laughter in celebration of our survival.

Roland Burkert, 1955 - 2013

3

THE IRON MAN OF YOSEMITE

By E.C. Joe

I had only been climbing for just over a year. In the autumn of 1975, while hanging out in front of the original Mountain Room Bar, then a hole in the wall between the Four Seasons Restaurant and the Mountain Room Broiler, I observed Warren Harding wandering about outside the bar, struggling with this huge backpack. I had recognized Harding from photos I had seen of him in books and magazines. However, the person I saw only matched in the face, but not in legend. Slight in stature, Harding was not the ten-foot-tall omnipotent climbing hero from urban legend. Instead, he was a small spindly one.

In 1958, when Warren Harding and his companions had completed the first ascent of the Nose Route on El Capitan, I was just four years old. By the time I had started climbing, most of Harding's major achievements were behind him. A voracious reader of climbing stories, I had quickly become aware of Harding, the "Iron Man of Yosemite." He reportedly had unprecedented tenacity, an independent style, and an ability to climb some of the most audacious route lines up a sheer rock face. Back in the day, the climbing world would debate the validity of his methods and style. I appreciated his "do your own thing" attitude.

Harding was a visionary, a climber ahead of his time. Many in the climbing community were not willing to accept his methods at the time, even though many of those methods became common today.

The locals seemed weary of Harding's wandering, but I was curious. So, I timidly introduced myself to him, "Hey, my name is Ed. Are you Warren Harding?"

"A matter of fact, I am," Warren replied, in a voice, matching his spindly stature.

We had a friendly conversation, and then he quickly invited my partner Joel Matta and I into the bar for a few rounds of drinks. I realized much later that what had occurred had been Warren's normal modus operandi to supplement his drinking habit. No big deal. This guy was one of my heroes! Harding "bought" us a round of drinks by writing us an I.O.U. for them. Classic!

We talked about climbing as one was supposed to while in the Mountain Room Bar. During the evening, fueled by alcohol and good times, Harding invited us on one of his dream projects located to the right of the Lost Arrow Spire. It then dawned on Joel and I that we weren't the only ones enlisted in his project. It turned out that he had invited just about the whole damn world to participate!

When queried about this, he replied, "Well," rubbing his chin, "with all these people coming with us, we have a problem."

"What's that, Warren?" we wondered.

"How do we haul all that wine?!" Harding exclaimed.

Well, we never took him up on his offer, and later in the night, we parted ways.

Years later, while I managed Sunrise Mountaineering in Livermore, CA, I got Warren to present a slideshow for us. Harding's show had one of the largest attendance of any show ever in the store's history. During the Q&A session afterward, someone asked how much force the rivets would hold that Warren frequently had used on his routes to pass blank sections of rock.

Warren says in classic Harding fashion, "Weeeaaall..., I've always wondered how much one of those things (rivets) would hold?"

Helping Warren out, I reiterated a story of when I had repeated his route, "The Wall of the Early Morning Light[1];" where one of my partners, Ed Sampson, took an outrageous 60-foot fall after a rivet sheared under his body weight. Having pulled a long string of anchor placements, the fall was finally held by another original Harding rivet, WITH the original swedged wire hanger on it!

"Warren," I said, "They hold everything and nothing."

Warren Harding, 1924 - 2002

4

ROYAL INSPIRATION

By E.C. Joe

W e were stuck, stuck in the Southern San Joaquin Valley with outdoor/climbing shops without real product depth. It was the early '70s. We made pilgrimages to Royal Robbins' shop in Modesto or Fresno, The Great Pacific Iron Works (aka GPIW) and to West Ridge Mountaineering in Southern California. West Ridge sold bolts & hangers, essential items for pioneering face climbs and the Iron Works had — well iron; pitons. The Robbins' shop was the most impressive with its extensive resource of climbing books, journals and maps. They didn't sell bolts & hangers, however the employees would never interrogate us of our intentions or "qualifications" like at West Ridge. Everyone at the Robbins' shop dealt in inspiration.

By the mid-'80s, I worked for a climbing shop, Sunrise Mountaineering (aka Sunrise Mountain Sports), in Livermore, CA. Back then, Sunrise was in an old Victorian building on First Street that had been a hardware store back in the day. It was a rustic old place, creaky wood floors and all. It was there that many a climber visited on the way to their adventures out of the Bay Area. I strived to offer that same kind of inspiration as I had experienced at the Robbins' shop.[1]

Through my association with Sunrise, I met Royal at an outdoor industry trade show. In the past, Royal had played a major role in the development of rock climbing in Yosemite. He also had published the *Basic and Advanced Rockcraft* books my generation learned from, and had his own clothing line as well as the stores that bore his name. At some point, he developed arthritis that kept him from climbing. But when I had the chance to grill him for climbing route information, I could tell that he had never left his spirit for adventure behind.

One day, back in the office, I answered the phone with the standard greeting, "Sunrise Mountaineering, can I help you?"

"Hello. This is Royal Robbins."

"Hi, Royal, this is Ed."

Royal, "I remember you."

It was not a social call but a sad announcement; Royal was closing his shop. It was the end of an era. Royal wanted to clean house and allowed Sunrise to purchase his remaining climbing inventory for cents on the dollar. Royal and some employees delivered the goods in person. I could sense that it was a bittersweet moment. Royal remarked that he had chosen Sunrise, as we would be the best to represent what his store had been. Wow...

During my years at Sunrise, I would take employees out on climbing trips. I suppose nowadays it would be called "team building." Unlike that, the trips weren't a required work activity. We just went out to have fun together climbing or cross country skiing. The climbing outings were premium adventures on routes like, "Travelers' Buttress" at Lovers' Leap, "The Great White Book," and Fairview Dome "Regular Route" in Tuolumne Meadows, and two classics at the Needles of Sequoia, "Strange Brew," and "White Punks on Dope." The Sunrise staff got some of the best hands on experience.

On one trip we headed to Yosemite Valley for the day. We arrived early in the morning at the base of The Nutcracker (Suite), a renowned classic climb on Manure Pile Buttress. Unlike what visions the name of the buttress the climb was on may invoke, The Nutcracker was a beautiful, moderate but challenging multi-pitch climb adorned with memorable passages throughout its 500-foot length. It was pioneered in the 1960s by Royal Robbins and his wife Liz — done in impeccable style without hammering pitons. The Nutcracker remains, by far, one of Yosemite Valley's most popular climbs, thus our crack o' dawn start.

As we were gearing up, an employee asked, "Who did the 1st ascent of this?"

"Royal Robbins," I replied.

At that moment, no shit, Royal walked out from behind the rock!

"As a matter of fact," I said, "Here he is."

"Hey, Royal, how's it going?"

"Good morning," he replied.

I introduced Royal to my astonished employees. I tried to make it like it was no big deal. Of course, I was as surprised as anyone but did not let on. I just rolled with it. It was like a scene from a television talk show where the host brings out the twin brother you never knew existed. But it wasn't staged. It was complete luck.

After the intros, Royal asks, "Hey, have you seen (Ron) Kauk around? I'm supposed to meet him here to climb (The Nutcracker)." Royal explained that after his long hiatus, he was going to climb again. Kauk eventually did show up, and they disappeared up the 5.9 finger crack variation to our right.

While we roped up for the 5.8 corner variation, my crew was so inspired they couldn't stop reflecting on our encounter. That sure was a special day.

Royal Robbins, 1935 - 2017

5

WHAT THE HELL DID YOU DO...?!

By E.C. Joe

The first time I met Yvon Chouinard was in the original Mountain Room Bar in 1975, the same autumn I had met Warren Harding. Yvon was with Dennis Hennek. My climbing partner and mentor, Joel Matta, knew Hennek from a previous trip to Pakistan to climb. Henneck had climbed the second ascent of the North American Wall on El Capitan and Yvon had been a huge influence on Yosemite climbing and its hardware. I was a neophyte climber and was admittedly a bit star struck. Curious, I asked Yvon about his then recent clean ascent (using no hammer-driven anchors) of the Nose of El Capitan with Bruce Carson. At that time, climbing a big wall without a hammer and pitons had never been done before. This bold feat upped the ante for the status quo at the time, eschewing the use of pitons. It was a statement that said that this is how routes should be climbed. It indeed made us all look at the rock differently. Yvon was friendly, understated, and inspirational.

Some ten years later, I was invited by Richard Leversee to join Yvon, James Wilson, and Alberto Bendinger on a trip to the Eastside of the Sierra to do a rare ice ascent of Split Mountain Gully from the base. It would be a rare ascent, mainly because Split Mountain is remote, and

more so because this was the Sierra, not the Rockies; ice climbing is a
novelty in Cali. It was late November during a long, cold, dry period after
an early snowfall. We were hoping that there was some ice to climb. By
that time, I had plenty of rock climbing experience, but this was to be
my second ice climb - ever. After a healthy 4WD ride to the trailhead, we
were off.

Yvon assumed the role of "chief," and we fell in line. We bivouacked
near Split Mountain below Red Lake. Yvon had plenty of yarns to tell
about climbing, surfing and had quite a few laughs that night huddled
around the campfire. Yvon had insisted on being our chef, cooking his
"special" soup. It was as if we were guests at his house. (thirty years later,
Yvon sells a version of that soup through his company Patagonia
Provisions®).

Pre-dawn, o'dark-thirty, Yvon was all business. He was packed and left
our asses in the dust. The lake was frozen solid and made our climb easy
to approach. By the time we made it to the base, Yvon had already soloed
up a rope length up a nice, thickly frozen ice apron that yawned from the
gully above. Yvon was already asking for someone to belay him on the
next pitch. I must have missed the memo, but everyone soloed up to
Yvon's position. I mentioned that I was in over my head soloing, and
thankfully, they tossed me a line for a belay.

The next lead (crux) was a bit steeper, and the ice was not completely
formed and had waves and pockets of exposed rock in it. Of course, Yvon
made short work of it. It was the most challenging ice I had done.
Above, the route became a long, exhausting gully slog that involved post-
holing deep snow the remainder of the distance to the summit ridge.

After reaching the summit, we made haste towards basecamp.
Chasing daylight, we packed and left camp ASAP. Again, Yvon was first
to hit the trail. James and I were exhausted and brought up the rear. We
navigated the seemingly endless switchbacks in the dark by headlamps. It
was so dark that the light from our headlamps created an eerie bubble of
light in the surrounding blackness. Traveling inside the bubble messed
with my mind because it made me feel like we were going nowhere and
was mentally punishing as the gully slog was physical.

James and I plodded forward and downward, drifting through what
outer space might be like. At some point, we could make out the faint
beam of a headlamp randomly scanning the sides of the canyon below. I

figured we were catching up with the others, but that couldn't be, as the others had to be way ahead.

Moments later, we hear a faint voice, "Hey, you guys, hold up!"

While we waited, there was some severe bush-thrashing, and cussing was going on. Alas! From the brush-choked ravine below appeared Yvon with his waining Chouinard/Lago Headlamp.

"Man! I'm glad you guys came by! I saw your headlamps! I got fucking lost!" exclaimed Yvon.

The day after returning to Ventura, Malinda, Yvon's wife, approached Richard in the Patagonia campus cafeteria to ask him, "What the HELL did you do to Yvon? He's been useless since you guys got back."

A postcard response to John McGee from Yvon Chouinard concerning the trashing of climbs in Yosemite Valley. Photo: E.C. Joe

6

GALEN ROWELL UNCHAINED

By E.C. Joe

Galen Rowell had been known worldwide for his unequaled wilderness photography and his advocacy for the ecology of our planet. Establishing over 100 first ascents, he was one of the first Sierra backcountry climbers known for pushing "light, fast, and free" of iconic Sierra climbs.[1] Galen was the quintessential master of backcountry climbing.

Galen had just finished up a peregrine falcon photo project at the upper Needles. Ron Felton and I spent a weekend accompanying Galen, Michael Sewell, Brian Allison, and Lee Aulman to show them the prime locations to view the birds. We set up a base on the summit of the Charlatan Needle. It was perfect, as it overlooked the Wizard and Sorcerer Needles and the airspace where the peregrines were most active. At some point, Galen wanted to wander to vantage points in the other steep gullies where the birds were soaring. Ron, Galen, and I scrambled about into some precarious spots where Galen got to work. As late afternoon arrived and the shadows grew long, we could barely keep up with him. He was like a man possessed. We ran about the climbers' trails with Galen's Nikon set on rapid fire for the alpenglow. And this continued until dusk.

Sunday was laidback, where we spent most of the time viewing the birds from our base. Galen had never visited the Needles before and had time for one climb before his departure. As the unofficial Needles ambassador, I was responsible for recommending THE route for us to do. Eager not to disappoint, the route had to represent typical Needles climbing, be iconic, be difficult, but not extreme, and be easily accessible from our base. The climb had to be a "one stop shop." Ask yourself, if you had but one chance to climb at the Needles, what route would you choose? The ONE climb, I thought would have to be "Igor."

Igor Unchained follows the crack system on the smooth west face of the Witch Needle, just left of the summit. Photo: Michael Sewell

The entire route name is Igor Unchained and one will realize that it is aptly named once you've witnessed someone on the first pitch. That initial corner leans leftward to force the climber to jam their hands in the crack over their head, feet groping below like a veritable Quasimodo. The final pitch of Igor by far, is the most striking line that climbers notice from the Needles Lookout. It's not the most difficult climb, but it undoubtedly is the most aesthetic line. Three pitches in length, the route is very balanced in its offerings which include cracks combined with face climbing, good protection, straightforward passages, and some devious ones, too. Unlike what the route name may imply, the variety of climbing requires more than brute force alone.

A team of three was to climb Igor Unchained: Galen, Ron Felton, and myself. On a previous attempt, Ron had failed to climb the most strenuous 1st pitch in impeccable style and he was eager to have a rematch. I told Galen that the 3rd pitch was the most remarkable, and I suggested he take that lead. That left me with the middle pitch, which was dark and dubious with scantily protected face climbing between usable cracks. As for routes I had done before, I would minimize a weighty rack of protection for a climb and bring only the necessary gear.

The first two leads went well; Ron made good on his challenge, and I swept through the second, reaching the cool alcove belay below the third lead. Galen grabbed the rack and deemed it heavy, "Do we need ALL this stuff?" Ron voiced his doubts about removing any piece from the rack as Galen "tossed" out several wide cams. I also cautioned against doing so, but hey, Galen is the MAN, and we weren't telling him shit about what to do!

Looming over the safety of our niche, the wall was ominous and seriously steep. The initial moves were capped by a sizable guillotine-like block that required mounting. I could tell by Galen's body language that he was apprehensive. He then asked us if the block was solid. The sharp, angular wing jutting precariously out of the crack certainly filled Galen's mind with suspicion that any well traveled backcountry climber would have. "Yeah, it's cool," we replied in chorus. Galen moved on cautiously, working the moves, and eventually disappeared beyond the bulging wall.

Ron and I looked at each other and shrugged as Galen remarked with remorse that he should have brought those big cams as the crack widened. Of course, Galen "cowboy'd-up" and rose to the occasion because sometimes, you HAVE NO CHOICE but to go. This was Galen's only visit to the Needles. It was a special day to have shared this classic climb with our brother Galen. You will be missed.

Galen A. Rowell, 1940 - 2002

Galen Rowell clowning around at Needlerock Creek. Photo: E.C. Joe

7

HOW I LEARNED TO STOP WORRYING
AND JUST RUN IT OUT

By E.C. Joe

I watched Steven Colbert interview Aaron Paul (Breaking Bad) one time, and he told a story about working with movie producer J.J. Abrams on a Tom Cruise *Mission Impossible* movie. Someone had told him to talk about magic since J.J. was into it, even though Aaron wasn't. So, he did that and admitted that he didn't know much except a few kid card tricks.

Then, J.J. brought over Cruise to introduce him and said, "Aaron IS A MAGICIAN." Then, everyone on the whole set was like, "Show us!" He couldn't back down, so he tried and failed miserably. Then, he finally performed a successful trick (like for a 3y/o) where Cruise goes, "Good job!" Aaron was so embarrassed.

That story reminded me of something similar that happened to me years ago. Dennis Carroll was a high school classmate who lived across the street from me. After graduation, he went to Orange County to college at CSU Fullerton. At some point, I had told him that I started rock climbing. Soon, Dennis called me up and said he had joined a climbing club and invited me to a club trip to Suicide Rock. I hadn't climbed there before and I was in for going. I was puzzled during the meet and greet upon my arrival. I didn't know what Dennis had told the trip leader, but somehow I was an "expert." AND everyone was speaking to me as if I had OWNED A CLIMBING SHOP!

Shit. I had only led one climb; I only owned six nuts, six carabiners, six slings, an 11 mm x 45-meter rope, a 20 foot-long, 1" tubular web swami belt, and some shoes. At that time, that was the limit of my climbing repertoire.

At the crag, I had all these college kids depending on me to lead climbs for them. I wasn't good with that, and I even stated so. I must have sounded like Charlie Brown's Mom because NOBODY WAS LISTENING! "Wah, Wah, Wah..." Begrudgingly, I led a 5.5 route and brought up several people. Good thing they had some of their own ropes.

Next, I got on this 5.7 route where I got strung out, climbing with big distances between my protection and risked taking big falls with no way to back down. All I could do is remain calm and climb! My "666" rack was quickly depleted and I set the belay with my last Hex and carabiner. It was mere chance that the only Hex I had left actual fit, and it was solid. There had been several hopeful climbers waiting for a turn at the base. Unfortunately, I had to disappoint them and relieve myself from being their fearless leader. With a sleight of hand, I told them that the climb was too difficult for them and that only Dennis should come up. "Good job!" That's how I learned how to stop worrying and just run it out.

A year or so later, I brought Dennis out to the Kern to do the 1st ascent of the main route on Elephant Knob, "Elephantiasis." There I was, running it out and drilling bolts on lead into the unknown. It was a great adventure away from the crowds where I was able to show Dennis the expert I was becoming.

Dennis Carroll on the summit of Elephant Knob. The Needles loom in the background.
Photo: E.C. Joe

8

"THE GUIDE SAYS IT'S ONLY 5.9?"

By Todd Vogel

I was completely tangled in a climber trap of manzanita and mountain laurel with some other strange scrub thrown in. It was an Alpine Jungle, rating at least T-3+ on the bushwhack rating scale. The bushwhack rating scale parallels the aid climbing scale; T-1 is the easiest and T-5 the hardest. T-3, by definition, means all hands and feet are off the ground, but chances of a fall are minimal. We were on our third hour of a "45-minute" approach. I could hear my partner's curses but could not see him as he avoided a short cliff by the only possible method: down climbing a tree. I reminded myself that we were here to climb rocks, not trees. Finally, we met at the base of the route. We simultaneously suggested that there might have been an easier approach.

Climbing at the Needles is strange. First, you crank out the 2.5-mile pre-approach, and then you do the approach. The first hike allows plenty of time for "karma-ponderation." "Oh, no! Did you see that dead mouse? Let's go bouldering instead! Or fishing..." Inevitably we ended up at the base of some radical-looking route. I have yet to figure out if the climbs in the Needles are underrated or if the approach takes one grade's worth of ability out of the prospective rock lemming. Whatever it is, "The guide says it's only 5.9!" was the 2nd most common sentence of our trip. The first was, "Waah!"

The rudimentary guide contributes to the uniqueness of Needles climbing. The book helps one find the start of the climb, but if more info is desired, it is found on the route. There is little or no info as to what sort of rack to carry, the nature of the climbing (crack, face, or?), where the crux is, or where the belays are. A typical description may be, "The 'S'Crack, 5.9, 9 pitches." A simple sketch showing the start relative to the main features is also included.

We saw "The 'S' Crack" in the book and immediately decided it was the route to do. Saying, "It is only 5.9, we'll flash it!" was our first mistake; the second was starting at noon. I was thinking about that dead mouse on the trail. The approach must have made me exceptionally tired because four hard pitches up, I decided 5.9 at the Needles only means there probably won't be much 5.11+ on the route. The fifth pitch was mine, and it made me wonder where the crux was or was going to be. Strange is the life of the rock lemming. I was doing all this wondering because I couldn't move. I was in a 5.9+ doublewaahsqueezechimney. One of those chimneys where you can't move your head and falling isn't the problem; suffocation is. The wind carried up a yell from my partner, "The guide says it's only 5.9!" "Waaaaah," I grunted back; it cost me three inches of movement too.

With one pitch left, it looked like rain, but it felt like snow. Because of the anticipated rate of ascent, we hadn't worn enough clothes, and for most of the climb, we'd been swapping a windbreaker at the belays. Now we just wanted off (OFFOFFOFF!). Rather than summiting, we traversed to the rappel/descent route. The epic was over — all we had to do was hike three miles back to Shangri-La, bean burritos, and a tent, alas! No beer!

Back at camp, safe and stomach full, we decided that it had been one of our best days of climbing in a long time. If the guide had a complete route description or if it had hinted about that chimney, I doubt we'd have done the climb. But our experience was all the better because of the sparse information. I hope that any subsequent Needles' guides show the way to the base as "well" as the present book, maintaining the tradition of being able to climb as if the route was being done for the first time.

Besides, as old Ellsworth Kolb has noted, *"...too much information would spoil the romance of such an adventure."*

Todd Vogel searching for answers on the 1st ascent of North of Eden, North Dome, Kings Canyon National Park. Photo: E.C. Joe

9

MEANWHILE, IN THE SIERRA NEVADA

Ramblings from the InterWeb

"*Burl and I were sitting alongside the trail between Lon Cheney's cabin and 3rd Lake, at a nice little crick. I'm sure you know the place, everyone stops there. We'd just concluded a low-key tribal rite involving native herbs and fire. Good thing, 'cause we were both fried otherwise. The previous day we'd done the U-Notch and had to bivy on a slab of rock when we failed to find our tent in the dark.*

Then, this faded purple pack ever so slowly comes into view, along with a gray wool knit cap. Of course, it was Fred (Beckey). He was taking his time, but he didn't seem to be shirking his load. 'Same pack as the one in the pic, I'm pretty damn sure, loaded to the top. 'Was probably around 2001, I'd have to check.

'Hey Fred, how's it going?' I asked as he came by. He stopped to puzzle the question. Then he interrogated me — wanted to know what we'd done, the gear we used, what else we'd seen. I asked him what he was up to, and he wouldn't say! F*#k all he's 80-something and still playing his cards close to the vest. Right ON! He was with E.C. Joe. Eddie wasn't any more forthcoming about their destination — "check out some stuff on Temple Crag.'

Then on up the trail, they went. My steps were one helluva lighter after that. Floated clear back to the trailhead." — Cheers, Dingus Milquetoast

"Who, this guy?" — ec

Fred Beckey at Mosquito Flat.
Photo: E.C. Joe

*"Hell yeah, Eddie! THAT day. 'Walking with legends.' Between the two of you,
what's that, 1.32 zillion first ascents? What did you guys end up doing anyway?"*
— Dingus Milquetoast

"If I told you, I'd have to kill you." — ec

Ed & Fred, 2001. Photo: Christy Joe

SECTION V

RITES OF PASSAGE

"Early on like maybe in '73, one of my first multi-pitch climbs was 'Arch Bitch-Up' at Dome Rock, which is like a four pitch route. We didn't know what the hell we were doing, and we spent an unplanned night on it. We had to bivy on it with no gear; an early character-building epic."
  — *Richard Leversee*

1

RITES OF PASSAGE

Richard Leversee was one of the foremost pioneers of classic backcountry rock climbs throughout California's Sierra Nevada Mountains. I had an interview with Richard over the phone about his life as an adventure climber, working for Chouinard/Black Diamond, guidebooks, his best adventures, and the "ones that got away." Editor's Note: *Eleven months after Richard and I had this chat, he passed away. I hope that this interview will instill those unfamiliar with Richard's legacy, his love and devotion to climbing and the Southern Sierra. To those who knew and loved Richard, perhaps this will be cathartic.* — *ecjoe*

ec: "I know you started climbing while you were in high school, but when exactly was that? Who taught you? Where did you first go?"

Richard: "Well I grew up in LA, and I hated being in LA; there was way too many people. So, I got into backpacking. Then I became a bored backpacker. To me, climbing was the obvious way to be in the mountains, but have some adrenaline with it. When I was a freshman in high school in 1972, I signed up for a basic rock climbing class through 'The Backpack Shop' in Pasadena. We went up to Mount Pacifico in the Angeles National Forest. I used to go hang out at that shop because they had technical climbing gear. They had this event I went to and saw a film by Rick Sylvester when he skied off of El Cap, which just blew my mind.

The people who came to see the film in this tiny mountain shop, were all climbers. I was like, 'Wow, these are my people! How do I join this club?'"

ec: "That's cool, wow…"

Richard: "Yeah, I went to Mt. Pacifico, and then after that I started bouldering at Stony Point. That was in '72. What was super cool Eddie, you'll probably remember this, 1972 was a huge transformational year in climbing, because the Chouinard Catalog came out and introduced nuts, stoppers and hexes. It had that classic Chinese rice paper cover and there were those articles by Yvon, Doug Robinson and Tom Frost. Everyone was saying, 'Stop using pitons, clean climbing is the way to go.' I had never pounded a piton. I didn't have any pitons. So, I just thought, wow, this is a really cool sport."

ec: "Huh, interesting. I started similarly with backpacking, then there was a shop in Bakersfield, and they had a rock climbing class. Actually, a backpacking buddy, a friend that I had gone to high school with, he got me to go because he was interested in it; at first, I really wasn't. The rest is history, as only two of us out of a class of a dozen people ended-up really climbing."

Richard: "Was that Bigfoot (Mountaineering)?"

ec: "No, it was actually called 'High Country.' There was a guy named Darryl Easter who ran that place, and he'd done a little climbing and he was instrumental in getting Chouinard Equipment to send someone out to Bakersfield, of all places, to do a class. Tex Bossier came out to instruct. That's how I got my start. You were in high school?"

Richard: "Yes, I was kind of a misfit in high school. I mean, I played little league, and Pop Warner football, and stuff, but when I got to high school, I wasn't a 'loadie' and I wasn't a jock and I wasn't a cool social kid, so I didn't really fit in any of the cliques. I was kind of geeky and awkward, but I loved climbing. It became my religion, my tribe, this was it; I felt at home.

When I got that Chouinard catalog, I was like, 'Oh, Wow!' There's all these crazy quotes in there from the whole psychedelic era. Yeah, it was super cool. I just remember that all of a sudden I was exposed to all this psychedelic music like 'Yes,' 'Genesis,' 'Hendrix,' Emerson, Lake and Palmer,' and 'Pink Floyd.' The psychedelic progressive rock music scene was in its glory days; the music of the time and rock climbing became my religion."

ec: "I remember you telling me you were getting class credit for physical education for school. What year of school were you in when you finagled that?"

Richard: "Let's see. I think I was a junior and my younger brother, John was also in the same physical education class under this one teacher. My brother was a hoodlum and a wild man and he always ditched PE. I followed the rules. I did enough PE to get a passing grade, like a 'B,' but every chance I could, I would ditch PE to go climbing. I would leave the campus; we had a boulder a half a mile away. I'd get more exercise bouldering than if I had gone to PE class, right.

When it came time for grades, the teacher who was actually the basketball coach, a part-time cop, and kind of a jerk, he gave my brother and I both the same grade, and back then grades were based upon attendance. And I was like, 'Hey, what the heck? I have enough attendance to show that I should have a B in PE.' He goes, 'Well, that's just not the case, John,' he called me by my brother's name. So, I went to the administrators and I said, 'Look, the PE coach gave, my brother and I both the same grade. My brother doesn't have the same attendance as me and the PE teacher doesn't know one of us from the other. That's why he gave us both the same grade. The fact is, that if you're concerned about the amount of exercise I'm getting, I'm doing all this climbing.' The administrator said, 'Well, if you want to, you can document all of your climbing hours, so you fulfill the number of hours for attendance and give us a presentation at the end of the semester, like a slideshow or something, then we'll let you count your rock climbing for PE credits."

ec: "Wow, I wish I could have done that!"

Richard: "Yeah, Well, it wasn't like they had that program going and plugged me in. They could see that the system wasn't working for me. That's when I was a junior, so I gave a climbing slideshow."

ec: "I bet they were looking at the picture sideways, lol."

Richard: "Well, I don't remember exactly how many hours that the state was requiring for PE credits. I don't know, let's say it was 40 hours, but I was so addicted to climbing that before the end of the semester, I had like a hundred bonafide hours."

ec: "Were your parents supportive of all this?"

Richard: "Yes and no, I mean they let me go climbing. My dad was not happy about it because my dad worked his tail off Monday through Friday, and then on the weekend he expected us kids to be home, so we could all do yard work. That was my dad. That's the way he communed with the family on the weekend, with mowing the lawn, etc. Obviously, that was not a good thing for my climbing. I negotiated with them and I said, 'Look, if you need me to do extra work during the week so that I can go climbing on the weekend, give me a list.' He gave me a list and I would do all my chores during the week. He wasn't happy about that, because that didn't satisfy his dream of how the family comes together on the weekend."

ec: "Bonding! Lol."

Richard: "Eddie, you could probably relate to this. My parents had no freaking idea what I was doing. I mean, if they could have gone out to Suicide Rock or Joshua Tree or the Needles and seen what we were doing, they would have pooped their britches. They supported it, but you know that they had no clue, which was fine with me."

ec: "Yeah, at one point I brought my mom to Yosemite Valley. She watched me climb Moby Dick Center at the base of El Cap. She wanted to hide her eyes at first, and then she's like, 'Wow, this is sorta cool.'"

Richard: "Well, I had the same experience. Many, many years later, way after high school when you, Ed Sampson and I were going to do the Dawn Wall and we had the trip planned and everything. Then my folks said, 'Well, we're coming out from Georgia,' where they had been living at the time. 'We want to see you.' I was like, 'I want to see you too, but I can't change the dates of this trip, and it's super-important. Why don't you just come to Yosemite and I'll see you there?' It didn't occur to me that it had been many, many years since they had seen me climb. Then, there we were, fixing the first few pitches of the Mescalito/Dawn Wall and my parents walked to the base and they about pooped their pants. Afterwards, my mom was in El Cap meadow, with her ankle length, wool skirt, and her button-up to the throat blouse, going up to random tourists and saying, 'That's my son up there!'"

ec: "Oh, man. Lol!"

Richard: "That's when they first got a glimpse of what was really going on."

ec: "That's when they went, 'Oh, it's too late now.' Did they have that cabin at Camp Nelson for all that time, or was it during your rock climbing that they ended up buying that?"

Richard: "They bought the cabin in about 1964 when I was around 8 years old. They sold it in about 1984. Let's see. Okay, I graduated high school in '76 and then I went to work at Sunrise (Moutaineering) in 1980, and was living at the cabin for a good chunk of that time between '76 and '80. Patrick Paul lived with me at the cabin in the late '70's. That's when the place became a total climbers' pad. Then after I was at Sunrise, my parents had it for a few more years after that."

ec: "Did you guys go up there as a family often, or what?"

Richard: "Oh, yeah, here's a funny story. When I figured out that my religion was climbing, I pretty much didn't want to have anything to do with the family if it cut into my climbing time. So, I was always gone. I was always climbing out at Stony Point mid-week and then on the weekends I'd go to Joshua Tree and Suicide-Tahquitz and my parents would say, 'Well, you're going to have to spend some time with the family. We're going up to the cabin for Thanksgiving, or we're going up to the cabin for Easter, and you're part of the family, so, you've got to come,' and I was like, 'Oh, no, this will cut into my climbing!'

It never even occurred to me. I had just completely forgotten that Dome Rock and the Needles were up there. I had hiked there when I was a little kid, but I just I forgot. I was a sophomore in high school getting dragged to the cabin by my parents and it's like, 'Okay, well, if I'm here with the family, let's go on a hike out to the Needles.' So, we go on a hike out to the Needles and I'm like, 'Holy, shit!' It was the first time I put two and two together, and the same thing with Dome Rock. All of a sudden, my whole world changed. It blew the lid off my whole idea about where to go climbing. That's when I started spending most of my time, going up to the cabin and climbing, at Dome Rock and the Needles. That's when I met you, probably."

ec: "Yeah, I think I met you around '75. In '75, was when we did the first ascent of 'Just Lovely.' We were walking the base by the 'Tree Route' area to go repeat it (Just Lovely). Then what happened was you guys dropped your bolt kit. That started the conversation after we dodged the bag, it was a big stuff sack, and we helped pick up all the stuff. After you realized that we had done that first ascent, we became friends."

Richard: "Yeah, I remember. I would be in L.A. and I'd had these friends who I would go to Joshua Tree, Tahquitz, and Stoney with. I was like, 'You're not going to believe the rock up in Sequoia. It's just insane. You got to come out.' I talked these guys into coming up and there was one guy I used to climb with, after he saw what you guys did on 'Just Lovely,' he was like, 'Oh, man! I thought everybody in Bakersfield were just rednecks.' He used to call you the 'Chinese Cowboy' or something."

Richard and E.C. at the Dome Rock parking area. Photo: Alan Boyle, E.C. Joe Collection

ec: "Yeah, I was the 'Chinese Cowboy.' That was Joe Mitchell. He's the guy we took up on the 'Romantic Warrior.' He had never jugged on a free hanging line before. I remember him swinging into space going, 'Whoa! Oh, Man! Shiiit!' I guess you decided to start doing new routes right away?"

Richard: "No, early on like maybe in '73, one of my first multi-pitch climbs was 'Arch Bitch-Up' at Dome Rock, which is like a four pitch route. We didn't know what the hell we were doing, and we spent an unplanned night on it. We had to bivy on it with no gear; an early character-building epic. We climbed the Arch Bitch-Up and then we climbed the 'Tree Route.' There were maybe 6 routes on Dome Rock at that time. Those two routes being a couple of them.

Then sometime after that, we started doing new routes, but basically what happened during '72 and '73, I was learning my chops. At some point the light turned on and I was like, 'I love adventure climbing.' Adventure climbing meant doing new routes, because, there's no information. Everything was adventure at that point, and I'm preaching to the choir here, but I love adventure, period. The marriage of adventure and climbing together just became my mantra and my reason to live. I don't know if you remember this quote, but we used to say, 'I'd rather do a shitty new route than a great one-hundredth ascent.'"

ec: "Who of the climbing 'masters' inspired you the most?"

Richard: "Galen (Rowell), Galen was clearly an adventure addict and he was definitely a guru for me. Of course, there were Yvon (Chouinard), Warren Harding, Royal Robbins, and the Stonemasters. I mean the climbing community was pretty small when we started. I would say that Galen really captured it for me, if I was to name one person, it was because he loved the Sierra backcountry and he loved doing new routes. He climbed at a fairly high standard for the times; he was doing five tens and five elevens when five twelve was the top end.

I remember at one point, you and I talked about freeing all of the old Rowell and Harding routes in the Sierra that had been put up in the backcountry; like Angel Wings, Keeler Needle, Castle Rock Spire, Tehipite Dome, Hermit Spire, Warlock Needle, etc. We were just ticking them off; trying to free them all."

ec: "Ron Felton and I were able to climb with Galen once. He came out to do a peregrine photo shoot at the Needles. We helped him locate some good photo shoot spots. That dude was hard to keep up with him running for the sunset shots. It was amazing to watch. On the last day he says, 'Oh, I want to climb with you guys.' Okay! I suggested that we do 'Igor Unchained.' Up on the route, Galen is like, 'Man, do we need all this stuff?' Ron goes, well, you know, Ed's got it pared down to exactly what we need. Galen goes, 'Man, I don't want these big cams.' On lead, Galen's going, 'Oh, I should have brought those big cams.' Of course, he just sucked it up and did it without pro; like the typical badass we had expected."

Richard: "I have a pretty funny Henry Barber story like that. Henry was famous, or more like legendarily notorious for refusing to use cams, not only when they first came out, but for quite a few years after that. I think I was working for Chouinard at the time. Henry came out to the Needles for the first time. I knew Henry's reputation. I knew he was going to refuse to use cams. Everybody used cams back then. They weren't new. It wasn't a big deal.

We're sitting, racking up at the Witch-Sorcerer notch and I knew what he was going to do. I opened my pack and pull out this rack of a double set of Friends. He looks at me and goes, 'What are those for?' We were going to do the Don Juan Wall, which is a pretty stiff route and a crack line, right? Then I was like, 'Well, you got a better idea?' He pulls out a double set of well-worn hexes and stoppers and goes, 'This is all we need.' I was like, 'Okay, you're on!' But really, inside I'm thinking, 'Uh, oh...What did I get myself into?' But it was super, it was really cool. As you know, I hadn't climbed with just hexes and stoppers for awhile and I was like, 'Okay, big boy, Game On!'"

ec: "He had no problem, right?"

Richard: "Yeah, pretty much, I think it was challenging for both of us, but he was a better climber than me, for sure.

I want to go back to what we were talking about with adventure climbing, because when you and I first had the brain child, 'We're putting together a guide book for the Needles, Dome Rock and the whole Kern Canyon (*Stonemasher Rockclimbing Guide to the Kern River Canyon and Environs*).' I think it's fair to say that you and I were both hopelessly addicted to adventure climbing at that point.

Remember when we started talking to people about doing a guide? There was definitely some pushback, and people were not happy. Herb wasn't happy, Mike and Mari and that crew weren't happy. They were like, 'No, we want to preserve the adventure and keep it from becoming popularized.'

I think one thing that most people don't know is that you and I designed the guidebook, especially the Needles part, so that it preserved the history of the area, like the route names, the first ascensionists, when they were done, how hard they were, and how many pitches there were. We didn't have detailed topos, and we didn't we didn't mark where the cruxes of the pitches were. We just said how hard the pitches were. There was still all this adventure that was preserved and spared the area from less adventurous climbers.

The history needed to be preserved because around that time, there were people who would go out to the Needles who were thinking that they were doing a first ascent, when in fact, they were probably doing a 6th or 7th ascent. We wanted to preserve the route names and so forth. Unfortunately, for us and for the guidebook, that same year, those really beautiful detailed, guides for Tuolumne Meadows came out, and I think for Joshua Tree. When our guide book came out, nobody really understood. It was like, 'Okay, great. I got the route name here, and I heard the route is 4 pitches and rated .10b, but that's all the information I have?!'"

ec: "It became a throwback, of sorts. There was a method to our madness. Some people, years later, gave us some kudos for that, believe it or not, because they saw the downside of what happened as a result of detailed guidebooks (i.e., crowds). Yeah, preserving the history and those names, I think that was important."

Richard: "If we hadn't done that, the names, and for sure the dates, and the first ascensionists, the accurate history would have indeed been lost. Inevitably, bolts would have been added to pre-existing routes through ignorance. We wanted the guide to help preserve the bold high ethical quality of these classic routes."

ec: "An example is like the Domeland 'Vernon-Mosher' guide. I'd go to Domeland and did new routes on several domes and just figured, 'Ain't nobody going to come out here.' I figured that documentation didn't matter and left it that way. It ended-up where others went and did a bunch of 'first ascents,' and the routes are listed in the guide. I'm like, 'Dude, I was there like eight years before you.'"

Richard: "Yes, especially at the Needles where most of the routes are crack climbs, or at least they used to be. With clean climbing, and when it's mostly a crack line, there's a good chance that you wouldn't know if somebody had climbed it before. Most of the people doing those routes back then were bold, badass mofos and they were not afraid to run it out, compared to nowadays. You have these routes that have been established, named and treasured, but some people wouldn't have known that they had already been climbed.

I just remember you and I kind of having a meeting of the minds, when we were like, 'What are we going to do here? How do we preserve the history of these bold incredibly classic routes without ruining the adventure?' We powwowed and then we're like, 'Okay, let's just hand draw the topos so people know where the route goes, we'll make circles where the belays were, we'll get the first ascent information, the name of the route, the difficulty, and note if it needs any special gear and we'll call it good.' That way we preserved the history and the ethical style of the first ascents.

In hindsight, I actually think that our unorthodox strategy of an 'adventure style' guidebook achieved those goals pretty well. The original route names, dates, first ascentionists were documented and preserved and the bold traditional style in which many of the routes were put up was also preserved. Very few extra bolts appeared. Without the guidebook, route names, dates, etc., and the legendary signature bold character of some of the routes would have been lost forever."

The 1st-Ever rock climbing guide to the Kern Canyon area, 1983.

ec: "What was the first route that you ever did at the Needles, beyond walking out there to the tower?"

Richard: "Black Magic, on the Magician."

ec: "Okay, that was pretty typical, The Magician."

Richard: "The Needles are a scary place. Especially back then, you'd be lucky if you saw any climbers out there. There was no guidebook, nobody knew what the fuck had been done unless one saw it written up in the American Alpine Journal, and there were very few entries. Most entries were from Fred Beckey, right? There was probably one or two routes on each of the summits, at best.

ec: "That's pretty close. I checked the existing first ascent records to see how many known routes there were prior to 1975, and there were maybe 20 at the Needles, and most of those were on the lower formations near the lower road. There were at least six known routes at Dome Rock, two on the Hermit, and 11 routes down the canyon.

Richard: "Talk about adventure, you know what it was like. Back then, running it out was the highest ethic; that's what everybody was trying to do in order to place as few bolts as possible. Our mentors, the 'Stonemasters,' were the Kings of that. I mean, Tobin (Sorenson) was the 'Grand Poobah' for running it out. Only notable people had climbed out there; Herb, Mike Lechlinski, Mari Gingery, Tom Gilje, Kris Solem, Tony Yaniro, Randy Leavitt, Ron Carson, and everybody who climbed there was a bonafide badass. Lechlinski/Gingery/Gilje/McClenahan routes, in particular, were legendary for long, hard, seriously bold runouts and struck fear into the hearts of many of us. This made it an intimidating place. The Needles had the finest stone that I've ever climbed on. It was the cleanest, purest Sierra granite with perfect cracks, spectacular summits, wild technicolor lichen, wind, and it was kind of scary; it was the 'Promised Land.'

ec: *"Yeah, the Needles puts everybody in their proper place, lol."*

Richard: "I mean, you could do a 5.9 at the Needles back in the day and it would probably be rated .10b now, as Needles ratings were notoriously stout."

ec: *"Did you have any problems getting climbing partners from LA to go to Sequoia?"*

Richard: "Yeah, I did. I had trouble getting partners. I would have climbed more if I had more steady partners."

ec: *"You'd probably got these one-offs where you'd get them up there and they realized they didn't want to climb ever again, right? Lol!"*

Richard: "Yeah, some partners were intimidated and dropped out, but then there were some people who were like, 'Holy crap, this is the best rock I've ever seen in my life!' and they became regulars."

ec: *"You had mentioned earlier about working for Yvon (Chouinard Equipment). That seemed to me like a dream job. Was it actually a dream job for you?"*

Richard: "Yes and no, I started working for Chouinard Equipment in '85. I had been working at Sunrise as you know and Rick Hatch was the Chouinard Sales Representative back then. He would come by like maybe once every year or two. We didn't see him that often, but I knew that Rick wanted to be a Patagonia rep and leave Chouinard.

In '82 I decided to go back to school and so I left Sunrise Mountaineering. I had worked there in '81 and '82 for two years, and I went to a junior college, did really well and finished up my degree there. I was going to go to UC Santa Cruz to become an English teacher. I was there for one semester and I was kinda lost. My dream was to be an English teacher.

Then, I realized that it wasn't the ideal profession that I thought it was, which is a long story. Anyway, I was talking to my sister and she said, 'Well, what are you going to do?' I said, 'Well, I'll see if I can go back to Sunrise,' because they had multiple stores back then. Maybe I could go work in the Walnut Creek store or something. My sister said, 'Is that really what you most want to do? You want to go back to where you were?' That's what I know. I love it and I have a home there.'

She asked, 'Well, what if you had a magic wand and you could just create your total dream job, what would you want to do?' Before I could even think about it, I said, 'Work for Chouinard Equipment.' She replies, 'Well, why don't you go for it?' I knew Mariah (Cranor) back then. Through her, I found out that they had been looking for a sales rep. They wanted a rep who could not only rock climb, but ski, because they were going to introduce a new ski line in the next year or two, and also one who could ice climb.

They had interviewed Duncan Ferguson who was a rock and ice 'God' from Colorado. He was going to take the job, but his wife didn't want to move to California at the last minute. Then, I think they talked to Lynn Hill about it, but she didn't ice climb or ski. There may have been someone else. Then they got frustrated. They stopped looking.

When I started inquiring with Mariah, they were pretty depressed about, or frustrated about looking for someone. The first question she asked on the phone to me was, 'Do you ski?' I said, 'Yeah,' she asked, 'backcountry skiing?' 'Yeah,' 'Do you ice climb?' It's like, 'Yeah.' Then she said, 'Let me get you an interview.' I was in the right place, at the right time plus, I had been a shop manager for one of their better accounts (Sunrise Mountaineering); all the stars aligned."

ec: "You said it was a dream job, and then not. What was the downside?"

Richard: "You know, Chouinard Equipment has a storied history as the biggest climbing gear company in the United States and maybe even the world at that time. There were only a couple of reps. As one of my friends said, 'Yeah, you got indoctrinated into 'Diamond C Royalty,' because back then it was kind of a dream job. It was a rockstar job, you get to travel around the United States and sell toys to your friends. If your job requirement is that you can climb and ski, that's pretty good, but it was a real job. I actually got a paycheck. I didn't make a ton of money, but, I had medical benefits, it was a real job. That's the good part. You got to be a rockstar and all that stuff; got to go all over the United States and climb with your dealers. But there were only three reps at the time to divvy up the entire United States and Canada.

Even though we were the biggest climbing gear company, we still didn't make very much money. We were selling climbing gear, we weren't selling t-shirts or something that's lucrative, and there was very little mark-up or profit margin. At that time, there weren't that many climbers in the United States, and even though the sport was growing; it wasn't growing that much. We had a lot of overhead, we paid rent in the Patagonia complex. The downside of that job was traveling all the time and there was never any routine. That's fine during the honeymoon phase for the first few years, you got this ideal job, you're cruising all over the place, there were some years that I traveled probably 10 months out of the year. Eventually, that gets old, and it starts to wear on you, the lack of sleep and not having any routine in life. Then when I got married to Cari, you know that's no way to have a relationship, she was a 'rep's widow'.

I worked for Chouinard/Black Diamond for 13 years and became an employee/owner. After 10 years or so, I was burned out from traveling. I just wanted to go home and sleep in the same bed with my wife for three nights in a row, go home and unpack my suitcase and not have to repack it for a week. I wanted to have like a gym membership or anything that resembled a routine. It was this awesome job that I'm very grateful for and fortunate to have had. Eventually, I was burnt. It was too much and I think that I wanted to do something to make the world a better place above and beyond selling adult adventure toys to my friends."

ec: "During that time, I bet, the positive part was that you got a lot of contacts?"

Richard: "Yeah, although I kind of kept it to a small, small group of friends, you included, who I went climbing with, because, if you're going climbing all the time and if all your contacts are because of work, it doesn't feel like your own time. You know, it feels like you're always still at work. There were some people who I climbed with a bunch. Here's a good example, you know, who Scott Thelen is from Truckee? I did a bunch of new routes with him at Patterson Bluffs. It was cool because my climbing partnership friendship with him had nothing to do with me being from Black Diamond (aka: Chouinard Equipment). No, it was a pure partnership. It wasn't somehow diluted by the fact that I knew him from work.

Patterson is about 1,500 feet high. There's some parts of the wall that are a little longer than others, but yeah, it's really good rock, south facing and you rappel in from the top. There's like a 10 minute casual walk from your car to the rap anchors. It's a pretty special place. We put up a lot of routes at Patterson. When I started climbing at Patterson, my feelings about the ethics of bolting had changed. Even though we were still bolting on lead, the approach to Patterson was from above, we would rap down, of course, you're inspecting the route all the way down, knocking off any loose blocks and we were using power drills. It was very different from the early days at Dome Rock and the Needles."

ec: "What was the one route that was burning in your mind the most on your hit list to climb?"

Richard: "'The Widow's Tears' in Yosemite. I waited many years for the ice to finally come into decent condition and attempted it twice before finally bagging it. Our ascent was one of the first 10 ascents. BIG adventure!"

ec: "That's ice climbing in California; you need to have someone on-site to give you the current conditions over the phone and a fast car! When I saw that Vitaliy (Musiyenko) on-sight, free soloed that, I was like, 'Wow, what the Hell?!' What was your most memorable climb?"

Richard: "Two of them, Crystal Bonsai on Bubbs Creek Wall, and Archangel on Cherubim Dome are my favorites; Cherubim Dome because everything just clicked. But even if things hadn't clicked, both those routes are way far back in the Sierra backcountry and they're on perfect stone. They're both like the perfect ideal long backcountry routes. They were both between one and two thousand feet tall, which means you could do them in a day, but you had to be on your game. They were full value days in the backcountry, with flawless stone, minimal bolts, on natural features, and pretty spicy, but not crazy.

Crystal Bonsai, I love that route. I mean, first of all, I did it with you. It was like you've said before, we were like 'Lennon and McCartney.' We put up many classic new routes together and that was one of our best creations, man. The whole route followed that spectacular crystal band and then there were those little bonsai plants. There were just so many classic pitches on that. For a time it was one of the longest Sierra backcountry routes, it was 2,000 feet. It's like bigger than Keeler. It had only one pitch or so of aid on it. It was a hard aid pitch and we did it clean; there was lots of hooking including inverted Leeper Cam Hooks on an expanding flake and there was like this one 30 or 40 foot section of all number zero and number one RPs."

ec: "That stuff (aid climbing) is totally under appreciated now. Because people just go out to do free climbs in the backcountry. We had a little niche going for big wall stuff in the backcountry. I think that's just totally lost at this point. I can't see anybody following our lead on that, lol. Are there any routes that you think that you regret that got away off the hit list?"

Richard: "Yeah, what I've been doing since I retired from climbing (2002), especially when Vitaliy Musiyenko showed up and he started doing all those routes up by Lodgepole, I got a hold of him through Facebook. I just said, 'Hey man, you don't know me, but I used to have this little black book. Most of the routes got done, but there's a couple that got away and you should go for it.' He goes, 'Well, why don't you come do them with me?' I was like, 'No, no, no, no, I'm not climbing anymore. I haven't climbed for a long time. These are for you.' The number one route that I gave him was to free the prow of the Watchtower in Sequoia."

ec: "Yeah, I've seen that route. Man, that thing's badass!"

Richard: "He had already seen the line of course, because he had done a bunch of climbing in that area. But he had never been on the Watchtower. He

Richard Leversee on Crystal Bonsai, Bubbs Creek Wall, Kings Canyon National park. Photo: E.C. Joe

Cherubim Dome. The Archangel Route follows the left skyline. Photo: E.C. Joe

knew that John Long had done 'All Along the Watchtower' and the route was somewhere in there. He also knew that I had gone out there with

(Scott) Cosgrove and Jay Smith and figured that it was above his head, you know, too hard. I was like, 'No, no, no.' Those attempts trying to free the prow, no one has freed the prow to the top. First of all, the prize is still there. Secondly, there's not very many sections that haven't been done. It's just more of a case where people thought since there was such a large number of people who had tried and failed, this actually kept them from going back and trying to do it. I gave him all the beta I possibly could. One thing about the Watchtower is the cracks initially are a little dirty, which stops some ground up attempts.

Anyway, Vitaliy went in there with this guy, Brian Prince. It turns out when I was talking to Vitaliy he asked, 'Where do you live?' I told him, 'I live in Morro Bay,' and he goes, 'Oh, that's where Brian lives; Brian's been on the Watchtower and he's really had his eye on that.' I ended up having lunch with Brian in Morro Bay. I never met him before and we brought out photos and the topo from the guidebook and I said, 'Man, that thing is waiting. It's a total plum.' Anyway, those guys went back like I dunno, probably three times to clean it up. So, that's one of the ones that got away from me. I had gone there with Jay Smith and again with Cosgrove...Okay! Then those guys did it. It's called 'Big Time.' Rated 5.12, it has a reputation as being 'the Astroman of Sequoia.' Then I said, 'Well, there's a route on North Dome in Kings Canyon that you should probably do. It's that ramp, to the left of original 'Frost/Herbert Route.'"

ec: "Right, that's the arête left on the edge of the ramp."

Richard: "Exactly, it sits in between our route ('North to the Bone') and the Frost/Herbert Route. Again, he was like, 'Oh, I don't know, man.' I sent him a few photos. In fact, I found this photo that he took from Grand Sentinel looking at North Dome where the whole buttress is totally lit up. I was like, 'That's the line right there.' He and Brian went and did that. Then there was another one that got away. When you're going into King's Canyon and you're driving in, and just before Boyden Cave there's that big limestone wall on the left, across the river."

ec: "That's the one that those old timers (Mark Powell, et al.) went and did something on it years ago."

Richard: "Yeah, they went and did that line. Then there's also a line on Patterson that I've been trying to talk him into finishing or doing. So, yeah, there's, there was probably a half a dozen in my little black book that got away and it makes my heart happy to see the young bucks getting after them."

ec: "Yeah, that's all right! I appreciate your time and doing this interview."

Richard: "Just to wrap up, Eddie, I would just say that those were some of the very best times of my life; you, and those other people from that time in my life, it was our sacred religion, man. We belong to a really small spiritual tribe. Thank you. I love you brother."

Richard and E.C. two pitches from the top of the Wall of the Early Morning Light, El Capitan, 1982. Photo: Ed Sampson, E.C. Joe Collection

CONTRIBUTOR BIOS

Linda E. Adams

Linda E. Adams *was born and raised in Dinuba, CA, in the 1950s & 1960s and has spent most of her entire life in Kernville, CA. In 1976, Linda was the Needles Lookout. The Needles Lookout was a spectacular place to live, despite some adjustments to what most people would consider their "normal" daily lifestyle. She worked as a GS3 for 10-12 hours per day, 7 days per week for 5 1/2 months, May to November, with no days off. Drinking water, propane, and trash pick-up were done by a helicopter crew. Linda's Monday night schedule would be to hike the 2 1/2 miles to the end of the road, drive over to Peppermint Heliport for a shower. The following day, she would hike back out to the Lookout with her clean laundry, a week's worth of fresh and frozen food, in her old, green-canvas knapsack. Linda considers herself lucky to have always lived & worked around the wild, high country of the Kern, Kaweah, & Kings Rivers — Heart of the Sierras.*

Kathy Allison

Kathryn Allison *spent 23 years as a Forest Service fire lookout and founded the Buck Rock Foundation, a non-profit organization that restores and staffs Southern Sierra fire lookouts. With her love of granite and the great outdoors, she found a commonality with climbers. During her years of tireless advocacy saving fire lookouts, she has worked closely with the climbing community and has enjoyed their enthusiastic support for preserving special places. Still involved in the lookout and climbing world, she is also an avid river rafter and enjoys gardening and traveling with her husband in their camper van.*

Lee Aulman

Lee Aulman*, Raptor Specialist & Wildlife Manager, has worked for the Santa Cruz Predatory Bird Research Group studying peregrine falcons on the coastal and Channel Islands cliffs, including much of the northern interior of California. He also participated in the high-priority California Condor Project. Lee moved on to an assignment to survey peregrine falcons throughout the entire length of the Sierra Nevada Mountain range from El Dorado National Forest, Kings, and Sequoia National Parks to the Sequoia National Forest. Currently, Lee performs non-lethal avian predator management (select trapping and translocation of raptor individuals that predate endangered species) at Vandenberg Air Force Base.*

Ron Carson

Ron Carson *is well known in the Southern Sierra. He has climbed with Tony Yaniro, Randy Leavitt, Mike Lechlinski, Tom Gilge, Herb Laeger, Richard Leversee, Ron Kauk, and Vino Kodas, to name a few. Any of these people can attest to his skill, power, and tenacity, and joyful exuberance on the rock. Of the first ascents Ron has done in the Southern Sierra, many remain landmark test pieces for another generation of climbers and a testimony of his skill. Among those were Bon Voyage - Sorcerer Needle - 5.11+, Severed Ties - Djin Needle - 5.10b (solo), The Caduceus - Wizard Needle - 5.12, Vanishing Point - Witch Needle - 5.12+, The Life Boat - Witch Needle - 5.11b, The Iceberg - Witch Needle - 5.12a, The Titanic - Warlock Needle - 5.12+, and Carson-Oma - 5.12 - Dome Rock. From the Needles, Dome Rock, Shuteye Ridge, The Castle Rocks in the Sequoia National Park, the list goes on and on*

David Hickey

David Hickey *spent the summers of his youth in Sequoia National Park, where his father worked as a Park Naturalist and also at his grandparent's cabin near Mineral King. The experience instilled his enduring love for the Southern Sierra. David's involvement in rock climbing became another way for him to enjoy the Sierra. He co-authored the first rock climbing guide to the Sequoia/Kings Canyon area and was a founding member of the Southern Sierra Climbers' Association. David is currently devoting all his time and talent to restoring classic sport and racing cars.*

E.C. Joe

Eddie, "E.C." Joe, *a native of Bakersfield started climbing in the Southern Sierra in 1974, and spent most of his free time exploring new climbing opportunities in the scattered locations in and around the Kern Canyon. He has established many first ascents and authored the Stonemasher Rock Climbing Guide to Kern Slabs (1981-82), and co-authored the Stonemasher Rock Climbing Guide to the Kern River Canyon and Environs (1983) with Richard Leversee. Back in the day, Eddie was generally regarded as the single most knowledgeable person for climbing information in the area. In the '90s, he assisted in the research of Southern Sierra peregrine falcons and was a founding member of the Southern Sierra Climbers' Association. After years of climbing, guiding, and teaching others the ropes, Eddie eventually worked as a commercial vehicle driver trainer, public transit supervisor, and a DMV Commercial License Examiner. He currently is retired an is attempting to make sense of it all by publishing this book.*

Richard Leversee

Richard Leversee *is known for being an adventure climber, and the foremost pioneer of classic backcountry rock climbs throughout the Sierra Nevada Mountains of California. He was the first resident climber in the Needles/Dome Rock area. Richard co-authored the original rock climbing guide to the Kern Canyon area and was a Chouinard Equipment, aka Black Diamond sales representative.*

Joe Metz

Joe Metz *is a weekend alpinist, enjoying hiking, backpacking, mountaineering, rock climbing, snow shoeing, and skiing whenever the opportunity comes up. He learned to love the outdoors at a young age and taught himself the basics of rockcraft as a teenager. His game stepped up considerably under the tutelage of John Fischer and Alan Bard at the Palisade School of Mountaineering and later under the guidance of E.C. Joe and many other mentors. Joe loves the focus and intensity that comes with climbing on lead and the camaraderie around the campfire when the day is done. Many of climbers he has met along the way have become lifelong friends, bound by the love for adventure in wild and beautiful places.*

Dave Ohst

Dave Ohst *fell into vertical rock and wilderness adventure after seven successful years of bicycle racing at consistently high levels. This was perhaps an ideal athletic transition during the explosive 1970s Stonemaster age in Yosemite Valley and beyond. In parallel with both, Dave earned an engineering degree from Cal Poly in San Luis Obispo, California, with later executive education at Stanford University and UC Berkeley. Despite the pull of professional cycling or career climbing, engineering and subsequently aerospace management prevailed as a long career. Across those early years and beyond to today - athletics and adventure have been and remain central tenets. A self-confessed "Flow" junkie, Dave continues to chase the ephemeral groove across motorsports, rowing, fitness training, cycling, and the mountains.*

Patrick Paul

Patrick Paul *grew up in Manhattan Beach, California. He surfed the shores of the Pacific from central Baja to Santa Cruz, the North Shore of Oahu, and various breaks on Maui and Kauai, Hawaii.*

In 1976 he was introduced to rock climbing by chance through an invitation while making a deal with a real estate agent in Long Beach, California. His first climb was on the Pope's Hat in Joshua Tree. His next climb was almost a year later in central Oregon while dating a girl who happened to have climbing equipment. They found an obscure crag, a short basalt cliff, near La Pine and unwittingly did a first ascent. Unfortunately, they could not top-out on the climb because a Bobcat was occupying a small ledge a few feet from the top and refused to let them pass.

Within a few months, Patrick moved from Oregon to Springville, CA, near The Needles, Dome Rock, and the other crags of the Kern Canyon area, where he met Richard Leversee and began climbing in earnest. His partnership with Leversee started him on the way to doing the first ascents, and he proceeded to put up many routes at the Needles, Dome Rock, Hermit Spire, Trilogy, and Parker Bluff. He would establish several routes in the Southern Sierra from Chiquito Dome to the Domeland Wilderness, Kern Canyon, and the Mojave Desert to the East.

During his 44 years of climbing, he has guided climbs and conducted climbing classes. Patrick was a member of the American Mountain Guides Association, a founding member and president of the Southern Sierra Climbers' Association, and co-authored the book Southern Sierra Rock Climbing: Needles, a guide to the superb climbing in the Southern Sierra and Kern River Canyon area.

Randy Powers

Randy Powers *AKA: PowerMan, while in high school at age 17, he wrestled in the Junior National Championships and the Junior World Championship. Randy started rock climbing at 20 and was a pioneer on many Southern Sierra first ascents with various climbers, including David Peck, E.C. Joe, Dr.Joel Matta, and Richard Leversee. His resume includes big wall ascents like Zenyatta Mondatta and The Shield on El Capitan in Yosemite. At the age of 68, Randy enjoys backpacking and fishing in the remote corners of the High Sierra.*

Kris Solem

Kristian Solem *discovered climbing during the 1970s at New York's Shawangunk cliffs. Ten years later, he moved to California. Bouldering regularly at Stoney Point, Kristian formed lifelong partnerships with the likes of Bob Kamps, Herb Laeger, Jan McCollum, and Guy Keesee. Over the next 25 years, he did numerous first ascents at Joshua Tree, Dome Rock, the Needles, Courtright Reservoir, and the Gorge of Despair. His focus was on doing difficult new routes in ground-up style. Highlights from his climbing career include having pioneered first ascents in the Gorge of Despair, and several at Courtright Reservoir, notably Seamstress and the Gold Standard.*

Additionally, Kristian led a free ascent of the regular route on Castle Rock Spire and redpointed Suicide Rock's notorious Pirate. Climbing with Jan McCollum, Kristian led the second ascent of Joshua Tree's Games Without Frontiers, a 5.13. In 2016 he authored a new guidebook for his favorite climbing area, The Needles.

Randy Steele

Randy Steele *"Redasian" began climbing at 22 on New Year's Day 1995, at the Pinnacles National Park, Central California, during a family outing. That summer, he first experienced Southern Sierra granite at the Needles by climbing the second ascent of Voodoo Chil. Since then, the norm became to set out after work with friends and gear, all crammed into his old 1987 Honda Civic to frequent his favorite crags of Sugarloaf and Lover's Leap. Randy graduated from Cal State University, Sacramento, in 1997 and had the pleasure of working the most desirable jobs known to man: agriculture, heavy construction, and supervising male penal colonies. All of which has left him with a firm belief that climbing has been his greatest escape from the mundane and known processes of everyday life. Climbing, baseball, snowboarding, hiking, or deciding what beer was on tap provided the variety and free will that he and his friends were seeking. Randy's core values are simple: God, family, work, and fun--especially in the company of his favorite climbing partners Phil, Jason, Kenny, and Isaac.*

Brandon Thau

Brandon Thau *became hooked on rock climbing after his father suggested taking a class at Joshua Tree National Park when he was 13. Climbing in the Southern Sierra for over 30 years, he pioneered numerous classic and difficult backcountry routes. Brandon remains impressed with the Southern Sierra's solitude, variety of climbs, and the unlimited potential for new route discovery in one of the country's most populated states. Brandon currently resides on the Central Coast of California with his wife Cristina and his two sons, Sebastian and Tristan.*

Todd Vogel

Todd Vogel *is a mountain guide, outdoor educator, and retail mountain shop owner from Bishop, California. Originally from Michigan, he moved to Bishop from Santa Cruz in 1988 to be closer to the mountains and the outdoors. His first job in Bishop was digging ditches for a local mountain resort — not the glamour job he was hoping for! His future wife-to-be also made the move with him and started working at the local mountain shop. Fast forward thirty-plus years, and now Chris and Todd both own that store, "Eastside Sports," having purchased it in 2012. The store employs fourteen people, and Todd currently serves as the book-keeper - a position he had there for a year in 1989 - advertising director, CFO, HR head, and maintenance supervisor (toilet cleaner); the joys of owning a small business.*

Todd is a well-regarded leader in the mountain guiding and outdoor education community, having served on the board of directors of the American Mountain Guides Association (AMGA) in the early 2000s and as the founding president of the thirty-four hundred member Professional Climbing Instructor's Association (PCIA) from 2005 to recently. Todd also serves with the Inyo County Search and Rescue team as a team captain and lead trainer and is an appointed member of the Inyo County Planning Commission.

Recognizing the importance of helping future generations learn about the outdoors, Todd founded the non-profit "Eastern Sierra Youth Outdoors," in part-nership with the local Rotary chapter, with grant funding in 2015.

Todd spends about 16 weeks a year out on outdoor programs. When he's not pretending to help run Eastside Sports or out on a program, he loves to run with his dog – sometimes ridiculous distances, bird watch, hike, and try to ignore all the house maintenance projects he really should be doing.

IMAGE DESCRIPTIONS & ATTRIBUTIONS

COVER: Full Metal Jacket, Moro Rock. Photo: René Ardesch

OPPOSITE TITLE PAGE: Granite with Purple Carabiner. Photo: E.C. Joe

OPPOSITE EPIGRAPH PAGE: Richard Leversee on the summit of the Warlock Needle, 1977. Photo: E.C. Joe

OPPOSITE FOREWORD: Climber over Cactus. Sketch by: Lulu

END OF PROLOGUE: Arch Bitch-Up. Sketch by Lulu

PAGE 1: Poem by E.C. Joe, 1977

PAGE 2: Ron Carson on The Avenger, 5.13 a/b, Sorcerer Needle. Photo: Greg Epperson

PAGE 7: The Rope. Photo: Ron Carson

PAGE 10: Mountain Magazine 145. Photo: Ed Hartouni

PAGE 11: Ron Carson on the 1st ascent of Chemo Therapy. Photo: Ron Carson Collection

PAGE 12: Dave Ohst ascends the rope on the Salathé headwall, El Capitan. Photo: Ed Sampson, Dave Ohst Collection

PAGE 14: Bishop Peak: Where It All Began
Jeff Lang in 1978 – Jeff also proved that he could solo 5.6 rotten stair. Photo: Dave Ohst

PAGE 16: Hollister Peak. Photo: Dave Ohst

PAGE 18: The Needles & Voodoo Dome from Dome Rock, The perpetrator Warlock is just left of Voodoo Dome. Photo: Kristian Solem

PAGE 20: Saytr 1st Ascent - Diamond Rock under a Diamond, Sky Dave Ohst on the 2nd Pitch – July 1980. Photo: Richard Leversee, Dave Ohst Collection

PAGE 21: The Last Pitch of the Nose on El Capitan – Enjoying the Exposure and Blissfully Unaware of Impending Dirt Doom. Photo: Gary Clark, Dave Ohst Collection

PAGE 22: A De Rigueur Rugby Shirt Summiting Warlock Needle after the S-Crack. Photo: Kim Grandfield, Dave Ohst Collection, Witch Needle – Igor Unchained Drop-Dead Blonde Stone Matches Gold Joy. Photo: Gary Clark, Dave Ohst Collection

PAGE 24: Sublime and Spectacular Alpine Gems – Unnamed Pillars above the North Fork of Lone Pine Creek. Photo: Dave Ohst

PAGE 25: Steve Roper's *Climber's Guide* and Hervey Voge's *Mountaineer's Guide to the High Sierra.* Photos: Dave Ohst

PAGE 26: The Start of the Harding Route, before Global Warming – August 1980, Complete with GPIW tee shirt as homage. Photo: Kim Grandfield, Dave Ohst Collection, Keeler Needle Topos. Photos: Dave Ohst

PAGE 27: Superb Sierra Granite – the 5.10 Roof on the 3rd Pitch. Photo: Kim Grandfield, Dave Ohst Collection

PAGE 28: The Red Dihedral – Arguably Never Better. Photo: Kim Grandfield, Dave Ohst Collection

PAGE 29: Dave Ohst ascends the rope on the Salathé headwall, El Capitan. Photo: Ed Sampson, Dave Ohst Collection

PAGE 30: Mt. Athabasca – North Face Ice Instead of Rock in 1981. Photo: Dave Ohst

PAGE 32: Richard Hershberger on the Magician Needle. Photo: E.C. Joe

PAGE 33: Needles Dawn. Photo: E.C. Joe

PAGE 34: The Needles Lookout. Photo: E.C. Joe

PAGE 36: The Needles. Sketch by Lotus Steele

PAGE 37: Kern Slabs. John McGee on the 1st Ascent of Just Lovely, Dome Rock. Joel Matta. Photos: E.C. Joe

PAGE 39: Guy Thompson. Photo: E.C. Joe

PAGE 40: Rack Du Jour. Photo: Joel Matta, E.C. Joe Collection

PAGE 44: The Wizard Needle, Yellow Brick Road follows the straight crack just right of center. Photo: Kristian Solem

PAGE 46: David Peck, 1971. Photo: Janet Peck, David Peck Collection

PAGE 47: Randy Powers. Photo: E.C. Joe, The Bottle. Photo: Steph Abegg

PAGE 48: Scodie Spire Bivouac. Photo: David Hickey

PAGE 50: The Canebrake. Richard Leversee, on the summit of White Dome. Church Domes are visible in the distance. Photos: E.C. Joe

PAGE 52: The "North Domes," Domeland Wilderness. Photo: E.C. Joe

PAGE 55: Kaopectate Blues. Photo: Richard Shore

PAGE 56: Columbia Dome, Domeland. Photo: Richard Shore

PAGE 58: The Splitter Crack of Return to Forever, Radiant Dome. Photo: Jim Marchesini, E.C. Joe Collection

PAGE 60: Richard Shore on the 5.11 start of Kaopectate Blues. Photo: Brandon Thau

PAGE 61: Kaopectate Blues. Photo: Richard Shore

PAGE 62: Brandon Thau on Kaopectate Blues. Photo: Richard Shore

PAGE 64: Brandon Thau on Immodium Ao. Photo: Richard Shore

PAGE 65: Updated Kaopectate Blues Topo adapted with permission from *Southern Sierra Rock Climbing Guide by Sally Moser and Greg Vernon.* Photo: E.C. Joe

PAGE 66: Parker Bluff. Photo: René Ardesch

PAGE 68: Eddie "EC" Joe. Photo: David Hickey

PAGE 69: James Cook, Moro Rock. Photo: E.C. Joe

PAGE 70: James Cook on Pitch 1 of King of Pain. Photo: René Ardesch

PAGE 71: Eddie Joe headed for the "Little Black Knob in the Sun Belay," (visible left of the center, on the horizon) on the 1st Ascent of King Of Pain. Photo: David Hickey

PAGE 73: David Hickey in the throes of "Jaws" at Parker Bluff. Photo: E.C. Joe

PAGE 74: Valhalla and Cherubim Dome, Sequoia National Park. Photo: René Ardesch

PAGE 77: E.C. Joe on the 1st ascent of Archangel, Cherubim Dome. Photo: Richard Leversee, E.C. Joe Collection

PAGE 78: Richard Leversee and E.C. Joe, Angel Wings. Photo: Ron Felton, E.C. Joe Collection

PAGE 80: Fred Beckey. Photo: David Hickey

PAGE 82: Richard, E.C., and Ron on the summit of Angel Wings, Just a Rock in the Park. Photo: E.C. Joe Collection

PAGE 83: Just a Rock in the Park Topo. Photo: E.C. Joe

PAGE 84: Fred Beckey at Mosquito Flat. Photo: E.C. Joe

PAGE 91: Fred and his green bowl. Photo: Joe Metz

PAGE 95: Joe Metz on the Northeast Ridge of Bear Creek Spire. Photo: Fred Beckey, Joe Metz Collection

PAGE 101: Bear Creek Spire from Treasure Lakes. The Northeast Ridge is marked by the sun-shadow line. Photo: Joe Metz

PAGE 104: Randy Powers topping out on Scodie Spire. Photo: E.C. Joe

PAGE 105: Frank and Ernest Cartoon used with the permission of the Thaves and the Cartoonist Group. All rights reserved.

PAGE 106: The Living Corner, Romantic Warrior. Photo: E.C. Joe

PAGE 109: Warlock Needle. Photo: E.C. Joe

PAGE 110: Randy Powers on pitch 1, Romantic Warrior. Photo: E.C. Joe, E.C. Joe on pitch 3, Romantic Warrior. Photo: Randy Powers

PAGE 112: Randy Powers on the original pitch 4, Romantic Warrior. Photo: E.C. Joe

PAGE 113: The View from Excess Reality Ledge. Photo: Randy Powers, E.C. Joe Collection

PAGE 114: The Book of Deception. Photo: Randy Powers, E.C. Joe Collection

PAGE 116: Patrick Paul and Herb Laeger. Photo: Ron Carson, Patrick Paul Collection

PAGE 121: Whipper Snapper. Photo: David Hickey

PAGE 125: Whipper Snapper. Photo: David Hickey

PAGE 126: Two Climbers on Lightning's Hand, Dome Rock. Photo: René Ardesch

PAGE 130: Homers Nose. Photo: René Ardesch

PAGE 133: Homers Nose. Photo: Dave Ohst

PAGE 134: Dave Ohst ascends a fixed rope. Photo: Richard Leversee, Dave Ohst Collection

PAGE 135: Richard Leversee near the top of pitch 2. John Tuttle belays. Photo: Dave Ohst

PAGE 136: John Tuttle, Richard Leversee, and Dave Ohst after the 1st ascent of The Dance of Topo Usha, Homers Nose. Photo: Dave Ohst Collection

PAGE 137: Dance of Topo Usha Topo. Photo: E.C.Joe

PAGE 138: Brandon Thau and Jody Pennycook following pitch 8 of El Niño during a break in the weather. Photo: Grant Gardner, Brandon Thau Collection

PAGE 140: Grant Gardner approaching the Great Half Moon, El Niño, Grant Gardner on pitch 2, El Niño. Photos: Brandon Thau

PAGE 141: Grant Gardner leads the "Trust Your Pecker" pitch on the 1st ascent of El Niño. Photo: Brandon Thau

PAGE 143: Brandon Thau leads a free pitch in the rain, hoping for a good bivy spot before the storm really hits. Photo: Grant Gardner, Brandon Thau Collection

PAGE 144: Brandon Thau and Jody Pennycook following pitch 8 of El Niño during a break in the weather. Photo: Grant Gardner, Brandon Thau Collection

PAGE 145: Happy to be Alive! Grant Gardner and Brandon Thau on the summit of El Niño, Moro Rock. Photo: Jody Pennycook, Brandon Thau Collection

PAGE 146: The Fin and Castle Rock Spire, Sequoia National Park. Photo: René Ardesch

PAGE 149: Patrick Paul and Richard Leversee as depicted in the Tule River Times at Sky Garden Wall, 1981. Photo: R. Baracco

PAGE 152: Silver Lining. Photo: David Hickey

PAGE 154: A climber approaches the great dihedral on Silver Lining. Photo: David Hickey

PAGE 155: Silver Lining. Photo: David Hickey

PAGE 158: Patrick Paul on Silver Lining. Photo: Ron Carson

PAGE 159: Silver Lining Topo. Photo: E.C. Joe

PAGE 160: The Gorge of Despair Photo: Herb Laeger Collection

PAGE 162: Mount Harrington. Photo: Guy Keesee

PAGE 164: The Silver Turret. Photo: Guy Keesee

PAGE 166: The view from the summit of the Silver Turret. Photo: Guy Keesee

PAGE 167: Rappelling off the Cobra Comandante Turret lies behind. In the distance, across the canyon, stands the massive Tehipite Dome. Photo: Guy Keesee

PAGE 169: Kristian Solem hanging from a small hook on an edge, drilling the hole for the third bolt Photo: Guy Keesee

PAGE 170: Kristian Solem leading *From Afar.* Photo: Guy Keesee

PAGE 178: Red Danskin tights? Check. Nikon sunglasses? Check. Booting up to get on the biggest wall in the Gorge of Despair? Priceless. Photo: Guy Keesee

PAGE 180: The summit. Photo: Guy Keesee

PAGE 181: Despairadoes: The undercling starts the third pitch. Pitch 5 climbs the Gorilla Face. The arrow marks the line of our escape rappels after Guy's injury in 1995. Photo: Guy Keesee

PAGE 182: Terror at 30,000 ft: Tehipite Dome, Kings Canyon National Park. Photo: Kim Grandfield

PAGE 185: Ron Felton on Hetch Hetchy dome. Photo: E.C. Joe

PAGE 186: Tehipite Valley. Photo: E.C. Joe

PAGE 187: The Middle Fork of the Kings River, Tehipite Valley. Photo: E.C. Joe

PAGE 189: Ron showing his cooking chops as Guy Zielski looks on. Photo: E.C. Joe

PAGE 192: Ron and Guy swelter in the Hot Pocket. Photo: E.C. Joe

PAGE 193: The Mausoleum. Photo: E.C. Joe

PAGE 194: Ron Felton on the Roof Traverse. Photo: E.C. Joe

PAGE 195: Guy and Ron at the Roof Bivy. Photo: E.C. Joe

PAGE 196: Guy Zielsky launches into space. Photo: E.C. Joe

PAGE 197: Guy Zielsky cashing in his reward air miles. Photo: Ron Felton, E.C. Joe Collection

PAGE 199: Ron Felton in the sea of granite. Photo: E.C. Joe

PAGE 201: E.C. Joe follows a difficult face pitch on the upper dome. Photo: Ron Felton, E.C. Joe Collection

PAGE 202: E.C. Joe near the summit of Tehipite Dome. Photo: Ron Felton, E.C. Joe Collection

PAGE 203: In the Niche of Time Topo. Photo: E.C. Joe

PAGE 204: E.C. Joe on a Moro Rock Peregrine Survey. Photo: René Ardesch

PAGE 205: Moth on Rope. Photo: Amos Clifford

PAGE 206: Southern Sierra Climbers' Association Logo

PAGE 209: No - 'Not a bust. SSCA members working with Rangers at Moro Rock in Sequoia National Park to clean up litter, including items discarded by tourists that ended up along the base of the rock. Photo: René Ardesch Collection

PAGE 210: Peregrine Falcon, Point.Arguello nest site, Vandenberg Air Force Base. Photo: Lee Aulman

PAGE 212: The Peregrines' Champions, Lee Aulman, Yvon Chouinard, and Shawn Hayes below the Lompoc Skull, 2021. Photo: Malinda Chouinard

PAGE 216: Abandoned Peregrine Eggs in an Aerie, Moro Rock, Sequoia National Park. Photo: E.C. Joe

PAGE 217: Ron Felton, E.C. Joe, Lee Aulman, and Galen Rowell observing peregrines at the Needles. Photo: Brian Allison, E.C. Joe Collection

PAGE 218: E.C. Joe, CTRL+ALT+ DELETE. Photo: Dory Ptak

PAGE 223: E.C. Joe demonstrates to the scouts how to tie-in. Photo: Joe Metz, E.C. Joe Collection

PAGE 232: Randy and Phil Steele with Randy's cousin Wendy at Sugarloaf, CA. Photo: Randy Steele

PAGE 239: Voodoo Chile Topo. Photo: E.C. Joe

PAGE 240: The Needle Lookout. Photo: René Ardesch

PAGE 243: Margee Kelly. Photo: René Ardesch

PAGE 246: The Needles Lookout, Sunset. Photo: E.C. Joe

PAGE 248: Moro Oro Headwall. Photo: David Hickey

PAGE 249: Jon Allen takes a morning celebratory Dragon Dance in the Canebrake. Photo: E.C. Joe

PAGE 250: Cams for Days. Photo: E.C. Joe

PAGE 253: Richard "Dick" Banner. Photo: Jane Banner Collection

PAGE 254: Roland Burkert on the South Face of Washington Column. Photo: E.C. Joe

PAGE 257: The Minarets. Photo: E.C. Joe

PAGE 259: "But we shall continue with style." — Anderl Meier, The Eiger Sanction Roland negotiating a Glacier Point slab, Yosemite Valley. Photo: E.C. Joe

PAGE 260: Wino Towers, El Capitan. Photo: Ed Sampson, E.C. Joe Collection

PAGE 264: Royal Robbins. Photo: René Ardesch Collection

PAGE 268: Yvon Chouinard on the 1st Full Ice Ascent of Split Mt Gully, Sierra Nevada, CA. Photo: E.C. Joe

PAGE 271: A postcard response to John McGee from Yvon Chouinard concerning the trashing of climbs in Yosemite Valley. Photo: E.C. Joe

PAGE 272: Galen Rowell on Igor Unchained. Photo: Michael Sewell

PAGE 274: Igor Unchained follows the crack system on the smooth west face of the Witch Needle, just left of the summit. Photo: Michael Sewell

PAGE 275: Galen Rowell clowning around at Needlerock Creek. Photo: E.C. Joe

PAGE 276: E.C. Joe running it out on the 1st ascent of Moro Oro, Moro Rock, Sequoia National Park. Photo: David Hickey

PAGE 279: Dennis Carroll on the summit of Elephant Knob. The Needles loom in the background. Photo: E.C. Joe

PAGE 280: E.C. Joe on S Crack, Warlock Needle. Photo: Randy Jewett, E.C. Joe Collection

PAGE 283: Todd Vogel searching for answers on the 1st ascent of North of Eden, North Dome, Kings Canyon National Park. Photo: E.C. Joe

PAGE 284: Dome Rock Tourist Sketch by Lulu

PAGE 286: Fred Beckey at Mosquito Flat. Photo: E.C. Joe

PAGE 287: Ed & Fred. Photo: Christy Joe, E.C. Joe Collection

PAGE 288: Richard Leversee and Brian Hodges check out El Capitan. Photo: Dave Ohst

PAGE 290: Richard Leversee on the Zodiac, El Capitan. Photo: Randy Powers, Richard Leversee Collection

PAGE 298: Richard and E.C. at Dome Rock. Photo: Alan Boyle, E.C. Joe Collection

PAGE 302: The 1st-Ever Rock Climbing guide to the Kern Canyon Area, 1983. Photo: E.C. Joe

PAGE 307: Richard Leversee on Crystal Bonsai, Bubbs Creek Wall, Kings Canyon National Park. Cherubim Dome. The Archangel Route follows the left skyline. Photos: E.C. Joe

PAGE 309: Richard and E.C. two pitches from the top of the Wall of the Early Morning Light, El Capitan, 1982. Photo: Ed Sampson, E.C. Joe Collection

PAGE 310: Roland Burkert on White Punks on Dope, Voodoo Dome. Photo: E.C. Joe

ENDNOTES

Prologue

1. William Harland Boyd et al., *The Chinese of Kern County* (Bakersfield, CA: Kern County Historical Society, 2002), pp. 127, 161, 180, 197, 201
2. Marjorie Lee et al., *Duty & Honor* (Los Angeles: Chinese Historical Society of Southern California, 1998), pp. 54, 124, 126
3. Boyd et al., *The Chinese of Kern County,* pp. *202, 205, 206*
4. Hervey Harper Voge, editor (1910-1990), *A Climber's Guide to the High Sierra* 1st ed. (Sierra Club, 1954)
5. Steve Roper, *The Climber's Guide to the High Sierra* (San Francisco: Sierra Club, 1976)
6. E.C. Joe, Dick Leversee, *Stonemasher Rockclimbing Guide to the Kern River Canyon and Environs* (California, 1983)
7. John Harlin III, *The Climber's Guide to North America, West Coast Rock Climbs* (Denver, CO: Chockstone Press, 1984)
8. Sally Moser, Greg Vernon, *Southern Sierra Rock Climbing* Domelands (Evergreen, CO: Chockstone Press, 1992)
9. Sally Moser, Greg Vernon, Patrick Paul, *Southern Sierra Rock Climbing The Needles* (Evergreen, CO: Chockstone Press, 1992)
10. Sally Moser, Greg Vernon, David Hickey, *Southern Sierra Rock Climbing Sequoia-Kings Canyon* (Evergreen, CO: Chockstone Press, 1993)
11. Kristian Solem, *The Needles Climbing Guide* (CA: K. Daniels Associates, 2016)

1. Genesis

1. *Mountain 145* (UK: Mountain Magazine Ltd. Globe Works, 1992)

2. Vertical and Wandering Flow

1. Csikszentmihalyi, Mihaly (1990). *Flow: The Psychology of Optimal Experience*. New York: Harper and Row. ISBN 0-06-092043-2
2. In the 1970s, John Long, an original member of the Stonemasters, was a key contributor to rising climbing standards in Southern California, Yosemite & beyond. See also Footnote 3.
3. The Stonemasters in the 1970s were a cadre of bold and talented California climbers. This irreverent group was responsible for pushing standards and adventure to new dimensions in Yosemite and well beyond. Tobin Sorenson was a dynamic and central contributor – one of the foremost Alpinists in the world. Reference: The Stone Masters, John Long & Dean Fidelman, © 2009, ISBN 978-0-9840949-0-5

4. Goodbye, Yellow Brick Road

1. Majka Burhardt, *Yellow Brick Road (5.9+) – Wizard Needle, California, Climbing* (05-20-2012) Retrieved 2021-08-09

7. The Gorge of Despair

1. Steve Roper, *The Climber's Guide to the High Sierra* (San Francisco: Sierra Club Books,1976)

8. In the Niche of Time

1. Kris Solem, *The Needles Climbing, A Complete Guide* (CA: K. Daniels Associates, 2016) pp. 162, 163
2. Solem, *The Needles Climbing, A Complete Guide* p 161
3. R. J. Secor, *The High Sierra, Peaks, Passes, and Trails* (Seattle, WA: The Mountaineers, 1992) pp. 162-163
4. Secor, *The High Sierra, Peaks, Passes, and Trails*, pp. 162-163
5. Bazelon, Emily; Phillip Carter; Dahlia Lithwick (2006-09-27). *"What Is Torture? An interactive primer on American interrogation"*. Slate. pp. *Taxonomy of Torture: Dietary Manipulation.* Retrieved 2021-14-08
6. Warren Harding, *Downward Bound, A Mad Guide to Rock Climbing* (Birmingham, Alabama: Menasha Ridge Press, 1975) pp. 36-37
7. Harding, *Downward Bound, A Mad Guide to Rock Climbing,* p.37
8. Harding, *Downward Bound, A Mad Guide to Rock Climbing,* pp. 141, 143

3. The Iron Man of Yosemite

1. Warren Harding, *Downward Bound, A Mad Guide to Rock Climbing* (Birmingham, Alabama: Menasha Ridge Press, 1975) p. 136

4. Royal Inspiration

1. Vaughn Schultz, "No Way Out." *Climbing 136,* Feb/Mar 1993, p.86

6. Galen Rowell Unchained

1. Rowell, G. (1977). *New Ways Up Old Walls, High Sierra.* The American Alpine Club Publications. Retrieved February 20, 2022, from https://publications.americanalpineclub.org/articles/12197707300

www.ingramcontent.com/pod-product-compliance
Lightning Source LLC
Chambersburg PA
CBHW071137130626
46553CB00004B/1406